The rights of the child According to the Ahl al-Bayt

(*Ḥuqūq Farzandān dar maktab Ahl al-Bayt* ﷺ)

Muḥammad Jawād Murawwajī Ṭabasī

Translator *Sayyid Athar Husain Rizvi*

Copy Editing *Mohammed Danish Inayatullah*

LANTERN PUBLICATIONS

Lantern Publications
info@lanternpublications.com
www.lanternpublications.com

NATIONAL LIBRARY OF AUSTRALIA
A catalogue record for this book is available from the National Library of Australia

Ordering Information:
Quantity sales. Special discounts are available on quantity purchases by corporations, associations, and others. For details, contact the distributor at the address below.

Shia Books Australia
www.shiabooks.com.au
info@shiabooks.com.au

ISBN- 978-1-922583-49-9

First Edition

Dedication

Dedicated to the teachers and mentors of the human beings, bearers of revelation, true interpreters of the Holy Qur'ān, protectors of Islam, the pure ones of Muḥammad ﷺ, true successors of the Holy Prophet ﷺ models and exemplars for humanity, that is: the twelve luminous stars in the sky of *Imāmah* and *Wilāyah*.

Table of Contents

Dedication **2**
Table of Contents **4**

Part One
The status of the child and the responsibility of the parents
Traditions and customs at birth **16**
1. Reciting the call to prayer in the child's ear 16
Blessings of the call to prayer 16
The Prophet's call to prayer into the ears of Ḥasan ﷺ and Ḥusain ﷺ 17
Imām Kāẓim ﷺ recited Adhān in the ear of Imām Riḍā ﷺ 18
2. Raising the child's palate 19
3. Circumcision of boys 21
Refrain from opposing the Sunnah of the Prophet 21
4. Shaving the child's head 22
Shaving the child's head on the seventh day 23
Ṣadaqah equal to the weight of a child's hair 23
5. Walīmah dinner or feeding people 23
6. ʿAqīqah ceremony 24
7. Choosing a name 30
The name of Muḥammad is auspiciousness and blessing for the house 36
The name of ʿAlī ﷺ and the Infallible A'immah ﷺ 38
Names of the prophets 40
Summary and analysis 45
Milk and its effect on the child's personality 47
A mother's reward for breastfeeding her child 47
The best milk 48
Choosing a wet nurse 49
The first category: foolish women 49
The second and third category: unchaste and insane women50
Fourth category: Nāṣibī females (enemies of Ahl al-Bayt ﷺ)50
Negative effects of impure milk 50

Part Two

Father and child relationship 52
Negative effects of lack or excess in love 57
Expression of love 58
Love for other children 64
Practice of Lady Zahrā ﷺ 67
Justice between son and daughter 77
Respecting the child while praying 81
Breastfeeding a child while praying 83
Not removing children from the congregation 84
Greeting the children 84
Not finding fault with children 85
Addressing the children nicely 85
Consulting with the youth 86
Social context for the development of children's talents 86
Prophet's ﷺ supplication for children 89
Prophet Ya'qūb ﷺ seeks forgiveness for his sons 90
Imām Ṣādiq's prayer on behalf of his children 90
Imām Zayn al-'Ābidīn's ﷺ prayer for his children 90
Three supplications are definitely fulfilled! 92
Increase in grades through parents' forgiveness 93
'Allamah Majlisī's supplication for his infant 93
The Holy Prophet ﷺ mourned his son, Ibrāhīm 94
Imām Bāqir ﷺ in mourning for his son 94
Imām Ṣādiq ﷺ mourned for Ismā'īl 95
All this impatience for a small calamity 96
The lives of the men of Allāh ﷻ 98
Impatience, before calamity 98
A conversation between Qutaybah 'Ashī and Imām Ṣādiq ﷺ 99

Part Three

Good upbringing and training of children 100
Providing good education 101
Role of education in human development 102
Most suitable time for education 103
Seven years of continuous training 104
Benefits of politeness in childhood and adolescence 105
Encouraging children 108
Benefits of encouragement 108
Encouragement of Allāh ﷻ 109

Encouragement of the Prophet ﷺ 110
Encouragement of Ibrāhīm ﷺ 110
Encouragement and praise in the conduct of Ahl al-Bayt ﷺ 111
Corporeal punishment of children 114
Instances when corporeal punishment of children is forbidden 114
Instances when beating is justified 115
Limits of corporeal punishment 116
Limitation of corporeal punishment 117
Proof of blood money 117
Reminder... 118
Methods of punishment 119
Being furious is the best solution..................................... 120
Ahl al-Bayt's ﷺ method of punishment 120
Teaching to read and write 121
Luqmān encouraged knowledge and wisdom 121
Military training 122
Teaching dinner etiquette 125

Part Four
The period of rebuilding the child's personality.............. 129
Removing corruption and deviance 130
A) Separating the sleeping place and taking permission to enter 130
B) Destroying the context of disobeying parents 134
C) Abstaining from forbidden food................................... 135
Connection between prohibited food and corruption 136
D) Creating a supportive environment 137
Remind your children of the enormity of sin 138
Vaccinating the children 144
A) Raising children on the love of Ahl al-Bayt ﷺ 145
Deceiving 'Alī's ﷺ friends 146
B) Arming the child against deviant thoughts 147
C) Discussing, inquiring, and justifying Islamic knowledge with children 147
Zayd's query and Imām Sajjād's ﷺ reply 149
Control of the friends 151
Friend: A perfect mirror 153
Duty of parents regarding friends of their children 153
1. Encouragement to choose a friend................................ 153
2. First the research, then the selection............................. 154
3. Maintaining relations with good friends........................ 154
4. Avoid unsuitable friends 155

Forbidden friendships 156

Part Five
Nurturing faith and religion 164
A) Children's relationship with Allāh ﷻ 164
Knowing Allāh ﷻ 164
Pondering on the signs of Allāh ﷻ 165
Ascribing partners to Allāh ﷻ 166
Relationship with Allāh ﷻ 167
Remember Allāh ﷻ everywhere 167
Creating a state of fear and hope 168
Fruits of the tree of religious cognition (Ma'rifat) 170
Good expectation from Allāh ﷻ 171
Know Allāh ﷻ by these attributes 172
B) Teaching religion and Islamic laws 172
The statement of 'there is no god, except Allāh ﷻ 173
Patience and perseverance 175
C) Practical training in Islamic laws 176
D) Encouraging children for worship and good deeds 178
Striving in obedience to Allāh ﷻ 179
Unexpected effort 179
Provision of the journey 180
Avoid laziness 180
Spiritual poverty 181
Arrogance in sin 181
Avoiding haughtiness and dereliction in worship 181
If Allāh ﷻ loves a person 182
Fulfilling the duties 183
E) Preaching and good advice 183
What is the implication of 'save yourself'? 185
F) Connection with the afterlife 185
The Infallible ﷺ are concerned about the Hereafter 188
The edifying effect of remembering resurrection in the life of young people 190
G) Giving importance to children's prayers 193
My son! Become steadfast in prayer 194
Pillar of religion 195
Advice of Imām Ṣādiq ﷺ at the time of his passing 195
Imām Riḍā ﷺ was surprised by the child leaving the prayer196
Prayer at the earliest hour 197

H) Preparing the children for prayer and fasting.............. 198
Practice of the Infallibles عليهم السلام regarding prayer of children. 199
From training to punishment 200
I) Giving importance to children's fasting......................... 202
J) Teaching the Qur'ān 203
Imām 'Alī's عليه السلام advice to memorize the Qur'ān 205
The reward of learning the Qur'ān on the Judgment Day. 206
Encouragement of the Qur'ān teacher 209
Encouraging children to recite the Qur'ān 210
1. Effects of Qur'ān recitation at home............................. 212
2. Effects of abandoning recitation of Qur'ān at home 213
K) Acquaintance with recommended acts 214
Bedtime supplication... 220
L) Commemoration of Islamic rites.................................. 222
Commemoration of the 'Āshūrā' uprising 222
Remembering the oppression of 'Alī عليه السلام and Zahra عليها السلام 223
M) Teaching informative and epic poetry.......................... 224
Teaching the instructive verses of Abū Ṭālib 224
Teaching 'Abdī's poems 225
N) Celebrating Islamic festivals.. 227
O) Preparing for Friday 228

Part Six
Children and society 232
A) Social interactions.. 232
Knowing one's personality 232
Expression of poverty 233
Vying what others have... 233
The honour of the believer 234
Avoid humiliation. 234
Honouring the world... 234
Respecting the personality of others 235
B) Interaction with scholars and intellectuals.................... 246
What are the signs of the scholar? 246
Benefits of the company of scholars 247
C) Foresight.. 249
1. Dealing with problems of life 251
Never despair of supplicating... 255
2. Prayers to solve problems 256
3. Patience and endurance.. 257
4. The practice of the Prophet ﷺ and his family عليهم السلام 262

5. Avoiding attachment to the world 264
The world is a deep sea 265
The deception of world worshipers 265
Do not depend on the world 266
The warning of Imām Zayn al-'Ābidīn ﷺ 267
Moderation in life 268
Think about the future 268
Bitterness of this world is sweetness of the Hereafter 268

Part Seven
Puberty and youth 272
A) Celebrating adulthood 272
The greatest feast of man 272
Statements Sayyid b. Ṭāwūs in the ceremony of his son's adulthood 273
Complain of Ibn. Ṭāwūs to the parents 273
B) Choosing a spouse 274
1. He should be righteous and honest 275
2. He should be God-fearing and pious 276
3. He should be religious and trustworthy 276
4. He should have good morals 278
'Alī b. Asbāṭ and Imām Bāqir ﷺ 279
5. Do not use poverty as an excuse 280
Same religion and caste 280
Don't marry your daughters to transgressors 281
Consulting ladies of the family 282
Consulting the girl 283
Prophet ﷺ consulted with Lady Fāṭimah Zahrā ﷺ 283
No compulsion 284
Urgency in marriage of the girl 284
C) Future of children 284
1. Choosing a profession 285
2. Transferring life experiences to children 287
3. Financial aid 288
4. Protecting children from the burden of society 288

Bibliography 290

Foreword by the teacher and researcher: Āyatullāh Ḥāj Shaykh Muḥammad Hādī Ma'rifat

One of the most important religious and social duties that must be fully observed in Islamic societies is the duty of parents regarding their children, which unfortunately is less observed, most parents believe that they have reserved their rights in relation to their children and rarely think that maybe the children have rights and obligations, that must be respected and not be shortchanged. Therefore, one of the duties of the educators of the Islamic society in every nook and corner of different countries of the world is to introduce parents to this truth and divine duty and encourage them to fulfill it.

It is a pleasure to know that one of the noble and generous people, a distinguished scholar and thinker, the honourable Ḥujjat al-Islam wal-Muslimīn, Ḥāj Shaykh Muḥammad Jawād Ṭabasī, son of the late Āyatullāh Ṭabasī Najafī – May Allāh ﷻ shade him with his mercy – who has the blessings of that noble father's soul - has addressed an aspect of this religious and moral duty and tried to introduce the general public to this aspect of human and social duty. To be fair, the book he has written in this regard is the most comprehensive and complete writing that has been compiled so far. I have observed that in terms of expressing the contents, strong arguments, clear testimonies, and mention of appropriate and valuable traditions, he has played a great role and brought good results. May Allāh ﷻ increase the *Tawfīq* (good sense) of this talented and honourable author and may the Islamic society benefit from his glorious writings.

With the grace of the Almighty and His bountiful care, if Allāh ﷻ wills

Qom - Muḥammad Hādī Ma'rifat 29/1/74

Translator's Preface

Since the task of writing a foreword this book was already accomplished by a prominent scholar and then a nice introduction was provided by the author, I thought there was no need for the English translator's preface. However, the publishers asked me to pen my experiences translating this book, hence here I wish to mention a few insights and remarks that came to mind while translating this book into English.

As we all know, there were already numerous books on the rights of parents, but no one inquired if the little ones also have any rights over their parents? Thus, this fact highlights the importance to this topic.

As mentioned in the preface, the author has accomplished a magnificent feat in compiling so many statements of the *Ahl al-Bayt* (as) regarding the subject of the rights of children. So when I was translating the book, I came across many issues about which we were of the opinion that we know every aspect of the matter, but when we read the discussions in this book we find that no matter how learned we might consider ourselves, we have to rely on the writings of our scholars, who have devoted their lives in the pursuit of knowledge and dissemination of the same.

Another remarkable quality of this work is complete reliance on the statements of the two most significant sources of Islamic laws and culture: that is: the Holy Qur'ān and the statements of the holy *Ahl al-Bay*t (as). There is very little discussion beyond these two sources, thus maximizing the importance of this work.

I am sure that it will go a long way in filling the gap that existed in this sphere and urge other writers to also pay attention to this topic as it will prepare the future generations to face the changing world and emerging challenges to religion and ethics.

Lastly, it is my duty to confess that though I have tried my best to convey with utmost accuracy whatever the author intended to express, if at any point any weakness or error has crept in, I must confess that it is my own doing, and the author is not at all liable for the same.

Sayyid Athar Husain Rizvi
(October 2023)

Introduction

The family is the first centre of a child's education and the primary architect of its personality. It is in this great training school that children gradually imitate their parent's behaviour. For several years, children act according to the principle of imitation. Since children are born with the innate divine nature, and they arrive in the world as God-fearing and righteous beings, if their educational environment and their behaviour are according to divine monotheism and the parents are familiar with their duties, they will also become monotheistic and pious, otherwise, they will deviate as the Prophet of Allāh ﷺ said:

كُلُّ مَوْلُودٍ يُولَدُ عَلَى الْفِطْرَةِ حَتَّى يَكُونَ أَبَوَاهُ يُهَوِّدَانِهِ وَ يُنَصِّرَانِهِ وَ يُمَجِّسَانِهِ

'All children are created on the pure nature of Allāh ﷻ unless his/her parents make him a Jew, a Christian, or a Magian.'

The responsibility of the family and parents is not only to provide children with food, clothes, and health; they should also be educated according to monotheistic and divine nature and have full control over their behaviour, speech, friends, worship, etc.

Parents attention on children makes them grow up safe, be cheerful and correct and saves them from the traps that the devils spread before them.

Not paying attention to children and abandoning them causes depression, wallowing in the mire of guilt, and hanging out with friends, ultimately leading to destruction. The poet, Shoqī says:

"An orphan is not one whose parents have passed away, leaving him alone, but a child whose mother is separated from his father and whose father is very busy with his work."

Children want peace of mind and a safe place. They seek love and affection, so we must learn the key to the correct upbringing of our children by knowing the instructions and guidance of the Infallibles and make the home a safe and peaceful place conducive to their intellectual development. We should not let them be confused, have an inferiority complex, anxiety, etc...

The parent should be a good friend for their children and guide them properly, instil self-confidence in them so that they become men and women of faith, strong of will, trustworthy and devoted, who are honest, humble, self-sacrificing, modest, benevolent and who will contribute positively to the community.

This book explains the facts and instructions that we seek for raising faithful children because it is based on the words and actions of the Infallibles and their advice to their own children. The only merit of this book is that it has tried to convey as much as possible, from the life of the Infallibles and the state of their interaction and association with their children to be presented as a final solution. Therefore, in most of the traditions mentioned here, the word "my child" is mentioned or a specific duty for the parents is stated.

The motivation and goal of writing it was to save, through the guidance of the Infallible leaders, the lives of millions of children and young people from the danger of deviance and to save thousands of families from collapse. Because the current climate of the world is such that moral corruption and ideological deviation have reached their peak and the sound of destruction is being heard; in addition, the satans, through numerous ways, have targeted children and teenagers to immerse them in the mire of corruption and annihilation. Therefore, every compassionate Muslim must do their best to save the children and protect the family. This motivation became stronger in me when, on occasion, I was reading the splendid books of *Wasā'il al-Shī'ah* and *Mustadrak al-Wasā'il* and other narrative texts. In this research, I came across traditions that stated the duties of parents towards their children. I was fascinated by these narrations and decided to compile them for parents by devoting more time and accuracy in order to present a relatively comprehensive course that includes the statements and acts of the Infallible A'immah about how to raise children.

Now that, by the grace of Allāh, the *Tawfīq* (good sense) of this humble service is given to this lowly servant, on the basis of the dictum, "He who does not thank the creature, does not thank the Creator ﷻ: I consider it necessary to express my heartfelt thanks and appreciation for the sincere efforts of the respected brothers in Bostan-e-Kitāb, of the Islamic Propagation Office, who put a lot of effort into the production of this book.

It is hoped that elders and scholars will bless us with their useful ideas so that with the help of Allāh ﷻ its defects will be ironed out and corrected in the subsequent editions.

From Allāh ﷻ is the success, and upon Him is the reliance.

Qom Seminary

Muḥammad Jawād Murawwajī Ṭabasī

15-3-73

24 Dhū al-Ḥijjah 1414

Part One

The status of the child and the responsibility of the parents

Traditions and customs at birth

1. Reciting the call to prayer in the child's ear

One of the recommended actions that the Prophet of Islam ﷺ and the Infallibles (عليهم السلام) strongly recommended is that after the birth of the child, the parents should recite the *Adhān* in the right ear and the *Iqāmah* in the left. Because, without a doubt, instilling the words: 'Allāh is the Greatest', and 'I bear witness that there is no god but Allāh, I bear witness that Muḥammad is the Messenger of Allāh', at the earliest stages of life, will make the child's ear familiar with the concept of monotheism and the monotheistic message. The pure and luminous scripture of the child's soul will reflect these messages in itself.

Yes, monotheistic messages, like the water of life, will irrigate his divine nature and make him more ready to tread the road to happiness, and as modern psychology has proved, the child's soul in the first six years of life is much more receptive, more sensitive, and more flexible than other periods of life. He absorbs what he has seen and heard, and it is difficult to remove their positive or negative effects in adulthood. Despite the popular misunderstanding of many people, that the child does not grasp anything at this age.

Blessings of the call to prayer

A) Reason for the Satan to be kept at a distance from the child

Sakūnī has narrated from Imām Ṣādiq (عليه السلام) that the Prophet ﷺ said:

مَنْ وُلِدَ لَهُ مَوْلُودٌ فَلْيُؤَذِّنْ فِي أُذُنِهِ الْيُمْنَى بِأَذَانِ الصَّلَاةِ وَلْيُقِمْ فِي الْيُسْرَى فَإِنَّهَا عِصْمَةٌ مِنَ الشَّيْطَانِ الرَّجِيمِ

"A person who has a child should recite the *Adhān* in his right ear and *Iqāmah* in his left ear, because this act protects the child from Satan."[1]

[1] *Wasā'il al-Shī'ah*, vol. 15, p. 136; *Mustadrak al-Wasā'il*, vol. 15, p. 137.

In a tradition, Imam 'Alī narrates this *Sunnah* from the Prophet, which also includes its explanation:

$$\text{فَإِنَّ ذَلِكَ عِصْمَةٌ مِنَ الشَّيْطَانِ الرَّجِيمِ وَ الْإِفْزَاعُ لَهُ}$$

"This action (saying the *Adhān* and *Iqāmah* in the child's ears) protects the child from the evil of Satan and also causes him not to be frightened in his sleep."[1]

B) He is not safe from the sting of Satan

The Prophet ordered Amīr al Mu'minīn:

$$\text{يَا عَلِيُّ إِذَا وُلِدَ لَكَ غُلَامٌ أَوْ جَارِيَةٌ فَأَذِّنْ فِي أُذُنِهِ الْيُمْنَى وَ أَقِمْ فِي الْيُسْرَى فَإِنَّهُ لَا يَضُرُّهُ الشَّيْطَانُ أَبَداً}$$

"O 'Alī! When you become the father of a son or a daughter, recite *Adhān* in his right ear and *Iqāmah* in his left, and he will be safe from Satan's harm forever."[2]

C) Protection from Umm al-Ṣibyān

Imām Ḥusain narrated from the Prophet:

$$\text{من وُلِدَ لَهُ ولدٌ فَأَذَّنَ فى أُذنِه الْيُمنَى وَأَقامَ أُذُنهِ الْيُسرىٰ لَمْ تَضُرَّهُ أُمُّ الصِّبيانِ}$$

"Whoever has a child and recites *Adhān* in his right ear and *Iqāmah* in his left, will never be affected by *Umm al-Ṣibyān* disease."[3]

The Prophet's call to prayer into the ears of Ḥasan and Ḥusain

Abū Rāfi' says:

---

[1] *Mustadrak al-Wasā'il*, Vol. 15, p. 138.
[2] *Tuḥaf al-'Uqūl*, p. 14.
[3] *Kanz al-'Ummāl*, vol. 16, p. 457, '*Umm al-Ṣibyān*' disease is a type of epilepsy that is specific to newborns and causes fainting. (*Farhang Jāmi'*, Vol. 1, p. 45.)

إِنَّ النَّبِيَّ اَذَّنَ فِى أُذُنِ الحَسَنِ والْحُسَيْنِ حِينَ وُلِدا وأَمَرَبه

"The Prophet ﷺ recited the call to prayer in the ears of Imām Ḥasan and Ḥusain ﵉ and ordered others to also do this (to newborns)."[1]

It is narrated from ʿAlī ﵇ in the book of *Daʿim al-Islām* that the Prophet ﷺ ordered:

أَمَرَ أَنْ يُفْعَلَ ذَلِكَ بِالْحَسَنِ وَ الْحُسَيْنِ وَ أَنْ يُقْرَأَ مَعَ الْأَذَانِ فِي آذَانِهِمَا- فَاتِحَةُ الْكِتَابِ وَ آيَةُ الْكُرْسِيِّ وَ آخِرُ سُورَةِ الْحَشْرِ وَ سُورَةُ الْإِخْلَاصِ وَ الْمُعَوِّذَتَانِ.

"The *Adhān* and *Iqāmah* should be recited in Ḥasan ﵇ and Ḥusain's ﵇ ears, and Sūrah Ḥamd, Āyat al-Kursī, the end of Sūrah al-Ḥashr, Sūrahs Ikhlās, Nās, and Falaq should also be recited."[2]

Imām Kāẓim ﵇ recited Adhān in the ear of Imām Riḍā ﵇

ʿAlī b. Mītham narrates from his father:

قَالَ سَمِعْتُ أُمِّي تَقُولُ سَمِعْتُ نَجْمَةَ أُمَّ الرِّضَا ع تَقُولُ فِي حَدِيثٍ لَمَّا وَضَعْتُ ابْنِي عَلِيّاً دَخَلَ إِلَيَّ أَبُوهُ مُوسَى بْنُ جَعْفَرٍ ع- فَنَاوَلْتُهُ إِيَّاهُ فِي خِرْقَةٍ بَيْضَاءَ فَأَذَّنَ فِي أُذُنِهِ الْيُمْنَى وَ أَقَامَ فِي الْيُسْرَى وَ دَعَا بِمَاءِ الْفُرَاتِ فَحَنَّكَهُ بِهِ ثُمَّ رَدَّهُ إِلَيَّ فَقَالَ خُذِيهِ فَإِنَّهُ بَقِيَّةُ اللَّهِ فِي أَرْضِهِ

He said: I heard from my mother that she said: Najmah, the mother of Imām Riḍā ﵇ used to say: When I gave birth to ʿAlī, my son, his father Imām Kāẓim ﵇ came to me. I handed to him my child, who was wrapped in a white cloth. So, he recited the *Adhān* in his right ear and the *Iqāmah* in his left. Then he asked for some water from the

[1] *Kanz al-ʿUmmāl*, vol. 16, p. 599.
[2] *Mustadrak al-Wasāʾil*, vol. 15, p. 137.

Euphrates and filled his mouth with that water and returned him to me. Then he said, "Take him; as he is the remnant of Allāh ﷻ on the face of the earth."¹

2. Raising the child's palate²

The second tradition that parents must follow upon the birth of a child is to lift the child's palate, which is one of the Islamic traditions of the *Ahl al-Bayt* ؑ and their commands. Those noble people sometimes lifted their children's palates with dates, sometimes with water from the Euphrates, and sometimes with the *Turbah* of Imām Ḥusain ؑ.

Lifting the palate of the newborn has a good effect on the child; it is the foundation for the child's attachment to *Ahl al-Bayt* ؑ.

Raising the palate of the children of Imām Ḥusain ؑ

Ḥusain b. Abī al-'Alā' says:

سَمِعْتُ أَبَا عَبْدِ اللَّهِ ع يَقُولُ حَنِّكُوا أَوْلَادَكُمْ بِتُرْبَةِ الْحُسَيْنِ ع فَإِنَّهُ أَمَانٌ

"I heard Imām Ṣādiq ؑ say: Lift the palate of your children with the *Turbah* of Ḥusain b. 'Alī ؑ; as it will be a source of safety for the child."³

Lifting the palate with water of Euphrates

Sa'dān narrates from Amīr al Mu'minīn ؑ:

أَمَا إِنَّ أَهْلَ الْكُوفَةِ- لَوْ حَنَّكُوا أَوْلَادَهُمْ بِمَاءِ الْفُرَاتِ لَكَانُوا شِيعَةً لَنَا

"If the people of Kufa lifted the palate of their children with Euphrates water, they would all be our *Shī'ah*."⁴

---

¹ *Wasā'il al-Shī'ah*, vol. 15, p. 138.
² It implies tapping the index finger on the *Turbah* of Imām Ḥusain ؑ or a date or... and then tapping the child's palate.
³ *Mustadrak al-Wasā'il*, vol. 15, p. 139.
⁴ *Wasā'il al-Shī'ah*, vol. 17, p. 212.

Ḥusain b. 'Uthmān narrated from Imām Ṣādiq that he said:

مَا أَظُنُّ أَحَداً يُحَنَّكُ بِمَاءِ الْفُرَاتِ إِلَّا كَانَ لَنَا شِيعَة

"I don't think that if anyone's palate is lifted with Euphrates water, except that he would be our *Shī'ah*."[1]

It is mentioned in the narration of Sulaymān b. Hārūn 'Ajlī from Imām Ṣādiq that he said:

اِلَّا أَحَبَّنَا أَهْلَ الْبَيْتِ

"Except that he would from the devotees of *Ahl al-Bayt*."[2]

Raising the palate of children with date

Abū Baṣīr narrates from Imām Ṣādiq and he from Amīr al Mu'minīn that he said:

حَنِّكُوا أَوْلَادَكُمْ بِالتَّمْرِ ، فَكَذَا فَعَلَ رَسُولُ اللهِ بِالْحَسَنِ وَالْحُسَيْنْ

"Raise the palates of your children with date, because the Prophet lifted the palates of Ḥasan and Ḥusain with dates."[3]

Raising the palate with rainwater

The late Kolaynī narrates the following in a narration:

حَنِّكُوا أَوْلَادَكُمْ بِمَاءِ الْفُرَاتِ وَ بِتُرْبَةِ قَبْرِ الْحُسَيْنِ ع فَإِنْ لَمْ يَكُنْ فَبِمَاءِ السَّمَاء

"Raise the palate of your children with Euphrates water and *Turbah* of Ḥusain b. 'Alī, and if these two are not found, raise their palate with rainwater."[4]

---

[1] *Mustadrak al-Wasā'il*, vol. 15, p. 139.
[2] *Mustadrak al-Wasā'il*, vol. 15, p. 139.
[3] *Wasā'il al-Shī'ah*, vol. 15, p. 138, vol. 17, p. 18; *Tuḥaf al-'Uqūl*, p. 120.
[4] *Wasā'il al-Shī'ah*, vol. 15, p. 138, vol. 17, p. 18; *Tuḥaf al-'Uqūl*, p. 120.

3. Circumcision of boys

The third tradition that must be observed in the first week of a boy's birth is his circumcision, which the Infallible A'immah have emphasized much. The seventh day of birth has been determined for this purpose and they have also expressed wisdom behind it, which is referred to in two narrations:

Imām ʿAlī عليه السلام narrates from the Prophet ﷺ, who said:

اخْتِنُوا أَوْلَادَكُمْ يَوْمَ السَّابِعِ- فَإِنَّهُ أَطْهَرُ وَ أَسْرَعُ نَبَاتاً لِلَّحْمِ وأَرْوَحُ لِلْقَلْبِ

"Circumcise your children on the seventh day of their birth, because this act is purer for the child, more effective in accelerating his physical growth and refreshing his soul."[1]

Likewise, Imām ʿAlī عليه السلام said:

اِخْتَنُوا أولادَكُمْ يَوْمَ السّابعِ، وَلا يَمْنَعكُم حَرٌّ ولا بردٌ؛ فَإِنَّهطُهْرٌ لِلْجَسَدِ

"Circumcise your children on the seventh day of their birth, and heat or cold should not stop you from doing this, because circumcision is a means of purification for the body."[2]

Refrain from opposing the Sunnah of the Prophet

ʿAbdullāh b. Jaʿfar wrote to Imām Ḥasan ʿAskarī عليه السلام:

أَنَّهُ رُوِيَ عَنِ الصَّادِقِينَ ع- أَنِ اخْتِنُوا أَوْلَادَكُمْ يَوْمَ السَّابِعِ يَطْهُرُوا فَإِنَّ الْأَرْضَ تَضِجُّ إِلَى اللَّهِ عَزَّ وَ جَلَّ مِنْ بَوْلِ الْأَغْلَفِ وَ لَيْسَ جَعَلَنِي اللَّهُ فِدَاكَ لِحَجَّامِي بَلَدِنَا حِذْقٌ بِذَلِكَ وَ لَا يَخْتِنُونَهُ يَوْمَ السَّابِعِ وَ عِنْدَنَا حَجَّامُو الْيَهُودِ فَهَلْ يَجُوزُ لِلْيَهُودِ أَنْ يَخْتِنُوا أَوْلَادَ الْمُسْلِمِينَ أَمْ لَا إِنْ شَاءَ اللَّهُ فَوَقَّعَ ع السُّنَّةُ يَوْمَ السَّابِعِ فَلَا تُخَالِفُوا السُّنَنَ إِنْ

---

[1] *Kanz al-ʿUmmāl*, vol. 167, p. 436; *Wasāʾil al-Shīʿah*, vol. 15, p. 165, with slight difference; *Mustadrak al-Wasāʾil*, vol. 15, p. 149.
[2] *Tuḥaf al-ʿUqūl*, p. 119.

شَاءَ اللَّهُ

It is narrated from Imām Bāqir ﷷ and Imām Ṣādiq ﷷ that they said: "Circumcise your children on the seventh day so that they become ritually pure, as the earth complains to Allāh ﷻ when the urine of an uncircumcised person falls on it."

(The Imām ﷷ was asked) May I be sacrificed on you: The circumcisers in our city are not skilled in circumcision and they do not perform it on the seventh day, but there are Jewish circumcisers in this city, can they circumcise Muslim children? If Allāh ﷻ wills.

The Imām ﷷ wrote in reply: "The *Sunnah* is to circumcise on the seventh day. Try not to oppose the traditions. If Allāh ﷻ wills."[1]

4. Shaving the child's head

Another tradition that should be followed by the parents at the time of birth is shaving the child's head, which is recommended to be done on the seventh day.

The late Shaykh al-Ḥurr al-'Āmilī, the author of *Wasā'il al-Shī'ah*, has narrated about 30 narrations in this context in the 15th volume of his book, which undoubtedly show a strong approval of this *Sunnah*. In addition, in some of these narrations, the word '*Sunnah*' is mentioned, and perhaps the reason for it is that this was the conduct and practice of the Infallibles ﷺ.

Imām Ṣādiq ﷷ narrates from his forefathers as follows:

أَنَّ رَسُولَ اللَّهِ ص أَمَرَ بِحَلْقِ الشَّعْرِ الَّذِي يُولَدُ بِهِ الْمَوْلُودُ عَنْ رَأْسِهِ يَوْمَ سَابِعِهِ

"The Prophet ﷺ ordered that the child's head must be shaved on the seventh day of birth."[2]

[1] *Wasā'il al-Shī'ah*, vol. 15, p. 161.
[2] *Mustadrak al-Wasā'il*, vol. 15, p. 142.

Shaving the child's head on the seventh day

'Alī b. Ja'far says: I asked my brother, Imām Mūsā ﷺ regarding a child whose head is shaved on the seventh day; he replied:

إِذَا مَضَى سَبْعَةُ أَيَّامٍ فَلَيْسَ عَلَيْهِمْ حَلْقُهُ

"If seven days have passed, there is no need to shave."[1]

Ṣadaqah equal to the weight of a child's hair

Imām Ṣādiq ﷺ says:

وَ حَلَقَتْ فَاطِمَةُ ع رُءُوسَهُمَا (الْحَسَنَ وَ الْحُسَيْنَ) وَ تَصَدَّقَتْ بِوَزْنِ شَعْرِهِمَا فِضَّةً

"Fāṭimah ﷺ shaved the head of her sons [Imām Ḥasan ﷺ and Imām Ḥusain ﷺ] and gave the weight of their hair in silver as charity."[2]

5. Walīmah dinner or feeding people

The fifth recommended act is that a father performs at the time of the birth of a child is to feed believers, friends, and acquaintances, which - without a doubt - lays the foundation for good social ties and a prelude to the acceptance of the child by the society. In addition to this, it also has blessed spiritual and physical effects for the child.

The practice and conduct of *Ahl al-Bayt* ﷺ were also as such. Rather, Imām Ṣādiq ﷺ fed the people for three days on the birth of his son, Imām Kāẓim ﷺ. Also, it is on the same basis that the late Shaykh al-Ḥurr al-'Āmilī in his *Wasā'il al-Shī'ah* has mentioned in the 'Chapter on the desirability of feeding people at the birth of the newborn in the third day' that Minhāl, the butcher said:

خَرَجْتُ مِنْ مَكَّةَ وَ أُرِيدُ الْمَدِينَةَ فَمَرَرْتُ بِالْأَبْوَاءِ وَ قَدْ وُلِدَ لِأَبِي عَبْدِ اللَّهِ مُوسَى ع

---

[1] *Wasā'il al-Shī'ah*, vol. 15, p. 169.

[2] *Wasā'il al-Shī'ah*, vol. 15, p. 169.

فَسَبَقْتُهُ إِلَى الْمَدِينَةِ وَ دَخَلَ بَعْدِي بِيَوْمٍ فَأَطْعَمَ النَّاسَ ثَلَاثاً ...

I had left Makkah and was heading to Madinah, when I passed by al-Abwā', where Imām Mūsā Kāẓim ﷷ was born to Imām Ja'far Ṣādiq ﷷ. Then I preceded him to Madinah, and he arrived on the following day. He then fed the people for three days for the birth of Imām Kāẓim ﷷ...[1]

Jābir says:

كان علىٌّ بنُ الحُسَيْنِ يُولِمُ فى الوِلادَة

The practice of 'Alī b. al-Ḥusain ﷷ was to serve *Walīmah* dinner at the birth of his child.[2]

6. 'Aqīqah ceremony

One of the traditions of Muḥammad ﷺ is that on the seventh day of the child's birth, after shaving the child's head, the father divides the sacrificial sheep among the poor, friends, and neighbours. This Islamic tradition is called 'Aqīqah.

In Islam, 'Aqīqah is very much emphasized, and its obligation remains on the father until the child reaches puberty, and after that it falls upon the person himself. This emphasis is due to the wisdoms hidden in it, and some of them are as follows:

1. Health insurance

Samrah narrates from the Holy Prophet ﷺ, who said:

كُلُّ غُلَامٍ رَهِينَةٌ بِعَقِيقَتِه

"Every child is insured with 'Aqīqah."[3]

---

[1] *Wasā'il al-Shī'ah*, vol. 1, p. 133.
[2] *Kanz al-'Ummāl*, vol. 1, p. 210.
[3] *Kanz al-'Ummāl*, vol. 16, p. 431; *Kanz al-'Ummāl*, vol. 1, pp. 216 and 433.

Imām Ṣādiq quoted his forefathers from the Messenger of Allāh saying:

كُلُّ مَوْلُودٍ مُرْتَهَنٌ بِعَقِيقَتِهِ فَكَّهُ وَالِدَاهُ أَوْ تَرَكَاهُ

"The health of every child depends on his 'Aqīqah, whether the parents release the child from 'Aqīqah or not."[1]

2. 'Aqīqah on the seventh day

Imām Ṣādiq said:

الْغُلَامُ رَهْنٌ بِسَابِعِهِ بِكَبْشٍ يُسَمَّى فِيهِ وَ يُعَقُّ عَنْهُ

"The health of every child depends on the sacrifice of a sheep that is chosen for him and is sacrificed on his behalf."[2]

3. 'Aqīqah of sheep

The Prophet of Allāh says:

إِذَا كَانَ يَوْمُ سَابِعِهِ فَاذْبَحْ عَنْهُ كَبْشاً

"Slaughter a sheep (ram) for the newborn on the seventh day."[3]

4. The Prophet performed 'Aqīqah on behalf of A'immah Ḥasan and Ḥusain

Imām Ṣādiq said:

سَمَّى رسول الله حسناً وحسيناً عليهم السلام يومَ سابِعهما، وشَقَّ مِن اسمِ الحسنِ الحُسينَ وعَقَّ عنهما شاة شاة...

---

[1] *Mustadrak al-Wasā'il*, vol. 15, p. 140.
[2] *Biḥār al-'Anwār*, vol. 43, p. 256.
[3] *Mustadrak al-Wasā'il*, Vol. 15, p. 143.

"The Prophet ﷺ named Ḥasan ؑ and Ḥusain ؑ on the seventh day and derived the name of Ḥusain ؑ from 'Ḥasan'. He performed their ʿAqīqah with a sheep for each of them."[1]

5. Lady Fāṭimah Zahrā ؑ did ʿAqīqah for Imam Ḥasan ؑ and Ḥusain ؑ

Imām Ṣādiq ؑ said:

عَقَّتْ فٰاطِمَة عَنْ اِبْنيها صَلَواتُ اللهُ عَلَيْهِمٰا وَ حَلَقتْ رؤوسَهُما فى الْيومِ السّابع

"Lady Fāṭimah Zahrā ؑ performed ʿAqīqah for her two sons on the seventh day and shaved their heads."[2]

6. ʿAqīqah of Imām Bāqir ؑ for his two sons

Muḥammad b. Muslim says:

وُلِد لأبى جعفر غلامانِ، فأمر زيدَ بنَ علىّ أن يَشتَرى له جزورينِ للعقيقة...

"Two sons were born to Imām Bāqir ؑ. So, he asked Zayd b. ʿAlī to purchase two camels for their ʿAqīqah."[3]

7. ʿAqīqah of Imām ʿAskarī ؑ for Imām Mahdī ؑ

Ibrahīm b. Idrīs says:

وَجَّهَ إِلَيَّ مَوْلَايَ أَبُو مُحَمَّدٍ ع بِكَبْشٍ وَ قَالَ عُقَّهُ عَنِ ابْنِي فُلَانٍ وَ كُلْ وَ أَطْعِمْ أَهْلَكَ ثُمَّ وَجَّهَ إِلَيَّ بِكَبْشَيْنِ وَ قَالَ عُقَّ هَذَيْنِ الْكَبْشَيْنِ عَنْ مَوْلَاكَ وَ كُلْ هَنَّأَكَ اللَّهُ وَ أَطْعِمْ إِخْوَانَكَ

My master, Imām Ḥasan ʿAskarī ؑ sent two sheep and wrote to me: In the name of Allāh, the Beneficent, the Merciful. 'Slaughter these

---

[1] *Biḥār al-'Anwār*, vol. 43, p. 257.
[2] *Biḥār al-'Anwār*, pp. 256-257.
[3] *Wasā'il al-Shīʿah*, vol. 15, p. 146.

two sheep for your master, Imām Mahdī ﷻ, and consume their meat, may you be satisfied, and feed your brothers as well.' I did that.[1]

8. 'Aqīqah is same for boys and girls

It is narrated from the Messenger of Allāh ﷺ that he said:

الْعَقِيقَةُ شَاةٌ مِنَ الْغُلَامِ وَ الْجَارِيَةِ سَوَاء

"'Aqīqah is sacrifice of a sheep; and boys and girls are equal in this regard..."[2]

9. 'Aqīqah or giving charity for the value of the animal

'Abdullāh b. Bakr says:

كُنْتُ عِنْدَ أَبِي عَبْدِ اللَّهِ ع فَجَاءَهُ رَسُولُ عَمِّهِ عَبْدِ اللَّهِ بْنِ عَلِيٍّ فَقَالَ لَهُ يَقُولُ لَكَ عَمُّكَ إِنَّا طَلَبْنَا الْعَقِيقَةَ فَلَمْ نَجِدْهَا فَمَا تَرَى نَتَصَدَّقُ بِثَمَنِهَا فَقَالَ لَا إِنَّ اللَّهَ يُحِبُّ إِطْعَامَ الطَّعَامِ وَ إِرَاقَةَ الدِّمَاء

I was in the company of Imām Ja'far Ṣādiq ؑ when a messenger of his uncle, 'Abdullāh b. 'Alī arrived and said: Your uncle says: "We searched for a sheep for 'Aqīqah sacrifice, but it was not found; what is your opinion? Shall we give its value in cash as charity?" Imām ؑ said, "No (don't do that) because Allāh ﷻ loves feeding people and shedding the blood of sacrifice."[3]

Muḥammad b. Muslim says:

وُلِد لأبى جعفر غلامانِ، فأمر زيدَ بن على أن يشترى له جزورينِ للعقيقة وكان زمَن غلاءٍ. فاشترَى له واحدة وعَسرَتْ عليه الأخرى، فقال لأبى جعفر عليه السلام قد عَسَرتْعَلَىّ الأُخرى، فأتَصدّقُ بِثَمَنِها؟ قال:(لا،أطلُبها ؛ فأنّ اللهَ عزّوجلّ يُحبّ اهراق الدماءِ واطعامَ الطعامِ)

[1] Muḥammad Jawād Ṭabasī, *Ḥayāt al-Imām al-'Askarī*, p. 80.

[2] *Mustadrak al-Wasā'il*, vol. 15, p. 142.

[3] *Wasā'il al-Shī'ah*, vol. 15, p. 146.

Two sons were born to Imām Bāqir ﷺ. The Imām ﷺ ordered Zayd b. 'Alī to buy two camels for 'Aqīqah. Those were hard times.

Zayd b. 'Alī bought a camel, but he could not find a second, so he asked the Imām ﷺ, "It is difficult for me to buy a second camel, can I give its value in charity?"

"No," said the Imām ﷺ, "Try to find it, because Allāh ﷻ likes shedding the blood of sacrifice and feeding people."[1]

Explanation

Allāh ﷻ loves serving food to others; therefore, sacrificing a sheep and dividing it among the neighbours and the poor is better than giving money to them. Importantly, there are many narrations about feeding and 'Aqīqah. In addition, it is good to give some of the meat of 'Aqīqah to the neighbours, as the Messenger of Allāh ﷺ, did when Imām Ḥasan ﷺ and Ḥusain ﷺ were born.[2]

It is recommended that some of the meat of 'Aqīqah be set aside to feed the believers and they should be invited and hosted; so that both the blessing of the presence of believers in the house of the child's father and the use of 'Aqīqah food will increase the blessing of the family. Also, prayers for the health of the child would be recited and the child will benefit from the supplications of the guests and get more spiritual and physical health.

Imām Bāqir ﷺ and Imām Ṣādiq ﷺ have hinted at this point and said:

إِنَّ اللَّهَ تَبَارَكَ وَ تَعَالَى يُحِبُّ إِهْرَاقَ الدِّمَاءِ وَ إِطْعَامَ الطَّعَامِ

"Allāh ﷻ loves shedding the blood of sacrifices, feasts and serving of food."[3]

10. Not depriving the midwife from 'Aqīqah meat

A very good tradition in the heritage of *Ahl al-Bayt* ﷺ is to give some of the 'Aqīqah meat to the midwife of the newborn. The Messenger of Allāh ﷺ sent a leg of 'Aqīqah sheep to the midwife during 'Aqīqah for Imām Ḥasan ﷺ and Ḥusain ﷺ.

---

[1] *Wasā'il al-Shī'ah*, vol. 15, p. 146.
[2] *Biḥār al-'Anwār*, vol. 43, p. 257; *Mustadrak al-Wasā'il*, vol. 15, p. 143.
[3] *Wasā'il al-Shī'ah*, vol. 15, p. 146.

Imām Ṣādiq said:

$$\text{سَمَّى رَسُولُ اللَّهِ ص حَسَناً وَ حُسَيْناً يَوْمَ سَابِعِهِمَا وَ عَقَّ عَنْهُمَا شَاةً شَاةً وَ بَعَثُوا بِرِجْلِ شَاةٍ إِلَى الْقَابِلَةِ}$$

"On the seventh day, the Prophet chose the name of Ḥasan and Ḥusain for them… and for each of them he sacrificed a sheep in 'Aqīqah and sent one (mutton) leg to the midwife."[1]

11. 'Aqīqah supplication of the Prophet

Imām Ṣādiq said: The Messenger of Allāh used to recite the following supplication during 'Aqīqah:

$$\text{بِسْمِ اللَّهِ عَقِيقَةٌ عَنِ الْحَسَنِ وَ قَالَ اللَّهُمَّ عَظْمُهَا بِعَظْمِهِ وَ لَحْمُهَا بِلَحْمِهِ وَ دَمُهَا بِدَمِهِ وَ شَعْرُهَا بِشَعْرِهِ اللَّهُمَّ اجْعَلْهَا وِقَاءً لِمُحَمَّدٍ وَ آلِهِ}$$

"In the name of Allāh, this is an 'Aqīqah from Ḥasan. O Allāh! Because of the bones, flesh, blood, and hair of the sacrifice, keep the bones, flesh, blood, and hair of Ḥasan in health. O Allāh! Make this sacrifice a means of protecting Muḥammad and the Progeny of Muḥammad."[2]

12. Opposing the false traditions of the period of ignorance

With the advent of Islam and the declaration of the mission of the respected Prophet of Islam, many of the rules and traditions of the period of ignorance were rejected, and some that were rational and desirable were approved and allowed.

Among the traditions that were accepted with some changes was 'Aqīqah. Though this trend was current during the period of ignorance, it was contaminated with superstitions. At the time, they only used to perform 'Aqīqah for boys, and it was done by soaking cotton wool with the blood of 'Aqīqah and applying it on the child's head after shaving his hair.

---

[1] *Biḥār al-'Anwār*, vol. 43, p. 257.
[2] *Biḥār al-'Anwār*, vol. 43, p. 257.

Abū Hurairah says:

انّ اليهود كانت تعقّ عن الغلامِ شاة، ولا يذبحون عن الجارية، فقال رسولُ الله:
اِذ بَحوا عن الغلامِ شاتينِ وعن الجارية شاة

Jews used to perform ʿAqīqah only for the male child; if it was a girl, they would not do ʿAqīqah for her. The Prophet ﷺ said: "ʿAqīqah is two sheep for a boy, and one for a girl."[1]

ʿĀʾishah says:

كانوا فى الجاهليّة اذا عَقّوا خَضَبواقُطنة بدمِ العقيقة، واذا حَلقُوا رأس الصّبىّ
وضَعوها على رأسِه. فقال النبىّ: اِجعَلُوا مَكان الدّمِ خَلوقاً

During the *Jāhiliyyah* period, whenever they performed ʿAqīqah, they dipped a piece of cotton in the blood of ʿAqīqah, and when they shaved the head of the newborn, they dabbed his head with it. To oppose this practice, the Holy Prophet ﷺ said: "Apply perfume instead of blood."[2]

In this way, the noble Prophet of Islam ﷺ purged this *Sunnah* from superstitions and popularized it as a good Islamic practice.

7. Choosing a name

Another tradition that parents should pay attention to at the birth of the child is choosing a name. Choosing a name is not a simple matter. Parents should know that the child would have to live with this name their entire life. His or her parents and others too will call him by this name, and the name will also reveal the child's personality. If the name is repulsive, people will hate him and he will be ridiculed, leading to mental suffering and emotional distress. It is natural that the child would consider these discomforts to be due to the ill decision of the parents. Therefore, they should be careful to choose good names.

---

[1] *Kanz al-ʿUmmāl*, vol. 1, p. 212.

[2] *Kanz al-ʿUmmāl*, vol. 16, p. 434.

As mentioned in traditional reports, one should choose the best names for one's children, and the best names are those that indicate servitude to the Lord ﷻ and are reminders of moral virtues. For this reason, the names of prophets, righteous persons and in the same way, names of the Infallible A'immah ﷺ and Lady Fāṭimah Zahrā ﷺ are most appropriate, which revive Islamic culture and rituals.

Yes, our infallible leaders ﷺ gave so much importance to the issue of name that since birth of a male child until the seventh day, they called him Muḥammad; so that from the very beginning, the soul, mind, and brain of the child were introduced to Prophet Muḥammad ﷺ. By mentioning Allāh's ﷻ name while calling the call to prayer in the ears of the child and repeating the name of Muḥammad ﷺ, his pure nature is awakened, and his limbs and bones also bear witness to the oneness of Allāh ﷻ and the mission of His Prophet.

Now we draw your attention to a selection of traditions in this regard:

1. Naming tradition

Imām Ṣādiq ﷺ said:

لاَ يُولَدُ لَنَا وَلَدٌ إِلاَّ سَمَّيْنَاهُ مُحَمَّداً فَإِذَا مَضَى لَنَا سَبْعَةُ أَيَّامٍ فَإِنْ شِئْنَا غَيَّرْنَا وَ إِنْ شِئْنَا تَرَكْنَا

"No child is born to us except that we first name him as Muḥammad and after seven days, if we want, we change his name, otherwise we continue with that name."[1]

2. A good name and the right of a child

Ibn 'Abbās narrates from the Prophet ﷺ who said:

حَقُّ الْوَلَدِ عَلَى الْوالِدِ أَنْ يُحْسِنَ اسْمَه وَيُحْسِنَ أَدَبَه

"It is the right of a child on his father to give him a good name and educate him in the best way."[2]

[1] *Mustadrak al-Wasā'il*, vol. 15, p. 127.

[2] *Kanz al-'Ummāl*, vol. 16, p. 477.

3. The best gift for a child

Amīr al Mu'minīn ﷺ said:

قَالَ رَسُولُ اللَّهِ ص: إِنَ أَوَّلَ مَا يَنْحَلُ أَحَدُكُمْ وَلَدَهُ الِاسْمُ الْحَسَنُ فَلْيُحْسِنْ أَحَدُكُمُ اسْمَ وَلَدِهِ

The Prophet ﷺ said: "The first gift that each of you gives to your child is a good name. So, choose the best name for your child."[1]

Mūsā b. Bakr narrates from Imām Abū al-Ḥasan ﷺ:

أَوَّلُ مَا يَبَرُّ الرَّجُلُ وَلَدَهُ أَنْ يُسَمِّيَهُ بِاسْمٍ حَسَنٍ فَلْيُحْسِنْ أَحَدُكُمُ اسْمَ وَلَدِهِ

"The first kindness of a man to his child is to choose a good name for him. So, use the best names for your children."[2]

4. Effect of a good name on the Judgment Day

Muḥaddith Nūrī says in *Mustadrak*:

وفى الخبر أنّ رجُلاً يُؤتىٰ فى القيامة واسمُه محمّد، فيقول الله له: ما استحييتَ أن عصيتَنى وأنت سَمِىُّ حبيبى، وأنا أستَحيى أن أُعذّبَك وأنتَ سمِىُّ حبيبى

وَ فِي الْخَبَرِ: أَنَ رَجُلاً يُؤْتَى فِي الْقِيَامَةِ وَ اسْمُهُ مُحَمَّدٌ فَيَقُولُ اللَّهُ لَهُ مَا اسْتَحْيَيْتَ أَنْ عَصَيْتَنِي وَ أَنْتَ سَمِيُّ حَبِيبِي وَ أَنَا أَسْتَحْيِي أَنْ أُعَذِّبَكَ وَ أَنْتَ سَمِيُّ حَبِيبِي

It is narrated that on the Judgment Day, a man will be brought whose name would be Muḥammad. He would be told by Allāh ﷻ: "Are you not ashamed of having sinned against me, while you were the namesake of My beloved (*Ḥabīb*)- the Messenger of Allāh ﷺ - and today I am ashamed to torment you while you are the namesake of My beloved."[3]

---

[1] *Wasā'il al-Shī'ah*, vol. 15, p. 122.
[2] *Wasā'il al-Shī'ah*, vol. 15, p. 126.
[3] *Mustadrak al-Wasā'il*, vol. 15, p. 130.

Imām Ṣādiq ؑ narrates from his forefathers:

إِذَا كَانَ يَوْمُ الْقِيَامَةِ- نَادَى مُنَادٍ أَلَا لِيَقُمْ كُلُّ مَنِ اسْمُهُ مُحَمَّدٌ فَلْيَدْخُلِ الْجَنَّةَ لِكَرَامَةِ سَمِيِّهِ مُحَمَّدٍ ص

"An announcer would call out on the Judgment Day: Let whoever is named Muḥammad, rise up and enter Paradise in honour of his namesake: Muḥammad ﷺ."[1]

5. People would be called by their names in resurrection

Imām Riḍā ؑ said:

اسْتَحْسِنُوا أَسْمَاءَكُمْ فَإِنَّكُمْ تُدْعَوْنَ بِهَا يَوْمَ الْقِيَامَةِ قُمْ يَا فُلَانَ بْنَ فُلَانٍ إِلَى نُورِكَ وَ قُمْ يَا فُلَانَ بْنَ فُلَانٍ لَا نُورَ لَكَ

"Enhance your names, because on the Judgment Day, you will be addressed with the same as: so-and-so child of so-and-so; get up and step towards your light and so-and-so, child of so-and-so, get up, you have no light."[2]

Explanation

There is no doubt that words and names, however good and pleasing they may be, cannot make a person successful alone, and the implications of the above narrations is that good names provide a psychological background and positive spiritual and social training that if the person who owns the name is placed in such atmosphere and is decorated with the morals of the Holy Prophet ﷺ and the manners of *Ahl al-Bayt* ؑ, it would align him with true morality and open the way of Paradise for him.

The important point in naming is that the name of each person and any meaning that is given to the child, by repeatedly mentioning it throughout life, the memory, and characteristics of that person and that meaning will affect the child's mind and psyche. A special bond

---

[1] *Wasā'il al-Shī'ah*, vol. 15, p. 128.
[2] *'Udat al-Dā'ī*, p. 78.

will be created between the two, which is effective in his being righteous or wretched.

6. The best name for boys

Many names for boys are mentioned in the narrations, but a few names have been emphasized as the best names.

Ibn. ʿUmar narrated that the Prophet ﷺ said:

أَحَبُّ الْأَسْمَاءِ إِلَى اللَّهِ عَبْدُ اللَّهِ وَ عَبْدُ الرَّحْمَن

"The names most liked by Allāh ﷻ are ʿAbdullāh and ʿAbd al-Raḥmān."[1]

Ibn. Ḥamīd consulted with Imām Ṣādiq ؑ regarding the name of his son. Imām ؑ said:

سَمِّهِ اسْماً مِنَ الْعُبُودِيَّةِ فَقَالَ أَيُّ الْأَسْمَاءِ هُوَ قَالَ عَبْدُ الرَّحْمَن

"Name him with a name denoting servitude to Allāh ﷻ."

What name do you imply?

ʿAbd al-Raḥmān, said the Imām ؑ.[2]

It is narrated from the Prophet ﷺ as follows:

مَنْ وُلِدَ لَهُ أَرْبَعَةُ أَوْلَادٍ لَمْ يُسَمِّ أَحَدَهُمْ بِاسْمِي فَقَدْ جَفَانِي

"Whoever has four sons and does not name any of them after me, he has wronged me."[3]

Abū Hārūn says: I lived near His Eminence, Imām Ṣādiq ؑ in Madinah. Once he did not see me for a few days and when I visited him after that he said:

---

[1] *Kanz al-ʿUmmāl*, vol. 16, p. 417.
[2] *Wasāʾil al-Shīʿah*, vol. 15, p. 125.
[3] *ʿUdat al-Dāʿī*, p. 77.

لَمْ أَرَكَ مُنْذُ أَيَّامٍ يَا أَبَا هَارُونَ فَقُلْتُ وُلِدَ لِي غُلَامٌ فَقَالَ بَارَكَ اللَّهُ لَكَ فَمَا سَمَّيْتَهُ قُلْتُ سَمَّيْتُهُ مُحَمَّداً- فَأَقْبَلَ بِخَدِّهِ نَحْوَ الْأَرْضِ وَ هُوَ يَقُولُ مُحَمَّدٌ مُحَمَّدٌ مُحَمَّدٌ- حَتَّى كَادَ يَلْصَقُ خَدُّهُ بِالْأَرْضِ ثُمَّ قَالَ بِنَفْسِي وَ بِوُلْدِي وَ بِأَهْلِي وَ بِأَبَوَيَّ وَ بِأَهْلِ الْأَرْضِ كُلِّهِمْ جَمِيعاً الْفِدَاءُ لِرَسُولِ اللَّهِ ص- لَا تَسُبَّهُ وَ لَا تَضْرِبْهُ وَ لَا تُسِئْ إِلَيْهِ وَ اعْلَمْ أَنَّهُ لَيْسَ فِي الْأَرْضِ دَارٌ فِيهَا اسْمُ مُحَمَّدٍ إِلَّا وَ هِيَ تُقَدَّسُ كُلَّ يَوْمٍ

"O Abū Hārūn! For how many days have I not seen you?" I said: A son was born to me. Imām ﷺ said: "May he be blessed, what will you name him?" I said: Muḥammad – as soon as he heard the name of Muḥammad - he bowed down and said: "Muḥammad, Muḥammad, Muḥammad and he bowed so much that his cheek almost touched the ground. Then he said: May my life, my child, my wife, my parents and all the people on earth be sacrificed on the Messenger of Allāh ﷺ. Never abuse or hit him, never be harsh on him."[1]

Abū Amāmah narrates from the Prophet ﷺ that he said:

من وُلِدله مولودٌ ذكرٌ فسمّى محمّداً حبّاً وتبرّكاً باسْمى، كان هو ومولوده فى الجنّة

"To whomsoever a son is born, and he names him Muḥammad out of love for me and to seek blessings from my name, both he and his child will be in Paradise."[2]

Jābir says quoting from the Messenger of Allāh ﷺ that he said:

مَا مِنْ بَيْتٍ فِيهِ اسْمُ مُحَمَّدٍ إِلَّا أَوْسَعَ اللَّهُ عَلَيْهِمُ الرِّزْقَ فَإِذَا سَمَّيْتُمُوهُمْ فَلَا تَضْرِبُوهُمْ وَ لَا تَشْتِمُوهُمْ

"There is no house that has someone named Muḥammad in it except that Allāh ﷻ widens the sustenance of (the folks of) that house.

[1] *Wasā'il al-Shī'ah*, vol. 15, p. 126.
[2] *Kanz al-'Ummāl*, vol. 16, p. 422.

So if you name your child Muḥammad, you must not beat or abuse him."[1]

The name of Muḥammad is auspiciousness and blessing for the house

Imām Riḍā ؑ said:

البيت الذى فيه محمّد يَصبح أهلُه بخيرٍ ويَمسون بخيرٍ

"Those living in a house with someone named Muḥammad will be happy and blessed day and night."[2]

The Prophet ﷺ said:

إِذَا سَمَّيْتُمُ الْوَلَدَ مُحَمَّداً فَأَكْرِمُوهُ- وَ أَوْسِعُوا لَهُ فِي الْمَجَالِسِ وَ لاَ تُقَبِّحُوا لَهُ وَجْها

"If you name your child Muḥammad, accord respect to him and make room for him in your meetings, and don't call his actions ugly and undesirable."[3]

Anas b. Mālik narrates from the Prophet ﷺ, who said:

تُسَمّون أولادَكم محمّداً ثمّ تَلعنونَهم

"How do you name your children Muḥammad and then curse them?!"[4]

Explanation

It is as if the Prophet of Islām ﷺ is amazed by the conduct some Muslims who call their children Muḥammad, but do not respect the sanctity of this name and curse and abuse them, while it is not

---

[1] *Majmū'ah Warrām*, p. 26.
[2] *Wasā'il al-Shī'ah*, vol. 15, p. 127.
[3] *Wasā'il al-Shī'ah*, vol. 15, p. 127; *Kanz al-'Ummāl*, vol. 16, p. 418.
[4] *Kanz al-'Ummāl*, vol. 16, p. 418.

appropriate for them to behave in this way with the name of the Messenger of Allāh ﷺ.

Abū Rāfi'says that I heard the Prophet ﷺ say:

إِذَا سَمَّيْتُمْ مُحَمَّداً فَلَا تُقَبِّحُوهُ وَ لَا تُجَبِّهُوهُ وَ لَا تَضْرِبُوهُ بُورِكَ لِبَيْتٍ فِيهِ مُحَمَّدٌ وَ مَجْلِسٍ فِيهِ مُحَمَّدٌ وَ رِفْقَةٍ فِيهَا مُحَمَّد

"If you name your child Muḥammad, do not demean his actions, do not reject his requests, and do not beat him. Blessed be the house in which there is someone named Muḥammad, and gatherings in which is someone named Muḥammad."[1]

Isḥāq b. 'Ammār says: I went to see Imām Ṣādiq ؑ and informed him that Allāh ﷻ has given me a son, he said:

أَلاَ سَمَّيْتَهُ مُحَمَّداً قَالَ قُلْتُ قَدْ فَعَلْتُ قَالَ فَلاَ تَضْرِبْ مُحَمَّداً وَ لاَ تَشْتِمْهُ جَعَلَهُ اَللَّهُ قُرَّةَ عَيْنٍ لَكَ فِي حَيَاتِكَ وَ خَلَفَ صِدْقٍ مِنْ بَعْدِكَ

"Did you name him Muḥammad?" "Yes," I replied. Imām ؑ said, "Do not beat Muḥammad and do not curse him, because as long as you are alive, Allāh ﷻ would make him the light of your eyes, and after your death he will be a righteous son and a righteous successor for you."[2]

Abū Rāfi' narrates that the Prophet ﷺ said:

إِذَا سَمَّيْتُمْ مُحَمَّداً فَلَا تُقَبِّحُوهُ وَ لَا تُجَبِّهُوهُ

"When you name your son Muḥammad, do not beat or deprive him."[3]

'Alī b. Hammām narrates through his chain of transmission from the Prophet ﷺ that he said:

---

[1] *Makārim al-'Akhlāq*, p. 25.
[2] *Wasā'il al-Shī'ah*, vol. 12, p. 19.
[3] *Kanz al-'Ummāl*, vol. 16, p. 218.

إِذَا سَمَّيْتُمُ الْوَلَدَ مُحَمَّداً فَأَكْرِمُوهُ وَ وَسِّعُوا لَهُ الْمَجَالِسَ وَ لَا تُقَبِّحُوا لَهُ وَجْهاً فَمَا مِنْ قَوْمٍ كَانَتْ لَهُمْ مَشُورَةٌ حَضَرَ مَعَهُمْ مَنِ اسْمُهُ أَحْمَدُ أَوْ مُحَمَّدٌ فَأَدْخَلُوهُ فِي مَشُورَتِهِمْ إِلَّا خِيرَ لَهُمْ وَ مَا مِنْ مَائِدَةٍ نُصِبَتْ وَ حَضَرَ عَلَيْهَا مَنِ اسْمُهُ أَحْمَدُ أَوْ مُحَمَّدٌ إِلَّا قُدِّسَ ذَلِكَ الْبَيْتُ فِي كُلِّ يَوْمٍ مَرَّتَيْنِ

"When you name your child Muḥammad, honour him, and hold ceremonies for him, and do not condemn his acts as ugly and detestable. Undoubtedly, if a group seeks counsel and there is a person named Muḥammad or Aḥmad among them and they make him a part of their consultation, it will be a good thing for them, and there is no such table where a person named Aḥmad or Muḥammad is present, but that house is sanctified twice a day."[1]

The name of 'Alī and the Infallible A'immah

Sulaymān Ja'farī says:

قَالَ سَمِعْتُ أَبَا الْحَسَنِ ع يَقُولُ لَا يَدْخُلُ الْفَقْرُ بَيْتاً فِيهِ اسْمُ مُحَمَّدٍ أَوْ أَحْمَدَ أَوْ عَلِيٍّ أَوِ الْحَسَنِ أَوِ الْحُسَيْنِ أَوْ جَعْفَرٍ أَوْ طَالِبٍ أَوْ عَبْدِ اللَّهِ أَوْ فَاطِمَةَ مِنَ النِّسَاءِ

I heard Abū al-Ḥasan say, "Poverty and destitution will never enter a house in which there is someone named Muḥammad or Aḥmad or 'Alī or Ḥasan or Ḥusain or Ja'far or Ṭālib or 'Abdullāh or Fāṭimah."[2]

'Abd al-Raḥmān b. Muḥammad 'Azar says:

اسْتَعْمَلَ مُعَاوِيَةُ مَرْوَانَ بْنَ الْحَكَمِ عَلَى الْمَدِينَةِ وَ أَمَرَهُ أَنْ يَفْرِضَ لِشَبَابِ قُرَيْشٍ فَفَرَضَ لَهُمْ فَقَالَ عَلِيُّ بْنُ الْحُسَيْنِ ع فَأَتَيْتُهُ فَقَالَ مَا اسْمُكَ فَقُلْتُ عَلِيُّ بْنُ الْحُسَيْنِ فَقَالَ مَا اسْمُ أَخِيكَ فَقُلْتُ عَلِيٌّ قَالَ عَلِيٌّ وَ عَلِيٌّ مَا يُرِيدُ أَبُوكَ أَنْ يَدَعَ أَحَداً مِنْ وُلْدِهِ

---

[1] *Mustadrak al-Wasā'il*, vol. 15, p. 130; Muḥammad Riḍā Ṭabasī, *Durar al-'Akhbār*, vol. 2, p. 103.
[2] *Wasā'il al-Shī'ah*, vol. 15, p. 129.

إِلَّا سَمَّاهُ عَلِيّاً ثُمَّ فَرَضَ لِي فَرَجَعْتُ إِلَى أَبِي فَأَخْبَرْتُهُ فَقَالَ وَيْلِي عَلَى ابْنِ الزَّرْقَاءِ دَبَّاغَةِ الْأَدَمِ لَوْ وُلِدَ لِي مِائَةٌ لَأَحْبَبْتُ أَنْ لَا أُسَمِّيَ أَحَداً مِنْهُمْ إِلَّا عَلِيّاً

Mu'awiyāh appointed Marwān b. Ḥakam as the governor of Madinah and ordered him to pay a fixed amount of stipend to the youth of Quraysh. Imām Sajjād ﷺ says: I also went to him, and he asked my name: I said: 'Alī b. al-Ḥusain.

He said: What is your brother's name? I said: 'Alī. He said: 'Alī and 'Alī! It's like your father is planning to name all his sons 'Alī! Then he decided a sum for me, and I left him and went to my father's ﷺ presence and told him the story. My father ﷺ said: Woe upon son of Marwān, the yellow-eyed tanner! Even if I had a hundred children, I would not like to name them with any other name than 'Alī.[1]

Rab'ī b. 'Abdullāh says:

قِيلَ لِأَبِي عَبْدِ اللَّهِ ع جُعِلْتُ فِدَاكَ إِنَّا نُسَمِّي بِأَسْمَائِكُمْ وَ أَسْمَاءِ آبَائِكُمْ فَيَنْفَعُنَا ذَلِكَ فَقَالَ إِي وَ اللَّهِ وَ هَلِ الدِّينُ إِلَّا الْحُبُّ

It was said to Imām Ṣādiq ﷺ: May I be sacrificed on you; we will name our children after you and your forefathers. Would this action be beneficial for us? The Imām said: Yes, by Allāh! Is religion anything but love and hatred?!

قَالَ اللَّه

Almighty Allāh ﷻ says:

... إِن كُنتُمْ تُحِبُّونَ ٱللَّهَ فَٱتَّبِعُونِى يُحْبِبْكُمُ ٱللَّهُ وَيَغْفِرْ لَكُمْ ذُنُوبَكُمْ...

'...*If you love Allāh, then follow me; Allāh will love you and forgive you your sins, and Allāh is all-forgiving, all-merciful...*'[2][3]

---

[1] *Wasā'il al-Shī'ah*, p. 128.
[2] Sūrah Āle-'Imrān 3:31.
[3] *Mustadrak al-Wasā'il*, Vol. 15, p. 129.

Names of the prophets

The Prophet ﷺ said:

$$\text{إِذَا كَانَ اسْمُ بَعْضِ أَهْلِ الْبَيْتِ اسْمَ نَبِيٍّ لَمْ تَنْزِلِ الْبَرَكَةُ فِيهِم}$$

"If any member of a family is named after a Prophet ﷺ, there will always be blessings among them."[1]

Aṣbagh b. Nubatah narrated on the authority of Imām ʿAlī ؑ from the Messenger of Allāh ﷺ as follows:

$$\text{مَا مِنْ أَهْلِ بَيْتٍ فِيهِمْ اسْمُ نَبِيٍّ إِلَّا بَعَثَ اللَّهُ (عَزَّ وَ جَلَّ) إِلَيْهِمْ مَلَكاً يُقَدِّسُهُمْ مِنْ صَلَاةِ الْغَدَاةِ إِلَى الْعِشَاء}$$

"There are no residents of any house that has someone with the name of a prophet among them, except that Allāh ﷻ sends an angel over them to sanctify them every morning and evening."[2]

Abū Wahab Jismī narrates from the Prophet ﷺ who said:

$$\text{تَسَمَّوْا بِأَسْمَاءِ الْأَنْبِيَاءِ ع وَ أَحَبُّ الْأَسْمَاءِ إِلَى اللَّهِ عَبْدُ اللَّهِ وَ عَبْدُ الرَّحْمَنِ وَ أَصْدَقُهَا حَارِثٌ وَ هَمَّامٌ وَ أَقْبَحُهَا حَرْبٌ وَ مُرَّةٌ}$$

"Choose the names of the prophets for yourself; the most liked names by Allāh ﷻ are: ʿAbdullāh and ʿAbd al-Raḥmān; and the ugliest of them are Ḥarb and Murrah."[3]

7. The best names for girls

Sakūnī says:

$$\text{دَخَلْتُ عَلَى أَبِي عَبْدِ اللَّهِ ع وَ أَنَا مَغْمُومٌ مَكْرُوبٌ فَقَالَ لِي يَا سَكُونِيُّ مَا غَمَّكَ فَقُلْتُ}$$

---

[1] *Mustadrak al-Wasāʾil*, Vol. 15, p. 129.
[2] *Wasāʾil al-Shīʿah*, vol. 157, p. 125.
[3] *Kanz al-ʿUmmāl*, vol. 16, p. 420.

لَهُ وُلِدَتْ لِي بِنْتٌ فَقَالَ لِي يَا سَكُونِيُّ ثِقْلُهَا عَلَى الْأَرْضِ وَ عَلَى اللَّهِ رِزْقُهَا تَعِيشُ فِي غَيْرِ أَجَلِكَ وَ تَأْكُلُ مِنْ غَيْرِ رِزْقِكَ فَسَرَّى وَ اللَّهِ عَنِّي فَقَالَ مَا سَمَّيْتَهَا فَقُلْتُ فَاطِمَةَ فَقَالَ آهِ آهِ ثُمَّ وَضَعَ يَدَهُ عَلَى جَبْهَتِهِ فَقَالَ قَالَ رَسُولُ اللَّهِ ص حَقُّ الْوَلَدِ عَلَى وَالِدِهِ إِذَا كَانَ ذَكَراً أَنْ يَسْتَفْرِهَ أُمَّهُ وَ يَسْتَحْسِنَ اسْمَهُ وَ يُعَلِّمَهُ كِتَابَ اللَّهِ عَزَّ وَ جَلَّ وَ يُطَهِّرَهُ وَ يُعَلِّمَهُ السِّبَاحَةَ وَ إِذَا كَانَتْ أُنْثَى أَنْ يَسْتَفْرِهَ أُمَّهَا وَ يَسْتَحْسِنَ اسْمَهَا وَ يُعَلِّمَهَا سُورَةَ النُّورِ وَ لَا يُعَلِّمَهَا سُورَةَ يُوسُفَ ع وَ لَا يُنْزِلَهَا الْغُرَفَ وَ يُعَجِّلَ سَرَاحَهَا إِلَى بَيْتِ زَوْجِهَا أَمَّا إِذَا سَمَّيْتَهَا فَاطِمَةَ فَلَا تَسُبَّهَا وَ لَا تَلْعَنْهَا وَ لَا تَضْرِبْهَا

I came to Imām Ṣādiq ؑ while I was sad and aggrieved. He said, "Sakūnī! Why are you distraught?" I said that a daughter is born to me.

The Imām said, "Sakūnī, her burden rests on the earth, her sustenance is upon Allāh ﷻ, her life is separate from yours, and the sustenance she gets is different from yours."

Sakūnī says: I swear to Allāh ﷻ! Sadness and sorrow left me. Then Imām ؑ asked, "What have you named her?" Fāṭimah, I replied, Imām ؑ said three times: "Ah, Ah, Ah," then he put his hand on his forehead...Then he said, "Now that you have named her Fāṭimah, don't curse her, don't insult her, and do not beat her."[1]

8. The names of kings and pharaohs

It is narrated from 'Umar that the brother of Umm Salmah, the Prophet's ﷺ wife, had a son, and they named him Walīd. When this was reported to the Prophet ﷺ, he said:

سمّيتموه باسمِ فراعنتِكم، غَيِّروا اسمَه، فَسمّوه عبدَالله

"You have given him the name of your pharaohs! Change his name. So they named him 'Abdullāh."[2]

It is narrated from Abū Hurairah that the Prophet ﷺ said:

---

[1] *Wasā'il al-Shī'ah*, vol. 15, p. 200.
[2] *Kanz al-'Ummāl*, vol. 16, p. 592.

سمّيتموه بأسامي فراعنتِكم، ليَكونَنّ في هذه الأ مّة رجل يقال له الوليد، وهو شرٌّ على هذه الأمّة من فرعون على قومِه

"You named him with the name of your pharaoh. Know that there will be a man in this nation called Walīd, whose harm and evil will be greater on this nation than Pharaoh on his own people.[1]

9. Shaytān is elated when children are named after the enemies of Ahl al-Bayt ﷺ

Jābir narrates from Imām Bāqir ﵇ that he asked a young child:

مَا اسْمُكَ قَالَ مُحَمَّدٌ قَالَ فَبِمَا تُكَنَّى قَالَ بِعَلِيٍّ فَقَالَ لَهُ أَبُو جَعْفَرٍ ع لَقَدِ احْتَظَرْتَ مِنَ الشَّيْطَانِ احْتِظَاراً شَدِيداً إِنَ الشَّيْطَانَ إِذَا سَمِعَ مُنَادِياً يُنَادِي يَا مُحَمَّدُ يَا عَلِيُّ ذَابَ كَمَا يَذُوبُ الرَّصَاصُ حَتَّى إِذَا سَمِعَ مُنَادِياً يُنَادِي بِاسْمِ عَدُوٍّ مِنْ أَعْدَائِنَا اهْتَزَّ وَ اخْتَال

"What is your name?" He said: Muḥammad. Imām ﵇ said: "What is your surname?" 'Alī, he replied. Imām ﵇ said: "You have built a fortress by means of this surname: the devil cannot reach you (you have protected yourself from the harm of the Satan). Whenever the devil hears the name of Muḥammad or 'Alī being called, he melts like lead, and whenever he hears someone being called by the name of one of our enemies, he becomes happy and proud of himself."[2]

10. Refraining from the name of the haters

Muḥammad b. Sinān narrates from Yāqūb Sarrāj:

Once I came to Imām Ṣādiq ﵇ and found him standing over his child, Imām Mūsā ﵇, who was in the cradle; and he was talking to him softly for a long time. I sat down in a corner until Imām Ṣādiq ﵇ finished speaking to his child. Then I arose from my seat, and he (the Imām) said:

ادْنُ إِلَى مَوْلَاكَ فَسَلِّمْ عَلَيْهِ فَدَنَوْتُ فَسَلَّمْتُ عَلَيْهِ فَرَدَّ عَلَيَّ بِلِسَانٍ فَصِيحٍ ثُمَّ قَالَ لِي

[1] *Kanz al-'Ummāl*, vol. 16, p. 430.
[2] *Wasā'il al-Shī'ah*, vol. 15, p. 126.

اذْهَبْ فَغَيِّرِ اسْمَ ابْنَتِكَ الَّتِي سَمَّيْتَهَا أَمْسِ فَإِنَّهُ اسْمٌ يُبْغِضُهُ اللَّهُ وَ كَانَتْ وُلِدَتْ لِي بِنْتٌ فَسَمَّيْتُهَا بِالْحُمَيْرَاءِ فَقَالَ أَبُو عَبْدِ اللَّهِ انْتَهِ إِلَى أَمْرِهِ تُرْشَدْ

"Come to your master and greet him." So I approached the child and greeted him. Imām Kāẓim ﷺ responded to my greeting nicely and said, "Go and change the name you gave to your daughter yesterday, because Allāh ﷻ hates that name." Yāqūb says: A daughter had been born to me and I had named her Ḥumayrā'.

Then Imām Ṣādiq ﷺ said, "Do what you are commanded as it has guidance for you."[1]

11. The Prophet changed repulsive names

'Allāmah Ṭarīḥī, in the book of *Muntakhab* in a detailed traditional report about the Christian, who came to the Messenger of Allāh ﷺ on behalf of the King of Rome, narrates that the Prophet ﷺ asked him:

ما اسمک؟ فقلت: اسمی عبدُالشمس ، فقال لی: بدّل اسمک فإنّی سَمّیتُک عبدَالوهّابِ

"What is your name?" 'Abd al-Shams, he replied. He said, "Change your name, and I name you as 'Abd al-Wahhāb."[2]

Sahl b. Sa'd says:

كان رجل من أصحاب النبى اسمُه أسودَ، فسمّاه رسولُ الله أبيضَ

"One of the companions of the Prophet ﷺ was named Aswad (black), the Prophet ﷺ changed his name to Abyaḍ (white).[3]

'Utbah b. Salmī says:

---

[1] *Mustadrak al-Wasā'il*, vol. 15, p. 128; *Biḥār al-'Anwār*, vol. 48, pp. 19 and 48.
[2] *Mustadrak al-Wasā'il*, vol. 15, p. 128.
[3] *Kanz al-'Ummāl*, vol. 16, Pg. 596.

كان النبىّ اذا أتاه الرجلُ وله اسمٌ لايُحبّه حَوَّله

If someone came to the Prophet ﷺ and did not have a good name, the Prophet ﷺ would change his name.[1]

Ibn 'Umar said:

انّ كثيرَ بن الصامتِ كان اسمُه قليلاً، فسمّاه النبى كثيراً، و أنّ مطيعَ بنَ الأسود كان اسمُه العاصَ، فسمّاه النبى مطيعاً، و أنّ أمّ عاصمِ بنِ عمرَ كان اسمُها عاصية، فسمّاها رسولُ الله سهلة، وكان يتفاَّلُ بالاسمِ

Kathir b. Ṣāmit was previously called 'Qalīl' (scanty) and the Prophet ﷺ changed his name to 'Kathīr' (abundant) and similarly the Muṭī' b. Aswad was al-'Āṣ' (disobedient) and the Prophet ﷺ named him Muṭī' (obedient) and the mother of Āṣim b. 'Umar was Āṣiyah (sinful) and the Messenger of Allāh ﷺ named her Sihlah (tranquil). The Prophet ﷺ usually took the names of people as good omen.[2]

Explanation

Perhaps the meaning of the Prophet's ﷺ taking omen is that he interpreted people's names in a good sense and disallowed people's names from being used as a means of humiliating and mocking them.

Ḥusain b. 'Alwān narrates from Imām Ṣādiq ﷺ from his forefathers who said:

انّ رسول الله كان يغير الاسماء القبيحه فى الرّجال والبلدان

"The Messenger of Allāh ﷺ used to change the ugly names of people and towns."[3]

12. Reviving the name and remembrance of the martyrs

Ibn. Qadāḥ narrates from Imām Ṣādiq ﷺ who said:

---

[1] *Kanz al-'Ummāl*, vol. 16, Pg. 591.
[2] *Kanz al-'Ummāl*, vol. 16, p. 591.
[3] *Wasā'il al-Shī'ah*, vol. 15, p. 124.

جَاءَ رَجُلٌ إِلَى النَّبِيِّ ص فَقَالَ يَا رَسُولَ اللَّهِ وُلِدَ لِي غُلَامٌ فَمَا ذَا أُسَمِّيهِ قَالَ سَمِّهِ بِأَحَبِّ الْأَسْمَاءِ إِلَيَّ حَمْزَة

A man came to the Prophet ﷺ and said: O Messenger of Allāh ﷺ! A son is born to me, what should I name him? The Prophet ﷺ said, "Ḥamzah is the name I like most."[1]

13. Reviving the name and remembrance of the righteous

Amīr al Mu'minīn ؑ narrates from the Prophet ﷺ, who said:

مامن قوم يكون فيهم رجلٌ صالحٌ فيموتُ فيُضلَف مولود فيُسمّون باسمِه الاّ أخلفَهم الله تعالى بالحسنى

"There is no nation that has a righteous man among them, and he passes away leaving a child among them and they name the child on the name of the righteous man, except that Allāh ﷻ returns to them what they lost in goodness."[2]

Summary and analysis

Following conclusions can be derived from the above narrations:

1. Having a good name is one of the rights of a Muslim child, at which many Shī'ah and Sunnī traditions hint, and in some terms of the traditions, words such as 'Nahlah' (gift) and 'Birr' (goodness), a subtle point is hidden. According to the Aimmah, a good name, in addition to having a significant psychological effect on the child's personality, is a good and lasting gift and kindness for him and the society.

2. The tradition of the A'immah ؑ is followed in such a way that when a child is born, if it is a boy, they first name him Muḥammad, and after seven days, if they want, they choose another name for him, otherwise, they continue with it.

---

[1] *Wasā'il al-Shī'ah*, p. 129; *Kanz al-'Ummāl*, vol. 16, p. 423.

[2] *Kanz al-'Ummāl*, Vol. 16, p. 419.

Perhaps this practice has been promoted by the A'immah ﷺ because with the blessing of Muḥammad's ﷺ name, from the very first moments of birth, Allāh ﷻ favours the parents, children and the family, and increases goodness and blessings of that home. It removes material and spiritual poverty.

3. One should choose the names of Prophets ﷺ, A'immah ﷺ, genuine leaders and names that are a sign of Allāh's ﷻ greatness, piety and servitude for their children, and avoid the names of pharaohs, oppressive kings, and those who promote false expressions and bring joy to Satan and Allāh's ﷻ enemies.

4. The names of the Holy Prophet ﷺ, 'Alī and Fāṭimah ﷺ have special effect that influences this world and the Hereafter. Therefore, the children named Muḥammad should not be insulted and disrespected. Of course, this does not mean that other children are disrespected or beaten, but this is an extraordinary respect for the holy names of the Holy Prophet ﷺ, 'Alī and Fāṭimah ﷺ.

Similarly, if we read in the traditions that if there was a person named Muḥammad, make him a party to your consultation. It does not mean that you should not consult with other people or children whose name is not Muḥammad, but it only shows that the holy name of Muḥammad ﷺ has a special sanctity, and it is natural that it leaves its special effect on the children named Muḥammad. A person who is called by this name tries to have more wisdom, planning, commitment, and piety and to be adorned with qualities worthy of this name.

5. It is an honour for a nation to treasure the memory and name of the epic protagonists of the battlefields who are forever alive, and one of the ways to keep fresh the memory of those pure and sincere warriors is to name our children after them. We should keep the spirit of bravery alive in our children.

6. It is mentioned in some narrations that choosing a name is a sign of love and friendship, which means that when parents choose a name for their child, they express their interest towards the original owner of that name. Therefore, care in choosing a name is one of the primary responsibilities of parents and one of their favourite ideals.

Milk and its effect on the child's personality

One of the points that mothers should observe is breastfeeding, despite the fact that some do not pay much attention to this crucial issue, however, Islam has attached great importance to it.

Often it so happens that the parents are good and pious in every respect, but their child deviates and when we investigate the root cause of his deviation, we find with great surprise that it is due to lack of the mother's attention to the issue of breastfeeding during the child's infancy. If he had received enough care, he would not have been like this; because during infancy, in addition to the physical structure of the child being strengthened, his mental structure is also developed and the behaviour, speech and food of the mother along with the milk have an effect on him. We refer to some of the narrations of the Holy Prophet ﷺ and the infallible A'immah ﷺ regarding the role of the mother in breastfeeding the child, as well as the importance of breast milk in the development and personality of the child and refraining to choose undesirable wet nurses.

A mother's reward for breastfeeding her child

Imām Ṣādiq ﷺ narrated from the Prophet ﷺ that he said:

أيّما امرأة دَفَعت من بيتِ. روجِها شيئاً من موضعٍ الى موضعٍ تُريد به صلاحاً، نَظرَ الله اليها، ومن نَظر الله اليه لم يُعذِّبه، فقالت أمّ سلمة: يا رسول الله؛ ذهب الرجال بكلّ خير، فأى شئى للنساءِ المساكينِ؟ فقال: بلى، اذا حَمَلت المرأة كانت بمنزلة الصائمِ القائمِ المجاهدِ بنفسه وماله وفى سبيل الله، فاذا وَضَعت كان لها من الأجر مالا يدرى أحد ماهو لعِظَمه، فاِ ذا أرضَعت كان لها بكلّ مصّة كعدل عتقٍ محرّرٍ من وُلد اِسماعيلَ، فاذا فرغت من رضاعِه ضرب ملک كريم على جنبِها وقال: استَأنفى العملَ فقد غَفرلکِ.

"Any woman who moves something in her husband's house to organize household affairs, Allāh ﷻ will cast a glance at her, and Allāh ﷻ never punishes anyone He glances at."

Umm Salamah said: O Messenger of Allāh ﷺ: Men have taken away all the good deeds, is there anything left for the poor women? The Prophet ﷺ said, "Yes, when a woman becomes pregnant, she is like a person who fasts all days and prays all night, who strives with her life and wealth in the way of Allāh ﷻ, and when she is pregnant, she has a reward that no one knows of its greatness, and when she breastfeeds her child; for every suckling of the child, she will receive a reward equal to freeing a slave from the descendants of Ismāʿīl ﷺ, and when she finishes breastfeeding her child, a noble angel will live on her side and say: Resume your actions, for Allāh ﷻ has forgiven you."[1]

In another narration, the Prophet ﷺ said to Ḥawla' Aṭārah:

فاِ ذا وَضَت حملَها وأَخذَت فى رضاعه فما يَمصّ الولدُ مصّة من لبن أُمّه الاّ كان بين يديها نوراً ساطعاً يومَ القيامة يَعجب من رآها من الأوّلين والآخرين، و كُتِبت صائمة قائمة...فاِ ذا فَطمَت ولدَها، قال الحقّ جلّ ذكرُه: يا أيتها المرأة: قد غفرتُ لكِ ما تَقدَّم من الذنوبِ ، فاستأنفى العَمَلَ

"After giving birth, when the mother starts breastfeeding the child, for every time he sucks the mother's milk, a bright light will appear in front of her on the Judgment Day, and everyone from the past and the future that sees it will be amazed and in her record of deeds she would be included among those who fast during the day and pray all night...So after she weans her child, Almighty Allāh ﷻ says to her: O woman! Know that I have forgiven all your sins, so you may continue your actions."[2]

The best milk

The Prophet ﷺ said:

---

[1] *Wasā'il al-Shīʿah*, vol. 15, p. 175.

[2] *Mustadrak al-Wasā'il*, vol. 15, p. 156.

$$\text{لَيْسَ لِلصَّبِيِّ خَيْرٌ مِنْ لَبَنِ أُمِّه}$$

"No milk is better for a child than its mother's milk."[1]

Imām Ṣādiq quotes from Amīr al Mu'minīn that he said:

$$\text{مَا مِنْ لَبَنٍ رَضَعَ بِهِ الصَّبِيُّ أَعْظَمَ بَرَكَةً عَلَيْهِ مِنْ لَبَنِ أُمِّه}$$

"No milk is more blessed to feed a child than its mother's milk."[2]

Choosing a wet nurse

It is preferable for the mother not to give the child except from her own milk, and considering the future of her child, she does this herself. But sometimes, if for some reason - a mother cannot breastfeed - either she resorts to powdered milk or a wet nurse. If a wet nurse is chosen to breastfeed the child, they should try to use chaste ladies or women of faith and piety, even though the compensation for breastfeeding them is more than others. If such a woman is not found, as far as possible, try to avoid some types of women to breastfeed the child, which will leave bad and unfavourable effects.

Although it is necessary to observe these issues in powdered milk as well, and we do not encourage and recommend mothers to use powdered milk, especially if the powdered milk comes from non-Islamic countries.

The first category: foolish women

'Alī narrates from the Prophet who said:

$$\text{إِيَّاكُمْ أَنْ تَسْتَرْضِعُوا الْحَمْقَاءَ فَإِنَّ اللَّبَنَ يُنْشِئُهُ عَلَيْه}$$

"Do not use a foolish woman to nurse your children, because milk is the basis of the child's growth and upbringing."[3]

---

[1] *Mustadrak al-Wasā'il*, vol. 15, p. 1567, quoted from *Ṣaḥīfah al-Riḍā*, p. 42.
[2] *Wasā'il al-Shī'ah*, vol. 15, p. 175.
[3] *Mustadrak al-Wasā'il*, vol. 15, p. 162.

The second and third category: unchaste and insane women

The Messenger of Allāh ﷺ said:

تَوقُّوا أولادَكم لبنَ البغيّة والمجنونة؛ فانّ اللبن يَعدى

"Avoid the milk of wanton and crazy women for your children, because milk leaves its mark."[1]

Fourth category: Nāṣibī females (enemies of Ahl al-Bayt ؑ)

Imām Ṣādiq ؑ said:

رَضَاعُ الْيَهُودِيَّةِ وَ النَّصْرَانِيَّةِ أَحَبُّ إِلَيَّ مِنْ رَضَاعِ النَّاصِبِيَّةِ فَاحْذَرُوا النَّاصِبِيَّةَ أَنْ تُظَائِرُوهُمْ

"The milk of a Jewish and Christian woman is better in my view than the milk of a Nāṣibī woman, so don't choose a Nāṣibī woman as wet nurse."[2]

Negative effects of impure milk

They asked the late noble martyr Ḥāj Shaykh Faḍlullāḥ Nūrī: Why one of your sons has become so evil from the aspect of the verse:

... يُخْرِجُ ٱلْحَىَّ مِنَ ٱلْمَيِّتِ...

"...He brings forth the living from the dead..."[3]

He said: You all have not seen, and you will not see what I have seen from him and which I can see. This child will be my killer and the one who stands at my feet to rejoice and cheer. They inquired: How did he get these characteristics? He replied: The milk he consumed was

---

[1] *Durar al-Akhbār*, vol. 2, p. 105.
[2] *Mustadrak al-Wasā'il*, vol. 15, p. 162.
[3] Sūrah al-'An'ām 6:95.

impure and evil, and the milk that reared him was unclean and polluted.

They said: Tell us his story. He said: When I was in Samarra, studying under the great teacher, Mīrzā Shirāzī, Allāh ﷻ granted me this boy. His mother was without milk, so we had to hire a wet nurse for him. We were compelled to hire a wet nurse for him for about two years. Later, it was found out that the woman was Nāṣibī and from the Khawārij and she fed him unclean milk for two years. Impurity and unlawful have their effect, even if we were in dark about it.[1]

---

[1] *Mardān al-'Ilm Dar Maydān al-'Āmāl*, vol. 1, p. 411, *Durar al-Akhbār*, Vol. 2, p. 106.

Part Two

Father and child relationship

Father and child relationship

1. Joy at the birth of a female

The false customs and traditions of *Jāhiliyyah* had not completely disappeared among the Muslims of early Islam, and even though some of them had become Muslims, the sediments of *Jāhiliyyah* thoughts and customs still remained in their minds. They used to frown when they heard about the birth of a girl and were very angry that the Prophet ﷺ placed a girl on his knee and treated her with kindness.

The Holy Qur'ān removed the veil from the thoughts and beliefs of *Jāhiliyyah*, although in *Jāhiliyyah* girls were slaughtered alive and they were ready to accept any kind of disgrace, but the disgrace of having a daughter was considered a disaster that no one was willing to accept. When it was reported that he had a daughter, his face would turn black with anger.

وَإِذَا بُشِّرَ أَحَدُهُم بِٱلْأُنثَىٰ ظَلَّ وَجْهُهُۥ مُسْوَدًّا وَهُوَ كَظِيمٌ ﴿٥٨﴾

"When one of them is brought the news of a female [newborn], his face becomes darkened, and he chokes with suppressed agony."[1]

These traces of the ignorant culture were still present in the thoughts and minds of the people, and the Prophet ﷺ stood against them and fought to remove them.

Once they gave the good news to the Messenger of Allāh ﷺ that a girl was born to him. At that time, the Prophet ﷺ looked at the faces of the companions and all their faces were drawn. The Prophet ﷺ said:

"What's wrong with you? She is a blossom with a pleasant fragrance, and her sustenance would be provided by Allāh ﷻ."[2]

This pure Muḥammadan morality should be lesson for all the parents of the Islamic society. They should love their daughters, and be affectionate to them, lest the rotten thoughts of *Jāhiliyyah*

[1] Sūrah al-Naḥl 16:58.
[2] *Makārim al-'Akhlāq*, p. 219.

contaminate them and they become depressed and sad for having daughters and daughters of daughters.

The retort of Imām Ṣādiq

The daughters of today are the mothers of tomorrow, and noble and righteous persons and creators of human culture. Under the shade of training and blessings of chaste and wise mothers, they develop and reach high degrees of evolution. This should tell you about the fateful role of girls in the future.

Once a man's wife gave birth to a girl, Imām Ṣādiq saw that the man was very angry and disappointed. He said, "What do you think? If Allāh sends a revelation to you and says: I will choose for you, or you choose for yourself; what would you say?"

He said, "I will say: Allāh, I am satisfied with whatever you choose for me."

He said, "Allāh has chosen this child girl for you."

Then he said, "The child who was killed by that learned man while traveling with Prophet Mūsā, whose story is mentioned in the Holy Qur'ān:

فَأَرَدْنَآ أَن يُبْدِلَهُمَا رَبُّهُمَا خَيْرًا مِّنْهُ زَكَوٰةً وَأَقْرَبَ رُحْمًا ﴿٨١﴾

"So We desired that their Lord should give them in exchange one better than him in respect of purity and closer in mercy."[1]

Instead of that boy, Allāh gave them a girl who gave birth to seventy Prophets.[2]"

To some extent these two events show the sensitivity of the people of that day on having daughters, but what caused them to give up those superstitions was the encouragement of Prophet and the honouring of daughters and exalting the status of women by the *Ahl al-Bayt*.

Numerous narrations have reached us in this regard, which the late author of *Wasā'il al-Shī'ah* has divided into several categories, some of which we mention here:

---

[1] Sūrah al-Kahf 18:81

[2] *'Udat al-Dā'ī*, Pg. 80.

Pleasing the daughters

The Prophet ﷺ said:

مَنْ دَخَلَ السُّوقَ فَاشْتَرَى تُحْفَةً فَحَمَلَهَا إِلَى عِيَالِهِ كَانَ كَحَامِلِ صَدَقَةٍ إِلَى قَوْمٍ مَحَاوِيجَ وَ لْيَبْدَأْ بِالْإِنَاثِ قَبْلَ الذُّكُورِ فَإِنَّهُ مَنْ فَرَّحَ ابْنَتَهُ فَكَأَنَّمَا أَعْتَقَ رَقَبَةً مِنْ وُلْدِ إِسْمَاعِيلَ وَ مَنْ أَقَرَّ عَيْنَ ابْنٍ فَكَأَنَّمَا بَكَى مِنْ خَشْيَةِ اللَّهِ وَ مَنْ بَكَى مِنْ خَشْيَةِ اللَّهِ أَدْخَلَهُ اللَّهُ جَنَّاتِ النَّعِيمِ

"Anyone who goes to the market and buys a gift for his family is like a person who distributes alms among needy people and if he wants to hand out what he took home he should start with the daughters, because whoever makes his daughter happy is like one who has freed a slave from the descendants of Ismāʿīl ؑ, and whoever makes a child happy, is like one crying out of fear of Allāh ﷻ, and whoever sheds tears out of fear of Allāh ﷻ, Allāh ﷻ will admit him into His bountiful gardens."[1]

Rewards for kindness to the daughters

It is narrated from the Noble Prophet of Islam ﷺ that he said:

مَنْ كَانَ لَهُ أُخْتَانِ أَوْ بِنْتَانِ فَأَحْسَنَ إِلَيْهِمَا كُنْتُ أَنَا وَ هُوَ فِي الْجَنَّةِ كَهَاتَيْنِ وَ أَشَارَ بِإِصْبَعَيْهِ السَّبَّابَةِ وَ الْوُسْطَى

"Whoever has two sisters and two daughters and does a good turn to them, I and he would be together in heaven like these two." And he joined his index and middle fingers.[2]

Raising a daughter is a shield against the flames of the fire of Hell

Ibn. Masʿūd narrates from the Prophet ﷺ, who said:

من كانت له ابنة فأدّبها وأحسن أدَبها، وَ عَلَّمها فأحسنَ تعليمَها. فأوسَع عليها من

---

[1] *Makārim al-'Akhlāq*, p. 221.
[2] *Mustadrak al-Wasā'il*, vol. 15, p. 118, *Kanz al-'Ummāl*, vol. 16, p. 448.

نِعَم الله التى أَسبغَ عليه، كانت له منعة ستراً من النار

"Whoever has a daughter, and he trains and educates her in the best way and confers upon her the blessings that Allāh ﷻ has bestowed on him, he has provided for himself a shield against the fire of Hell."[1]

Respecting the daughters

Ibn. 'Abbās narrates that the Prophet ﷺ said:

من كانت له أنثى فلم يُؤذها ولم يُهِنْها ولم يُؤثِر ولدَه عليها أدخَلَه الله الجنة

"Allāh ﷻ will admit into Paradise whoever that has a daughter and who does not harm and disrespect her and does not prefer his son over her."[2]

Wishing for the death of the female children

Imām Ṣādiq ؑ said:

مَنْ تَمَنّى مَوْتَهُنَّ حُرِمَ أَجْرَهُنَّ وَ لَقِيَ اللَّهَ عَاصِيا

"Whoever wishes for the death of his daughters will be deprived of the reward of having daughters and will meet Allāh ﷻ while he is a sinner."[3]

2. Love for the child

The duty of the parents is not only to feed, clothe and take care of the child, but beyond that it is to water the fields of their hearts with the life-giving water of love and affection.

---

[1] *Kanz al-'Ummāl*, vol. 16, p. 452.
[2] *Kanz al-'Ummāl*, vol. 16, p. 447; *Kanz al-'Ummāl*, vol. 1, p. 234; *Mustadrak al-Wasā'il*, vol. 15, p. 118.
[3] *'Udat al-Dā'ī*, p. 80.

Love and affection are the natural desires of a child because he needs a warm and reassuring centre in which his talents can flourish and find a well-developed personality and get to know the world full of love, affection, and confidence. It gives courage and self-confidence and makes his spirit strong against problems. The elixir of love is a medicine for many mental and even physical ailments of a child. He becomes calm and cheerful with love and the bud of his heart blossoms. Lack of love is the basis of many mental and physical diseases of children such as anorexia, insomnia, bedwetting, unnecessary imitations, unreasonable behaviours, disturbed dreams, depression, anger, and violence, to name a few.

Negative effects of lack or excess in love

The lack of love, especially at the age of preparation, provides the ground for anxiety, confusion, and deviation of the child.

Children who feel less loved by their parents seek refuge in anyone to make up for this deficit.

Nervousness and restlessness should be looked for in lack of love, which creates an inferiority complex in one's being.

The secret of the deviation of many girls and boys lies in this issue. For example, a girl who is full of family love, in the environment of the society, she will never be influenced by the infatuation of the lustful youth and will not go out of the boundaries of chastity and purity and will not step on the path of sin.

It should be noted that affection and love should not go to extremes, because excessive love also has irreparable loss, such as weak sense of responsibility in the child, reduction of intellectual development, spoiling, violation of the rights of others, selfishness in everything and so on...[1]

[1] 'Alī Qā'imī, *Naqs-i-Mādar dar Tarbiyat*, pp. 91-95; Muḥammad Taqī Falsafī, *Kūdak*, vol. 1, p. 265 (Summary).

Expression of love

Love must be expressed from the heart through the tongue and actions so that the child may perceive it with all his or her being. It is possible for the parents to love their child in their hearts, without expressing it. Such love does not have much effect, on the contrary sometimes it has a negative effect, and the child would not feel the love and affection of the parents, and as a result, thinks that he is all alone and that he is not the object of parental attention. Therefore, he develops contemptuous opinions about himself. It is for this reason parents should show their love in various ways.

Now let us examine some traditions of *Ahl al-Bayt* ﷺ about compassion for children.

1. The best action

Imām Ṣādiq ؑ said:

يَا رَبِّ أَيُّ الْأَعْمَالِ أَفْضَلُ عِنْدَكَ فَقَالَ حُبُّ الْأَطْفَالِ فَإِنِّي فَطَرْتُهُمْ عَلَى تَوْحِيدِي فَإِنْ أَمَتُّهُمْ أَدْخَلْتُهُمْ بِرَحْمَتِي جَنَّتِي

"Mūsā ؑ asked: O Lord ﷻ, which deeds are best in your view? He replied: Love for children, because I have created their nature based on monotheism, and if they die, I will bring them into heaven with my mercy."[1]

2. Allāh's ﷻ mercy in loving a child

Imām Ṣādiq ؑ said:

إِنَّ اللَّهَ لَيَرْحَمُ الرَّجُلَ لِشِدَّةِ حُبِّهِ لِوَلَدِهِ

---

[1] Shaykh al-Ḥurr al-ʿĀmilī, *al-Jawāhir as-Saniyyah*, p. 71; *Mustadrak al-Wasā'il*, vol. 15, p. 114.

"Allāh, the Mighty, the Sublime has mercy on a person because of the intensity of his love for his child."[1]

3. Expression of love

It is not enough to just love a child, but the educational effects of this friendship will appear when the affection of the heart is transformed into affection, love and sincerity in words and deeds, so express your love and say to them: "I love you" or express it practically. Conduct in such a way that your child feels and understands this love with all his heart. Here we hint at three examples of good behaviour in the lives of three A'immah ؑ :

A) The expression of the love of Amīr al Mu'minīn ؑ for Zaynab and 'Abbās ؑ

It is mentioned in traditions:

قيل : لمّا كان العباس وزينب-ولدى عليّ-صغيرين قال عليّ للعباس: قل: واحد
فقال: واحد، فقال: قل :اثنان، قال: أستَحيي أن أقول باللسان- الذى قلت واحد-
اثنان، فقبّل:على عينيه، ثم التفتَ الى زينب- وكانت على يساره والعباس على
يمينه- فقالت: يا ابتاه؛ أتحبّنا؟ قال: نعم يا بنى، أولادُنا أكبادُنا، فقالت: يا أبتاه؛
حبّان لا يجتمعان فى قلب المومن: حبُّ الله و حبُّ الأولاد، و ان كان لا بدّلنا،
فالشفقة لنا و الحبّ لله خالصاً،فازداد عليّ بهما حبّاً

When 'Abbās and Zaynab ؑ - the two children of 'Alī ؑ - were young, once 'Alī ؑ said to 'Abbās ؑ: My son! Say: 'one'. 'Abbās ؑ said: One. Imām ؑ said: Say: 'two'. 'Abbās ؑ said: I am ashamed to say two with the tongue with which I said 'one'. Imām was very pleased with his son's intelligence and perception. He kissed his child's eyes. Then he looked at Zaynab al-Kubra ؑ, who was on his left. Zaynab ؑ said: Father dear, do you love us? "Yes, my daughter," the Imām replied, "Our children are dearest to us."

---

[1] *Thawāb al-'Āmāl*, Pg. 182; *Wasā'il al-Shī'ah*, vol. 15, p. 201; *'Udat al-Dā'ī*, p. 78, *Makārim al-'Akhlāq*, p. 219.

Zaynab ﷺ said: Father dear, two kinds of loves: 'love of Allāh ﷻ' and 'love of children' cannot be gathered in the heart of a believer. 'Alī ﷺ said: "My dear child, I love you because it is Allāh's ﷻ command to love one's children. In loving you, I love Allāh ﷻ." This increased 'Alī's ﷺ love and affection for the two children.[1]

B) The love of Imām Ṣādiq ﷺ for his son

Muḥammad b. Mas'ada Baṣrī says:

كان لجعفر بنِ محمّد ابنٌ يحبّه حبّاً شديداً. فقيل: مابلغ من حبّک له؟ قال: لی ابناً آخر، فینشر له فی حبّی

Imām Ṣādiq ﷺ had a son whom he loved very much; he was asked: How much do you love him?

He said, "My love for him is so great that I don't want to have another son to whom my affection reaches."[2]

C) The love of the seventh Imām ﷺ for Imām Riḍā ﷺ

Mufaḍḍal b. 'Umar says:

دخلتُ علی أبی الحسن موسی بن جعفر علیه السلام وعلیّ ابنُه فی حجره، وهو یُقبّله و یَمصّ لسانَه ویَضَعه علی عاتِقه و یَضمّه الیه ویقول: بأبی أنت ما أطیب ریحک وأطهرخلقک وأبینَ فضلک

I came to Imām Mūsā Kāẓim ﷺ and saw that His Eminence ﷺ had seated his son, 'Alī (b. Mūsā al-Riḍā) ﷺ on his lap and was kissing him, sometimes putting him on his shoulder and sometimes hugging him and saying, "May my father be sacrificed for you! What a pleasant smell you have, and what pure morals, and how clear and obvious is your grace and knowledge."[3]

---

[1] *Mustadrak al-Wasā'il*, vol. 15, p. 215.
[2] *Kanz al-'Ummāl*, vol. 1, p. 315.
[3] *Wasā'il al-Shī'ah*, vol. 18, p. 557.

Practice of the Prophet ﷺ

The Prophet's love for 'Alī ؑ

'Alī ؑ himself said:

وَ قَدْ عَلِمْتُمْ مَوْضِعِي مِنْ رَسُولِ اللَّهِ ص بِالْقَرَابَةِ الْقَرِيبَةِ وَ الْمَنْزِلَةِ الْخَصِيصَةِ وَضَعَنِي فِي [حَجْرِهِ] حِجْرِهِ وَ أَنَا وَلَدٌ [وَلِيدٌ] يَضُمُّنِي إِلَى صَدْرِهِ وَ يَكْنُفُنِي فِي فِرَاشِهِ وَ يُمِسُّنِي جَسَدَهُ وَ يُشِمُّنِي عَرْفَهُ وَ كَانَ يَمْضَغُ الشَّيْءَ ثُمَّ يُلْقِمُنِيهِ وَ مَا وَجَدَ لِي كَذْبَةً فِي قَوْلٍ وَ لَا خَطْلَةً فِي فِعْلٍ وَ لَقَدْ قَرَنَ اللَّهُ بِهِ ص مِنْ لَدُنْ أَنْ كَانَ فَطِيماً أَعْظَمَ مَلَكٍ مِنْ مَلَائِكَتِهِ يَسْلُكُ بِهِ طَرِيقَ الْمَكَارِمِ وَ مَحَاسِنَ أَخْلَاقِ الْعَالَمِ لَيْلَهُ وَ نَهَارَهُ وَ لَقَدْ كُنْتُ أَتَّبِعُهُ اتِّبَاعَ الْفَصِيلِ أَثَرَ أُمِّهِ يَرْفَعُ لِي فِي كُلِّ يَوْمٍ مِنْ أَخْلَاقِهِ عَلَماً وَ يَأْمُرُنِي بِالاقْتِدَاءِ بِهِ

"You know very well my kinship with the Prophet ﷺ and the special position I had with him.

I was a young child when the Messenger of Allāh ﷺ would put me on his lap, hold me in his arms, and hold me to his chest. Sometimes he would make me sleep in his bed, and out of love and affection rub his face on my face and make me smell his exquisite scent. For me, every day he raised a standard from his best dispositions and commanded me: I practically follow the morals of His Eminence ﷺ."[1]

The Prophet's ﷺ attachment to A'immah Ḥasan and Ḥusain ؑ

'Anas narrates:

أَنَّهُ دُعِيَ النَّبِيُ إِلَى صَلَاةٍ وَ الْحَسَنُ مُتَعَلِّقٌ بِهِ فَوَضَعَهُ النَّبِيُّ مُقَابِلَ جَنْبِهِ وَ صَلَّى فَلَمَّا سَجَدَ أَطَالَ السُّجُودَ فَرَفَعْتُ رَأْسِي مِنْ بَيْنِ الْقَوْمِ فَإِذَا الْحَسَنُ عَلَى كَتِفِ رَسُولِ اللَّهِ ص فَلَمَّا سَلَّمَ قَالَ لَهُ الْقَوْمُ يَا رَسُولَ اللَّهِ لَقَدْ سَجَدْتَ فِي صَلَاتِكَ هَذِهِ سَجْدَةً مَا كُنْتَ تَسْجُدُهَا كَأَنَّمَا يُوحَى إِلَيْكَ فَقَالَ لَمْ يُوحَ إِلَيَّ وَ لَكِنَّ ابْنِي كَانَ عَلَى كَتِفِي

[1] *Kūdak*, vol. 1, p. 277.

فَكَرِهْتُ أَنْ أُعَجِّلَهُ حَتَّى نَزَلَ

Once, the Prophet ﷺ was praying while Imām Ḥasan ؑ was in his arms. The Messenger of Allāh ﷺ placed Imām Ḥasan ؑ on the floor in front of him and started praying. When he prostrated, he prolonged the prostration.

The narrator says: I lifted my head from prostration - to see why the Prophet's prostration was prolonged - suddenly I saw Imām Ḥasan ؑ sitting beside the Prophet ﷺ.

When the Prophet ﷺ concluded the prayer, people said: O Messenger of Allāh ﷺ, you prostrated long in this prayer, which you have not done before, as if a revelation was revealed to you. The Prophet ﷺ said, "No revelation was revealed, but my son was sitting on me, and I did not want to hurt him, so I waited until he came down from my shoulder."[1]

'Abdullāh narrates from his father:

كان النبيّ صلى الله عليه وآله اذا صلّى وَثَبَ الحَسَنُ والحُسَينُ عَلى ظهرِه، فا ذا، أراد أن يَجْلِس قَالَ بِيَده هكذا على ظَهرِه حتّى لايَقَعانِ[2]

When the Prophet ﷺ prayed, Imām Ḥasan and Ḥusain ؑ would jump on his back, and when he wanted to lift his head from prostration and sit down, he would put his hand on their back so that they do not fall.[3]

Love for the maternal grandchildren

Abū Qatādah says:

---

[1] *Biḥār al-'Anwār*, vol. 43, p. 294; *Kitāb al-'Ayāl*, vol. 1, pp. 383 and 384; *Mustadrak al-Wasā'il*, vol. 1, p. 433 (with slight difference).

[2] *Kitāb al-'Ayāl*, vol. 1, p. 283; Ibn. 'Asākir, *al-Imām al-Ḥusain*, p. 85 (with slight difference).

[3] *Biḥār al-'Anwār*, vol. 43, pp. 283 and 295; *Kitāb al-'Ayāl*, vol. 1, pp. 379 and 401; *Wasā'il al-Shī'ah*, Vol. 2, p. 1008.

انّ النبى صلى وهو حامل أمامة بنت زينب، فاذا ركع وَضَعها، فا ذا قام رَفَعها

The Prophet ﷺ was praying while holding 'Amāmah bt. Zaynab in his arms, and when he wanted to bow, he would put her on the floor, and when he wanted to get up, he would hold her in his arms again.[1]

Jew's surprise at the Prophet's ﷺ affection towards children

Layth b. Sa'd says:

أَنَ النَّبِيَ ص كَانَ يُصَلِّي يَوْماً فِي فِئَةٍ وَ الْحُسَيْنُ صَغِيرٌ بِالْقُرْبِ مِنْهُ فَكَانَ النَّبِيُّ ص إِذَا سَجَدَ جَاءَ الْحُسَيْنُ فَرَكِبَ ظَهْرَهُ ثُمَّ حَرَّكَ رِجْلَيْهِ وَ قَالَ حَلْ حَلْ فَإِذَا أَرَادَ رَسُولُ اللَّهِ ص أَنْ يَرْفَعَ رَأْسَهُ أَخَذَهُ فَوَضَعَهُ إِلَى جَانِبِهِ فَإِذَا سَجَدَ عَادَ عَلَى ظَهْرِهِ وَ قَالَ حَلْ حَلْ فَلَمْ يَزَلْ يَفْعَلُ ذَلِكَ حَتَّى فَرَغَ النَّبِيُّ ص مِنْ صَلَاتِهِ فَقَالَ يَهُودِيٌّ يَا مُحَمَّدُ إِنَّكُمْ لَتَفْعَلُونَ بِالصِّبْيَانِ شَيْئاً مَا نَفْعَلُهُ نَحْنُ فَقَالَ النَّبِيُّ ص أَمَا لَوْ كُنْتُمْ تُؤْمِنُونَ بِاللَّهِ وَ رَسُولِهِ لَرَحِمْتُمُ الصِّبْيَانَ قَال فَإِنِّي أُومِنُ بِاللَّهِ وَ بِرَسُولِهِ فَأَسْلَمَ لَمَّا رَأَى كَرَمَهُ مَعَ عِظَمِ قَدْرِهِ

Once, the Prophet ﷺ was praying with the people. Imām Ḥusain ؑ, who was a young child, was sitting near him, and when the Prophet ﷺ prostrated, he sat on the Prophet's ﷺ back and shook his legs and said: "*Ḥal, Ḥal*! When the Prophet ﷺ wanted to lift his head from prostration, he lifted and placed him next to himself, but as soon as he prostrated, Imām Ḥusain ؑ once again mounted his back and repeated the words: *Ḥal Ḥal*, until the Prophet's ﷺ prayer was over. A Jew [who watched the Prophet's ﷺ kindness to Imām Ḥusain ؑ] remarked: O Muḥammad ﷺ! You treat your children in a way that we would never do! The Prophet ﷺ said, "If you also believed in Allāh ﷻ and His Messenger, you would undoubtedly be kind to your children." The Jew said: I hereby believe in Allāh ﷻ and His Messenger ﷺ; and he

---

[1] *Kitāb al-'Ayāl*, vol. 1, p. 391.

converted to Islam, because he observed how the Prophet ﷺ behaved nicely with children.[1]

Love for other children

1. Abū Sa'īd says:

جاءَ صَبِيٌّ- قَدْ سَمّاه- الى رَسُولِ اللهِ وَهُوَ ساجِدٌ فرَكِبَ عَلَى ظَهْرِهِ فَأَمَسَكَه بِيَدِه ثُمَّ قامَ وَهُوَ عَلى ظَهْرِهِ ثُمَّ رَكَعَ ثُمَّ أَرْسَلَه فَذَهَبَ

Once a child came to the Prophet ﷺ and while he was in prostration, he immediately sat on the Prophet's ﷺ back. The Holy Prophet ﷺ, out of kindness, held him and stood up in the same position, while the child was still on his back, then he bowed, and after that he released the child and the child left.[2]

2. It is narrated from Imām Ḥasan ؑ or Jābir b. 'Abdullāh that he said:

صَلَّيْتُ مَعَ رَسُولِ اللهِ الظُّهْرَ أو العَصْرَ فَلمّا سَلَّمَ قالَ لنا: عَلى أماكِنِكُمْ، قالَ: جَرَّة فيها حلوى فَجَعَلَ يأتي عَلى رَجُلٍ فيَلعقُه لعقه حتّى أتى عَلَيَّ- وأنَا غُلامٌ- فألعَقَني لعقة ثمّ قال: أزيدك؟ قلت: نعم، فألعقني أخرى لصغرى فَلم يَزَل كذلك حتّى أتى على آخرِ القومِ

I prayed the Noon or Afternoon Prayer in the company of the Messenger of Allāh ﷺ. As soon as he greeted us, he said: "Don't stay where you are," and said: "There is a jar with some sweetmeat." Then he told Jābir to distribute it among the worshipers and he gave to each a portion until it reached me. I was a child. His Eminence ﷺ gave me some; then asked: Do you want more? Yes, I replied. He gave me

---

[1] *Biḥār al-'Anwār*, vol. 43, p. 296.
[2] *Kitāb al-'Ayāl*, vol. 1, p. 380.

another portion because I was young, and he continued like that until everyone was given his share of the sweetmeat.[1]

3. 'Usamah b. Zayd says:

كان نبّى الله صلى الله عليه و آله ليَاخذنى ويُقعِدنى على فَخِده، ويُقعدِ الحسنَ على الاُ خْرى ثم يَضمّنا،ثم يقول: اللّهمّ،ارْحَمهما، فانّى أرحمهُما

Sometimes it so happened that the Prophet of Allāh ﷺ used to take me and make me sit on one of his lap, and Ḥasan ﵇ would sit on the other, then he would take us in his arms and say, "O Allāh ﷻ, have mercy on them, as I love both of them."[2]

4. 'Ā'ishah says:

قال لى رسول اللهُ اغسلى وجه أسامة، فنَظرالىّ وأنا أنقيه، فَضَربَ يدى ثم أخذه فغَسل وجهَه ثم قبَّلَه

The Prophet ﷺ said to me: Wash 'Usamah's face. Then he looked at me and I was cleaning 'Usamah. The Prophet ﷺ removed my hand aside and got up and washed 'Usamah's face and then kissed him.[3]

5. The late Ṭabarsī says:

وَ كَانَ رَسُولُ اللَّهِ ص يُؤْتَى بِالصَّبِيِّ الصَّغِيرِ لِيَدْعُوَ لَهُ بِالْبَرَكَةِ أَوْ يُسَمِّيَهُ فَيَأْخُذُهُ فَيَضَعُهُ فِي حَجْرِهِ تَكْرِمَةً لِأَهْلِهِ فَرُبَّمَا بَالَ الصَّبِيُّ عَلَيْهِ فَيَصِيحُ بَعْضُ مَنْ رَآهُ حِينَ يَبُولُ فَيَقُولُ ص لَا تُزْرِمُوا بِالصَّبِي فَيَدَعُهُ حَتَّى يَقْضِيَ بَوْلَهُ ثُمَّ يَفْرُغُ لَهُ مِنْ دُعَائِهِ أَوْ تَسْمِيَتِهِ وَ يَبْلُغُ سُرُورُ أَهْلِهِ فِيهِ وَ لَا يَرَوْنَ أَنَّهُ يَتَأَذَّى بِبَوْلِ صَبِيِّهِمْ فَإِذَا انْصَرَفُوا غَسَلَ ثَوْبَهُ بَعْدَهُ

---

[1] *Kitāb al-'Ayāl*, vol. 1, p. 403.
[2] *Kitāb al-'Ayāl*, vol. 1, p.398.
[3] *Kitāb al-'Ayāl*, vol. 1, p. 394.

Sometimes a child was brought to the Prophet ﷺ that he may pray for him or choose a name for him. To honour his parents, he would hold the child in his arms, and sometimes the child would urinate on him, and some of those who witnessed the incident shouted at the child, but the Holy Prophet ﷺ would say, 'Don't stop him,' and he would leave the child alone until he finished, then he would pray for him. He would choose a name for him and in this way make the child's parents happy and they would not feel that the Prophet ﷺ was upset with their child's urination. After they would leave, he would go and wash his clothes.[1]

6. Faiḍ al-Kāshānī writes:

One of the characteristics of the Prophet of Islam ﷺ was that whenever he returned from a trip and met the children of the people on the path, he would stop to show respect to them. The people would summon the children and lift them up and give to His Eminence ﷺ. The Holy Prophet ﷺ used to take some in his arms and place some on his shoulders and tell his companions, "Hug the children and place them on your shoulders."

The children were extremely happy at this delightful scene and erupted with joy and happiness. They would never forget these sweet memories. Often, they would gather and retell each other the story; and one of them would say out of respect and pride: The Prophet ﷺ lifted me in his arms and placed you on his shoulders.

Another said: The Prophet ﷺ ordered his companions to place you on his shoulders.[2]

7. Caressing the head of the martyr's child

When Ja'far Ṭayyār was martyred at the battlefield, the Messenger of Allāh ﷺ went to his house and said to Asmā' bt. 'Umays, Ja'far's wife: Bring Ja'far's children here. When they arrived, he embraced and kissed them. 'Abdullāh, son of Ja'far says: I remember well that once the Prophet ﷺ came to my mother and mentioned to her the news of

---

[1] *Makārim al-'Akhlāq*, p. 25.

[2] *Rabitah Dustī wa Muḥabbat*, pg. 171 quoting from *Muḥajjat al-Baiḍā*, vol. 3, p. 366.

my father's martyrdom. Then he passed his affectionate hand over my head.[1]

8. Prophet's ﷺ fatherly conduct with the child of Rafāʿh

It is mentioned in *Tafsīr Kashf al-Asrār Mībdī* that once the Prophet ﷺ was passing through the streets of Madinah with some of his companions. At one place some children were playing, and next to them was child dragging himself on the ground and crying.

The Holy Prophet ﷺ noticed that child and sat down beside him. Then he lifted him up and asked why he was crying. He said: I am the son of Rafāʿh Anṣārī. My father was martyred in Battle of ʿUhud. I had a sister who got married and my mother also got married and threw me out. Now, I am left alone and abandoned. The children ridicule me and do not play with me.

The Prophet ﷺ was very upset, and tears flowed from his eyes. He placed him on his knees and said: Don't be upset, from today I am your father and my daughter Fāṭimah is your sister. The child was happy. He rose up and shouted: Children! Don't tease me anymore because my father is better than yours. Then the Prophet ﷺ took him by the hand to the house of his daughter, Fāṭimah عليها السلام and said: Daughter, this child is our child and your brother, take care of him. Fāṭimah عليها السلام covered him with a clean garment, anointed his head with oil, and placed a bowl of dates before him and called out: "Ḥasan عليه السلام and Ḥusain عليه السلام; come and have your dinner together."

After the passing of the Prophet ﷺ, that boy used to throw dust on his head and bewail: "O my father, I became an orphan today," and all the people cried because of his wailing.[2]

Practice of Lady Zahrā عليها السلام

Lady Zahrā عليها السلام used to toss Imām Ḥasan عليه السلام up and down and play with him while reciting:

أشبِه أباک یا حسن   واخْلَع عن الحقِّ الرسَنَ

[1] *Kūdak...*, vol. 1, p. 274.
[2] Sayyid Mahdī Shams al-dīn, *Akhlāq Islāmī*, p.30.

وَاعبُدْ الهاً ذامنن ولاتُوالِ الاحَنِ

"Ḥasan dear, be like your father and bring the truth out of bondage and worship Allāh ﷻ who is full of grace and kindness and do not follow the malicious enemies."[1]

Kindness to children

Kissing the child

There are many ways to express love: the best of them are hugging, caressing, speaking gently and pleasantly, playing with children, and kissing them.

A child's pure heart is a shining mirror: the parents' showing love to the child, especially kissing him, brightens the child's soul. In other words, parental care guarantees child's mental health and emotional balance.

Perhaps the philosophy of Islam's strict orders to kiss children is also concealed in this important point.

Some ways of expressing love were mentioned in the above narrations, and some aspects of the life of the Infallibles ﵃ were also observed in this regard. Now, due to the importance of kissing children, we mention some narrations about it:

Kissing one's children is a virtue

Faḍl b. Abī Qurah narrates from Imām Ṣādiq ﵇ who narrates from the Messenger of Allāh ﷺ that he said:

مَنْ قَبَّلَ وَلَدَهُ كَتَبَ اللّٰهُ عَزَّ وَ جَلَّ لَهُ حَسَنَةً

"Allāh ﷻ records a good deed for whoever that kisses his child."[2]

Ibn 'Umar narrates from the Prophet ﷺ that he stated:

[1] *Manāqib Ibn. Shahr Āshūb*, vol. 3, p. 389.
[2] *Wasā'il al-Shī'ah*, vol. 15, pp. 194 and 202; *'Udat al-Dā'ī*, p. 79.

اَلقُبْلَة حَسَنَة وَ الْحَسَنَة عَشَرَة

"Kissing (a child) is a good deed and the reward for every good deed is tenfold."[1][2]

Spiritual Effects of kissing children

The Prophet ﷺ said:

قَبْلَةِ أَوْلَادِكُمْ فَإِنَّ لَكُمْ بِكُلِّ قُبْلَةٍ دَرَجَةً فِي الْجَنَّةِ مَا بَيْنَ كُلِّ دَرَجَةٍ خَمْسُمِائَةِ عَام

"Kiss your children, because every kiss has a rank in heaven and the distance between two ranks is 500 years."[3]

The Prophet's ﷺ love and affection for children was so great that it never remained concealed and sometimes while talking to people, he expressed his affection for his children and kissed them frequently.

'Anas b. Mālik says:

مار أيت أحداً كان أرحمَ بالعيال من رسول الله كان ابراهيم مسترضعاً له في عوالي المدينة وكان ظِئره قيناً، فكان يأتيه وأنّ البيت لَيُدخَّنُ فَيَأخُذُه فقبَّله

I have never seen anyone more kind to his family than the Prophet ﷺ. During the infancy of his son, Ibrāhīm, the Prophet ﷺ had hired a wet nurse for him from the suburbs of Madinah. Her house was full of soot due to her husband's blacksmithing job, but the Prophet ﷺ still visited that place to see his child and kiss him.[4]

Explanation

---

1 A reference to the verse "*Whoever brings virtue shall receive ten times its like...*" Sūrah al-An'ām 6:160.

2 *Kanz al-'Ummāl*, vol. 16, p. 445.

3 *Makārim al-'Akhlāq*, p. 220, *Wasā'il al-Shī'ah*, vol. 15, p. 203.

4 *Kitāb al-'Ayāl*, vol. 1, p. 338.

Suburbs of Madinah refer to the villages around Madinah. It is interesting that the Prophet ﷺ was so affectionate and loving towards his children that he would travel from afar and visit his child again and again and kiss him.

Ibn. ʿAbbās says:

كنتُ عندالنبى وعلى فخذِه الأيسر ابنُه ابراهيم، وعلى فَخذِه الأيمنِ الحسينُ بنُ علىّ وهو تارة يُقبّل هذا و تارة يُقبّل هذا

I was in the company of the Prophet ﷺ while his son Ibrāhīm was sitting on his left knee and Ḥusain b. ʿAlī ؑ on his right; sometimes he kissed this one and sometimes that one.[1]

Abū Hurairah says:

خَرَجَ عَلَيْنَا رَسُولُ اللَّهِ ص وَ مَعَهُ الْحَسَنُ وَ الْحُسَيْنُ هَذَا عَلَى عَاتِقِهِ وَ هَذَا عَلَى عَاتِقِهِ وَ هُوَ يَلْثِمُ هَذَا مَرَّةً وَ هَذَا مَرَّةً حَتَّى انْتَهَى إِلَيْنَا فَقَالَ لَهُ رَجُلٌ يَا رَسُولَ اللَّهِ إِنَّكَ لَتُحِبُّهُمَا فَقَالَ مَنْ أَحَبَّهُمَا فَقَدْ أَحَبَّنِي

Once, the Holy Prophet ﷺ came out to us with Ḥasan ؑ and Ḥusain ؑ perched on each of his shoulders, and he ﷺ kissed them one after the other until he reached us. One of the companions remarked: O Messenger of Allāh ﷺ, you love these two very much![2]

He said, "Whoever loves these two has definitely been affectionate to me."

A man who never kisses his children

Ḥasan b. ʿAlī b. Yūsuf Azdī narrates from a man from Imām Ṣādiq ؑ that a person came to the Prophet ﷺ and said:

---

[1] *Manāqib Ibn. Shahr Āshūb*, vol. 3, p. 234.
[2] *Biḥār al-ʾAnwār*, vol. 43, p. 281.

مَا قَبَّلْتُ صَبِيّاً قَطُّ فَلَمَّا وَلَّى قَالَ رَسُولُ اللَّهِ هَذَا رَجُلٌ عِنْدِي أَنَّهُ مِنْ أَهْلِ النَّار

O Messenger of Allāh ﷺ! So far, I haven't kissed any of my children. When he went away - the Prophet ﷺ, who was surprised by his cruelty and unkindness – said, "This fellow is from the people of Hell."[1]

Abū Hurairah says:

أبصر أقرعُ بنُ حابسٍ النبّى وهو يُقبّل حسيناً، فقال: انّ لى عشرة من الوَلَد ما قبّلتُ واحداً منهم، فقال النبى: انّه من لا يَرحَم لا يُرحَم

Once, Iqrā b. Ḥābis witnessed the Prophet ﷺ kiss Imām Ḥusain ؑ and said: I have ten children, and I have never kissed anyone of them. The Prophet ﷺ said, "Whoever is not affectionate, will not receive mercy."[2]

3. Playing with children

Another way to express parental love to the child is to provide appropriate toys and entertainment for the young one according to his or her age. Additionally, one should play with the child sometimes, or respond positively to the child's request to play with him, because participation of parents in the children's game, although it takes a little time, has very good effects, in addition to being very joyful and exciting for the children. The game will also be a source of development of their talents and refinement of their emotions. If the game is regular and healthy it develops the child's mind. That is why it is said that games develop the child's thinking process.

The respected Prophet of Islam ﷺ and *Ahl al-Bayt* ؑ while stressing and commanding this matter much, used to play with their children or at least supervise their games and encourage them.

---

[1] *Wasā'il al-Shī'ah*, vol. 15, p. 202.
[2] *Kitāb al-'Ayāl*, vol. 1, p. 340; *Wasā'il al-Shī'ah*, vol. 15, p. 203.

Likewise, Shaykh Ṣadūq narrates from the Prophet ﷺ in the book of *Man Lā Yaḥḍuru al-Faqīh* that he said:

مَنْ كَانَ عِنْدَهُ صَبِيٌّ فَلْيَتَصَابَ لَهُ

"Whoever has a child should treat him like a child."[1]

Ibn. Abī Najīḥ says:

كَانَ الْحَسَنُ وَ الْحُسَيْنُ يَرْكَبَانِ ظَهْرَ النَّبِيِّ ص وَ يَقُولَانِ حَلْ حَلْ وَ يَقُولُ نِعْمَ الْجَمَلُ جَمَلُكُمَا

Imām Ḥasan ؑ and Ḥusain ؑ used to mount the Prophet's ﷺ back and say: *Ḥal Ḥal!* While the Prophet ﷺ would remark: "You have a nice camel as your mount."[2]

'Alqamah has narrated from Abū Salamah that he said:

أَنَّ رَسُولَ اللَّهِ ص كَانَ يَدْلَعُ لِسَانَهُ لِلْحَسَنِ وَ الْحُسَيْنِ ع فَيَرَى الصَّبِيُّ لِسَانَهُ فَيَهَشُّ إِلَيْهِ فَقَالَ عُيَيْنَةُ بْنُ بَدْرٍ الْفَزَارِيُّ وَ اللَّهِ لَيَكُونُ لِيَ الِابْنُ رَجُلًا قَدْ خَرَجَ وَجْهُهُ وَ مَا قَبَّلْتُهُ قَطُّ فَقَالَ رَسُولُ اللَّهِ ص مَنْ لَمْ يَرْحَمْ لَا يُرْحَمْ

The Prophet ﷺ stuck out his tongue for Ḥasan ؑ and Ḥusain ؑ and as soon as the child's eyes fell on the Prophet's ﷺ tongue, they ran to him.

A man named 'Ubaynah b. Badr Fuzārī (who witnessed this sweet act) said out of surprise: I swear to Allāh ﷻ! My son has matured into a man and has grown facial hair, yet I have not kissed him even once.

The Prophet ﷺ, who was astounded by 'Ubaynah's hardheartedness, said, "Whoever does not show kindness would not be loved."[3]

---

[1] *Wasā'il al-Shī'ah*, vol. 15, p. 203.
[2] *Kitāb al-'Ayāl*, vol. 2, p. 797, *Biḥār al-'Anwār*, vol. 43, p. 285 (with slight difference).
[3] *Majmū'ah Warrām*, p. 80.

عَنْ يَعْلَى الْعَامِرِي : أَنَّهُ خَرَجَ مِنْ عِنْدِ رَسُولِ اللَّهِ ص إِلَى طَعَامٍ دُعِيَ إِلَيْهِ فَإِذَا هُوَ بِحُسَيْنٍ ع يَلْعَبُ مَعَ الصِّبْيَانِ فَاسْتَقْبَلَ النَّبِيُّ ص أَمَامَ الْقَوْمِ ثُمَّ بَسَطَ يَدَيْهِ فَطَفَرَ الصَّبِيُّ هَاهُنَا مَرَّةً وَ هَاهُنَا مَرَّةً وَ جَعَلَ رَسُولُ اللَّهِ يُضَاحِكُهُ حَتَّى أَخَذَهُ فَجَعَلَ إِحْدَى يَدَيْهِ تَحْتَ ذَقَنِهِ وَ الْأُخْرَى تَحْتَ قَفَاهُ وَ وَضَعَ فَاهُ عَلَى فِيهِ وَ قَبَّلَهُ

A man named Ya'lī al-'Āmirī left the gathering of the Holy Prophet ﷺ to go to the banquet he had been invited to. Suddenly he saw Ḥusain ؑ playing with the children. It didn't take long for the Messenger of Allāh ﷺ to leave the house with his companions. When the Prophet ﷺ noticed Ḥusain ؑ, he left his companions and went to his child and reached out to embrace him. The child ran away laughing, and the Prophet ﷺ also went after him laughing, and finally caught up with him. He placed one hand under his chin and the other behind his neck; then kissed him on his cheeks.¹

عَنْ عَلِيٍّ ع قَالَ: بَيْنَمَا الْحَسَنُ وَ الْحُسَيْنُ يَصْطَرِعَانِ عِنْدَ النَّبِيِّ ص فَقَالَ النَّبِيُّ ص هَيَّ يَا حَسَنُ فَقَالَتْ فَاطِمَةُ يَا رَسُولَ اللَّهِ تُعِينُ الْكَبِيرَ عَلَى الصَّغِيرِ فَقَالَ رَسُولُ اللَّهِ ص جَبْرَئِيلُ يَقُولُ هَيَّ يَا حُسَيْنُ وَ أَنَا أَقُولُ هَيَّ يَا حَسَنُ

It is narrated from Amīr al Mu'minīn 'Alī ؑ that he said, "Once Ḥasan ؑ and Ḥusain ؑ wrestled with each other in the presence of the Prophet ﷺ. The Prophet ﷺ was cheering and encouraging Imām Ḥasan ؑ and telling him to take hold of Imām Ḥusain ؑ. I said: Why do you cheer Ḥasan ؑ who is older? The Messenger of Allāh ﷺ said: I am cheering Ḥasan ؑ, because Jibra'īl ؑ is cheering Ḥusain ؑ, and he is telling Ḥusain ؑ to take hold of Ḥasan ؑ."²

---

[1] *Mustadrak al-Wasā'il*, vol. 15, p. 176; *Biḥār al-'Anwār*, vol. 43, p. 271.
[2] *Biḥār al-'Anwār*, vol. 43, pp. 263 and 291; Ibn 'Asākir, *al-Imām al-Ḥusain*, p. 80; *Manāqib*, vol. 3, p. 393.

4. Fulfilling the promise

Another Islamic commandment for parents is to fulfill the promises they make to their children. Because by not acting on these words, they humiliate their children's character and teach them to lie, and with their inaction, they discredit the statements they will issue in the future. Undoubtedly, this way of dealing with children is rejected in the traditions, and parents who make baseless promises to their children are condemned.

The Prophet ﷺ says:

أَحِبُّوا الصِّبْيَانَ وَ ارْحَمُوهُمْ فَإِذَا وَعَدْتُمُوهُمْ فَفُوا لَهُمْ فَإِنَّهُمْ لَا يَرَوْنَ إِلَّا أَنَّكُمْ تَرْزُقُونَهُمْ

"Love the children and be kind to them. If you promise them something, fulfill the promise, because they regard their sustenance to be in your hands."[1]

'Alī ؑ narrates from the Prophet ﷺ, who said:

اذا وعدأحدكم صَبِيَّه فليُجِز

"If any of you make a promise to your child, you must definitely fulfill it."[2]

Ḥārith 'Āwar narrates from 'Alī ؑ, who said:

لَا يَصْلُحُ مِنَ الْكَذِبِ جِدٌّ وَ لَا هَزْلٌ وَ لَا أَنْ يَعِدَ أَحَدُكُمْ صَبِيَّهُ ثُمَّ لَا يَفِيَ لَهُ إِنَّ الْكَذِبَ يَهْدِي إِلَى الْفُجُورِ وَ الْفُجُورَ يَهْدِي إِلَى النَّار

"It is not proper to lie, be it seriously or as a joke, and it is not proper for one of you to make a promise to his child and then not

[1] *Makārim al-'Akhlāq*, p. 219; *Wasā'il al-Shī'ah*, vol. 15, p. 201.
[2] *Mustadrak al-Wasā'il*, vol. 15, p. 170.

fulfill it. Lying leads to transgression and transgression leads to the fire of Hell."[1]

Imām Kāẓim ﷺ said:

إِذَا وَعَدْتُمُ الصِّغَارَ فَأَوْفُوا لَهُمْ فَإِنَّهُمْ يَرَوْنَ أَنَّكُمْ أَنْتُمُ الَّذِينَ تَرْزُقُونَهُمْ وَ إِنَّ اللَّهَ لَا يَغْضَبُ بِشَيْءٍ كَغَضَبِهِ لِلنِّسَاءِ وَ الصِّبْيَانِ

"If you make a promise to your children, you must fulfill it, because they think that their sustenance is in your hands. Indeed, Allāh ﷻ is not infuriated at anything except for the sake of women and children."[2]

Summary of these narrations

1. It is not necessary to promise anything to your child, but if you make a promise, you must fulfill it.

The negative effects of breaking a promise are the same for big or small promises, and the phrases saying: 'Then fulfill it' denote that it is obligatory to fulfill the promise.

2. Just as you do not expect Allāh ﷻ and even His servants to break their promises, your children also do not expect you not to break any promise you make to them.

3. In the traditions, not fulfilling promises is considered a violation of the child's rights, and since the child cannot defend his right, violating his right will provoke the wrath of Allāh ﷻ as Allāh ﷻ is the supporter of the deprived and the weak.

4. As a result of not fulfilling false promises, you open a door of falsity for your children, the first result of which is the emergence of the spirit of hypocrisy and lying in them. Because children learn more from their parents' actions than from their words, and in this way, they think that there is nothing wrong in lying and that it is not necessary to fulfill promises and agreements. Also, that there is no problem in making promises just to maintain appearances and show

---

[1] *Al-'Amālī, al-Ṣadūq*, p.376.

[2] *'Udat al-Dā'ī*, p. 75; *Wasā'il al-Shī'ah*, vol. 15, p. 202.

our care to others and with thousands of excuses and apologies you can continue to indefinitely defer the fulfillment of promises.

But without any doubt, this type of unsavoury behaviour will be the basis for various deviations in the children and distance them from purity and honesty.

5. Justice and equality between children

Another moral duty of parents is to observe justice and equality between children, and to never give priority to a son over a daughter or a son over other sons, or over other children. Do not make one of them the sole target of your love and endearment. If you kiss, you should kiss all the children. If you buy presents, you should buy for all of them.

It is obvious that the parents would not remain careless with the bitter fruits of this discrimination and the children's trust is taken away from them. In addition, the fire of jealousy, enmity, and malice is ignited by their own hands.

Nuʿmān b. Bashīr narrates from the Holy Prophet ﷺ, who said:

اتّقوا اللّه واعْدِلُوا بَيْنَ أَوْلَادِكُمْ كَمَا تُحِبُّونَ أَنْ يبرّوكم

"Fear Allāh ﷻ and treat your children with justice as you would like them to treat you well."[1]

Now, with the help of Allāh ﷻ, let us study the instructions and guidelines of the infallible leaders ؑ about this very important training issue:

ʿAyyāshī has narrated from Masʿadah from Imām Ṣādiq ؑ that he said, My father [Imām Bāqir ؑ] said:

وَ اللَّهِ إِنِّي لَأُصَانِعُ بَعْضَ وُلْدِي وَ أُجْلِسُهُ عَلَى فَخِذِي (وَ أُفْكِرُ لَهُ فِي الْمِلْحِ) وَ أُكْثِرُ

[1] *Kanz al-ʿUmmāl*, vol. 16, p. 445, *Makārim al-ʾAkhlāq*, p. 220 (with slight difference).

لَهُ الشُّكْرَ وَ إِنَّ الْحَقَّ لِغَيْرِهِ مِنْ وُلْدِي وَ لَكِنْ مَخَافَةً عَلَيْهِ مِنْهُ وَ مِنْ غَيْرِهِ لِئَلَّا يَصْنَعُوا بِهِ مَا فَعَلُوا بِيُوسُفَ إِخْوَتُهُ وَ مَا أَنْزَلَ اللَّهُ سُورَةَ يُوسُفَ- إِلَّا أَمْثَالاً لِكَيْ لَا يَحْسُدَ بَعْضُنَا بَعْضاً كَمَا حَسَدَ يُوسُفَ إِخْوَتُهُ وَ بَغَوْا عَلَيْهِ فَجَعَلَهَا حُجَّةً وَ رَحْمَةً عَلَى مَنْ تَوَلَّانَا وَ دَانَ بِحُبِّنَا (حُجَّةً عَلَى) أَعْدَائِنَا وَ مَنْ نَصَبَ لَنَا الْحَرْبَ

"I swear to Allāh ﷻ! Sometimes I am too gentle and tolerant with one of my children. I put him on my knees and play with him, and I praise and laud him; while I know that my other children also deserve. But I fear lest the story of Prophet Yūsuf ﷺ and his brothers may also happen to him. And in fact, Almighty Allāh did not reveal this Sūrah except as a lesson for us. Because some of us are jealous of others, just like Yūsuf's ﷺ brothers were jealous of him, and they oppressed him.

Allāh ﷻ made this story as a proof and divine mercy for our followers and devotees and proof against our open enemies."[1]

Justice between son and daughter

The Messenger of Allāh ﷺ was very sensitive about discriminating between boys and girls.

An example of this sensitivity is as follows:

عن الحسن قال: بينا رسولُ الله يُحدِّث أصحابَه اذ جاء صبّى حتّى انتهى الى أبيه فى ناحية القول، فمَسح رأسَه وأَقعدَه على فَخذِه اليمنى، قال: فلَبثَ قليلاًفجاء ابنة له حتّى انتهت اليه، فمَسح رأسها و أقعدَها فى الارض، فقال رسول الله :فهلّا على فخذك الأخرى، فحَملها على فخذه الأخرى فقال: الآنَ عدلتَ.

Once, the Prophet ﷺ had a warm conversation with his companions. A little boy arrived and headed to his father who was seated in a corner. His father passed his hand on his head and placed him on his right knee. After a while, the young daughter of that man

[1] *Wasā'il al-Shī'ah*, vol. 13, p. 344, *Mustadrak al-Wasā'il*, vol. 2, p. 626.

also came and went to her father. The man caressed her head and placed her on the floor next to him.

The Prophet of Allāh ﷺ (who saw this discrimination and injustice) said, "Why didn't you make her sit on your left knee?"

That man (who realized his wrong behaviour and followed the Prophet's ﷺ order) placed his daughter on the other knee. Thus the Messenger of Allāh ﷺ said, "Now you have observed justice."[1]

Justice in kissing children

Kissing a child is a sign and secret of love and affection; in this case also, discrimination between children is not allowed.

Nuʿmān b. Bashīr narrates from the Prophet ﷺ, who said:

إنّ اللّه تعالى يحبّ أن تعدلوا بين أولادكم حتّى في القبل

"Allāh ﷻ wants you to observe justice between your children, even in kissing them."[2]

It is narrated from the Holy Prophet ﷺ that he said:

أَنَّهُ نَظَرَ إِلَى رَجُلٍ لَهُ ابْنَانِ فَقَبَّلَ أَحَدَهُمَا وَ تَرَكَ الْآخَرَ فَقَالَ النَّبِيُّ ص فَهَلَّا سَاوَيْتَ بَيْنَهُمَا

Once the Prophet ﷺ saw a man, who had two children; he kissed one and left the other. The Messenger of Allāh ﷺ said, "Why did you not observe equality between your two children?"[3]

Justice in giving gifts to children

Although the gift is often a material item, it indicates the affection and love of the giver. The love that remains hidden in the

---

[1] *Kanz al-ʿUmmāl*, vol. 1, p. 173.
[2] *Kanz al-ʿUmmāl*, vol. 16, p. 445.
[3] *Makārim al-ʾAkhlāq*, p. 220; *Wasāʾil al-Shīʿah*, vol. 15, p. 204.

heart and is not manifested is lost, or its existence is doubted. Give a gift to be loved. It is mentioned in the statements of *Ahl al-Bayt* ﷺ that you must gift each other so that you earn love and affection.

Children have a sensitive and gentle spirit, and parents' giving gifts to them is a true proof of their love for their children; but in this regard too, excesses, discriminations and differences are not allowed as instead of being beneficial, they would cause jealousy and discord between the children.

1. Nuʿmān b. Bashīr narrates from the Prophet ﷺ, who said:

اعدِلوا بين أولادكم فى النحل كما تُحِبّون أن يَعدلوا بينَكم فى البرِّ واللطفِ

"Treat your children with justice in giving gifts, just as you would like them to treat you with kindness and affection."[1]

2. Ibn ʿAbbās narrates from the Messenger of Allāh ﷺ, who said:

ساووابين أولادكم فى العطيّة، فلو مفضِّلاً أحداً لفضّلتُ النساءَ

"When you give a gift to your children, observe equality between them, and if I were to prefer someone over another, I would definitely prefer females."[2]

This narration shows that it is not permissible to discriminate between children. If at all we prioritize one child over others, girls are more deserving.

3. Muḥammad b. Nuʿmān and Ḥamīd b. ʿAbd al-Raḥmān narrate that:

انّ بشير بن سعد جاء بالنعمان بن بشير الى رسولِ الله فقال: انّى نَحلتُ ابنى هذا العبدَ فقال رسول الله: وكلّ ولدک نحلتَ؟ قال: لا.قال: فارْدُدْه.

[1] *Kanz al-ʿUmmāl* Vol. 16, p. 444; *Kanz al-ʿUmmāl*, vol. 1, p. 172.
[2] *Kanz al-ʿUmmāl*, p. 446.

Once, Bashīr b. Sa'd brought his son, Nu'man to the Prophet ﷺ and said: I gave to this son a servant as a gift. The Messenger of Allāh ﷺ asked: "Have you given all your children similar gifts?" No, he replied. The Messenger of Allāh ﷺ said: "Take back what you gave him."[1]

4. Jābir narrates that:

قالت امرأة بشير: انحل ابنى غلاما واشهِد لى رسولَ الله، فأتى رسولَ الله فقال: انّ ابنة فلان سالتنى ان انحل ابنها غلاما، قالت: اشهد الى رسول الله فقال له؟ قال: نعم. قال: فكلّهم أعطيتَ مثلَ ما أعطيتَ؟ قال: لا، قال: فليس يصلح هذا وانّى لا أشهد اِلّا على حَقٍّ

Bashīr's wife said to her husband: Give a servant to my son and let the Messenger of Allāh ﷺ be a witness to this gift. Bashīr came to the Prophet ﷺ and said: So-and-so's daughter asked me to give her son a servant and I will take you as a witness for this. The Prophet ﷺ asked, "Does this mean that the servant will belong to this child?"

I said: Yes. The Prophet ﷺ then inquired, "Have you given such a gift to all your children?"

No, said I. The Prophet ﷺ said, "It is not lawful; and without a doubt, I don't bear witness except for what is right."[2]

6. Respecting the child

No matter what age your children are, they have personality and self-respect. They yearn for attention to their personality and desire to be respected and cherished; therefore, it is worthy for parents to pay attention to this natural tendency and nurture children's spirit with self-respect and self-confidence; and to train and strengthen them. In parties and family and public gatherings, they should respect and praise them in a wise way and avoid any kind of humiliation and

[1] *Kitāb al-'Ayāl*, vol. 1, p. 175.
[2] *Kitāb al-'Ayāl*, p. 176.

mockery and exposing their faults and mistakes. Do not forget this point even in the home environment.

Like a flower, a child's spirit is very delicate and sensitive and may fade with the slightest abnormal movement. Some parents imagine that because they have become parents, they have the right to exert any kind of oppressive and domineering opinion on their children and treat them in any way they want. While the fact is that there is a narrow boundary and it has Islamic, educational, and moral standards, which shows that if parents have authority over their children, it is an authority that includes the welfare of all the members covered by it, and it is nothing but the rule of love, affection, knowledge, and lofty human training.

The words and actions of the Aimmah ﷺ teach us the greatest and finest lessons: that is to accord greatness to the personality of our children, and to instil a sense of self-discovery and confidence in their being in order to clarify and strengthen their development and self-confidence in the society and social relationships.

The Noble Prophet of Islam ﷺ says:

أَكْرِمُوا أَوْلَادَكُمْ وَ أَحْسِنُوا أَدَبَهُمْ يُغْفَرْ لَكُم

"Respect your children, and improve their manners, and you will receive mercy and forgiveness."[1]

Respecting the child while praying

Sometimes young children get impatient when their parents are praying, or because their prayers are too long, or because of hunger, and they tend to mount the necks of their parents and ride on their backs and play. The parents are puzzled what to do. Should they break the obligatory prayer and respond positively to their child's requests, or continue the prayer and listen to the wails and bawling of their children?

---

[1] *Wasā'il al-Shī'ah*, vol. 15, p. 195; *Makārim al-'Akhlāq*, p. 222.

From the conduct of the Prophet ﷺ and the Holy A'immah ؑ it can be concluded that one should neither forgo the remembrance of Allāh ﷻ and neglect Prayer, nor provide love and affection to the child and his needs be forgotten. The best way is that the Prayer should be completed attentively, but it can be interspersed briefly with responding to the needs and emotions of the children.

'Abdullāh b. Sinān narrates from Imām Ṣādiq ؑ that he said:

صَلَّى رَسُولُ اللَّهِ ص بِالنَّاسِ الظُّهْرَ فَخَفَّفَ فِي الرَّكْعَتَيْنِ الْأَخِيرَتَيْنِ فَلَمَّا انْصَرَفَ قَالَ لَهُ النَّاسُ هَلْ حَدَثَ فِي الصَّلَاةِ حَدَثٌ قَالَ وَ مَا ذَاكَ قَالُوا خَفَّفْتَ فِي الرَّكْعَتَيْنِ الْأَخِيرَتَيْنِ فَقَالَ لَهُمْ أَمَا سَمِعْتُمْ صُرَاخَ الصَّبِي

The Messenger of Allāh ﷺ performed the Noon Prayer with the people in congregation and finished the last two units quickly. After the prayer, people asked: O Messenger of Allāh ﷺ; did something happen during prayer? "What happened?" asked the Prophet ﷺ. They said: You prayed the last two units of the prayer quickly. The Prophet ﷺ said, "Did you not hear the crying of the child?"[1]

'Anas b. Mālik said:

كان رسولُ الله يَسمع الصبىَ مع أمّه وهو فى الصَّلاة فيقرأ بالسورة الخفيفة أو القصيرة

"When the Prophet ﷺ, while praying, heard the cry of a child who was with his mother, he recited light and short Sūrahs."[2]

It is narrated that the Prophet ﷺ called the people to prayer and Imām Ḥasan Mujtabā ؑ the young child of Lady Fāṭimah Zahra ؑ was also with him. The Prophet ﷺ placed the child down and stood up to pray, and during the prayer, he prolonged a prostration more than usual. The narrator says: I raised my head from prostration and

[1] *Wasā'il al-Shī'ah*, vol. 15, p. 198, vol. 6, p. 503; *'Udat al-Dā'ī*, p. 79; *Kitāb al-'Ayāl*, vol. 1, p. 422.
[2] *Kitāb al-'Ayāl*, vol. 1, p. 353.

saw Imām Ḥasan عليه السلام perched on the Prophet's ﷺ shoulders. When the prayer was over, the worshipers asked: O Messenger of Allāh ﷺ; we never saw such a (long) prostration. We thought that perhaps a revelation was being revealed to you. He (the Prophet ﷺ) said, "It was not a revelation. My child, Ḥasan عليه السلام had climbed on my back and I did not like to make haste and put down the child. So, I waited until he came down of his own volition."[1]

Breastfeeding a child while praying

ʿAmmār Sābāṭī narrates from Imām Ṣādiq عليه السلام:

لَا بَأْسَ أَنْ تَحْمِلَ الْمَرْأَةُ صَبِيَّهَا وَ هِيَ تُصَلِّي أَوْ تُرْضِعَهُ وَ هِيَ تَتَشَهَّدُ

"There is nothing wrong with a woman holding a child while praying and breastfeeding him while reciting *Tashahhud*."[2]

ʿAlī b. Jaʿfar, the brother of Imām Mūsā b. Jaʿfar عليه السلام says:

سَأَلْتُهُ عَنِ الْمَرْأَةِ تَكُونُ فِي صَلَاةِ الْفَرِيضَةِ وَ وَلَدُهَا إِلَى جَنْبِهَا فَيَبْكِي وَ هِيَ قَاعِدَةٌ هَلْ يَصْلُحُ لَهَا أَنْ تَتَنَاوَلَهُ فَتُقْعِدَهُ فِي حَجْرِهَا وَ تُسْكِتَهُ وَ تُرْضِعَهُ قَالَ لَا بَأْس

I asked the Imām عليه السلام regarding a woman praying an obligatory prayer while her child is crying next to her; that is it allowed for her to hold her child in her arms while she is sitting and place him on her lap and calm him down and breastfeed him? He said, "There is no problem."[3]

---

[1] Muḥammad Ṭaqī Falsafī, *al-Ḥadīth*, vol. 3, p. 65, quoted by *Biḥār al-'Anwār*, vol. 10, p. 82.
[2] *Wasā'il al-Shīʿah*, vol. 4, p. 1274.
[3] *Wasā'il al-Shīʿah*, vol. 4, p. 1274.

Not removing children from the congregation

Some worshipers are quick to react negatively and angrily when they see young children in the rows of congregational prayers and push them away or expel them from the *Masjid*. These wrong attitudes, which occur due to ignorance, weaken the religious spirit of children and make them disinterested towards religious practices and worship centres, whereas seeds of faith and religious orientation should be planted in the hearts of children from childhood so that they gradually become interested in religious ceremonies and worship centres, and the moments they spend in *Masjids* and religious gatherings are connected with joy, praise and encouragement, and become part of children's sweet memories.

Jābir says:

سَأَلْتُهُ عَنِ الصِّبْيَانِ إِذَا صَفُّوا فِي الصَّلَاةِ الْمَكْتُوبَةِ قَالَ لَا تُؤَخِّرُوهُمْ عَنِ الصَّلَاةِ وَ فَرِّقُوا بَيْنَهُم

I asked Imām Bāqir ﷷ about children who participate in congregational prayer. Imām ﷷ said, "Do not send them back to the last rows; rather separate them by standing between."[1]

In this way, the respect of children is preserved and also that the *Masjid* is prevented from being turned into a place for the children to only play and have fun.

Greeting the children

Greeting the children is a sign of humility and magnanimity, a cause to exalt the children's personality and prophetic temperament; and a fine Muḥammadan practice (*Sunnah*).

The noble Prophet of Islam ﷺ never forgot this good tradition as long as he was alive, and he constantly greeted the young and the old and said:

---

[1] *Majmu'ah Warrām*, p. 359.

خمسٌ لا أدعُهنّ حتّى المماتِ....والتسليمُ على الصبيانِ ليكونَ سنّة من بعدى

"There are five things that I will not leave till the moment of death... One is greeting children until it becomes a tradition (among Muslims) after me."[1]

Not finding fault with children

Hishām b. 'Urwah narrates from his father: Once, a man found fault with what his son had done in the presence of the Prophet ﷺ. The Prophet ﷺ told him:

انّما ابنک سهمٌ من كنانتِک

"Your child is an arrow from your quiver."[2]

That is: your child is a part of your body and the treasure of the future, and you - by insulting his character - are hurting yourself and weakening someone who will help and support you in the future, and you will also enjoy the rewards of every good deed that he does.

Addressing the children nicely

Another way to respect and honour children is to call them with good and worthy titles during childhood. Names and titles are nice which indicate affection and love and remind you of goodness and virtue. Calling a child with such names and titles, in addition to intensifying and sealing relationships, encourages and stimulates children's personality to grow up to be good and perfect, and instils a special greatness in their souls, whose good effects will not be forgotten.

The Prophet ﷺ said:

---

[1] *Kanz al-'Ummāl*, vol. 16, p. 584.
[2] *Kanz al-'Ummāl*, vol. 16, p. 584.

بادروأولادكم بالكُنى قبل أن تَغلِبَ عليهم الألقابُ

"Before ugly nicknames get over your child, give them good titles."[1]

Consulting with the youth

One of the clear examples of respect and honouring children is to consult them from early adolescence. This kind of attention and care to young people enriches their thoughts and way of thinking, and nurtures intellectual talents in their beings towards creativity and academic innovation, intellectual independence and giving opinions on various issues.

Consulting with children on various issues of life and family and seeking their opinion on academic and social topics gradually reveals their potential abilities and makes them aware and empowered in managing their lives in the future.

The late Ṭabarsī narrates from the Prophet ﷺ in *Makārim al-'Akhlāq* as follows:

الْوَلَدُ سَيِّدٌ سَبْعَ سِنِينَ وَ عَبْدٌ سَبْعَ سِنِينَ وَ وَزِيرٌ سَبْعَ سِنِينَ

"A man's child is a ruler and boss in the first seven years of his life; in the next seven years (7-14), he is obedient and submissive, and in the next seven years (15-21), he is the minister of the family and an advisor to his parents."[2]

Social context for the development of children's talents

There are extraordinary talents hidden in children and teenagers and the blossoming of these talents needs a foundation. Parents can accelerate the development of children's talents by creating socially effective backgrounds. For example, if a child recites the Qur'ān

[1] *Kanz al-'Ummāl*, vol. 16, p. 419.
[2] *Wasā'il al-Shī'ah*, vol. 15, p. 195.

beautifully at home, he should be asked to recite the same verses and Sūrahs in public gatherings. Or if he knows a poem, a discourse, or an art, he is asked to display his knowledge and skill to friends and relatives and in family and social gatherings. This would make the children confident in their abilities and they would feel happy and mature and become more interested in cultural issues and get rid of inferiority complex which is the reason for the stagnation of talents.

Shaykh Ṣadūq narrates:

Once, Amīr al Mu'minīn ؑ addressed the people in the *Masjid* and said:

سَلُونِي قَبْلَ أَنْ تَفْقِدُونِي

"Ask me before you lose me."

However, no one stood up to pose a question.

So Amīr al Mu'minīn ؑ, after reciting divine praise and glorification and invoking blessings on the Holy Prophet ﷺ glanced at Imām Ḥasan Mujtaba ؑ and said: My son, Ḥasan ؑ; arise and go to the pulpit and say something so that after me the Quraysh may not consider you young and say: Ḥasan ؑ does not know anything.

Imām Ḥasan Mujtaba ؑ said: Father, how can I go to the pulpit and give a speech while you are seated among the people; and you will hear my words and look at me?

Amīr al Mu'minīn ؑ said: May my parents be sacrificed for you! I will hide myself and listen to you and see you while you speak, whereas you will not see me.

Imām Mujtabā ؑ followed his father's order, went to the pulpit; and after praising Allāh ﷻ and saluting the Prophet ﷺ and his family ؑ, said: People! I heard from my grandfather, the Messenger of Allāh ﷺ that he said, "I am the city of knowledge and 'Alī ؑ is its gate. Is it possible to enter the city of knowledge without passing through the gate? Then he came down from the pulpit. Amīr al Mu'minīn ؑ stood up and hugged his child. Then he said to his other son, Imām Ḥusain ؑ, "My son! You too arise, mount the pulpit, and speak so that the Quraysh will not think less of me and say that Ḥusain b. 'Alī ؑ does not know anything, but speak in such a way that it is a continuation of your brother's speech."

Imām Ḥusain ؑ followed his father's order, went to the pulpit; and after praising Allāh ﷻ and praying for the Prophet ﷺ and his family ؑ, said: O people, I heard the Messenger of Allāh say, "'Alī ؑ is the city of guidance, so whoever enters it will be saved, and whoever avoids it will perish."

Imām 'Alī ؑ arose and while hugging him said to the people: O people, witness these two children of the Messenger of Allāh ﷺ. They are a trust that the Holy Prophet ﷺ entrusted to me, and I leave these two as a trust between you. People: know that the Prophet ﷺ will ask you about these two (what have you done with them?).[1]

In another narration of Imām Bāqir and Imām Ṣādiq ؑ it is mentioned that Amīr al Mu'minīn ؑ said to his son, Imām Ḥasan Mujtabā ؑ, "Speak!" Imām Ḥasan ؑ wanted to excuse himself saying, "How can I speak while my gaze falls on your face." So [Imām 'Alī ؑ] gathered his maidservants and said to them, "Get up and listen to my son's speech." Then he concealed himself so that he could only listen to the words of Imām Ḥasan ؑ; and at the end of the sermon, he stood up and kissed his son's head and said, "May my parents be sacrificed on you!" And then he recited this verse:

ذُرِّيَّةً بَعْضُهَا مِن بَعْضٍ ۗ وَاللَّهُ سَمِيعٌ عَلِيمٌ ﴿٣٤﴾

"some of them are descendants of the others, and Allāh is all-hearing, all-knowing."[2]

7. Supplication of the parents for children

Children should pray for their parents and ask Almighty Allāh for their forgiveness. The Holy Qur'ān says:

---

[1] al-*'Amālī al-Ṣadūq*, p. 307.

[2] *Biḥār al-'Anwār*, vol. 43, pp. 350 and 351; Sūrah āl-'Imrān 3:34.

...رَّبِّ ٱرْحَمْهُمَا كَمَا رَبَّيَانِى صَغِيرًا ﴿٢٤﴾

"*...My Lord! Have mercy on them, just as they reared me when I was [a] small [child]!*"[1]

But the children themselves need the prayers of their parents more because they are in the beginning of their life and they urgently need the help of their parents, and the prayers of parents for their children are speedily answered. Therefore, if we see that some are among righteous and wise, they did not reach these positions without influence of their parents' prayers; and if some are involved in calamities, perhaps it is the result of their parents' displeasure that has befallen on them. Therefore, the prayer of parents for their children has an effective and decisive role. Prophets ﷺ and the Holy A'immah ﵈ have taught us this lesson practically. They invoked Allāh ﷻ for help and prayed for the good future of their child.

Prophet Ibrāhīm ﵇ prays for himself and his children:

رَبَّنَا وَٱجْعَلْنَا مُسْلِمَيْنِ لَكَ وَمِن ذُرِّيَّتِنَآ أُمَّةً مُّسْلِمَةً لَّكَ...

"*Our Lord, make us submissive to You, and [raise] from our progeny a nation submissive to You...*"[2]

Now that we know the importance of parents' prayers for the health and happiness of their children, let us examine its reality in the life and sayings of *Ahl al-Bayt* ﵈:

Prophet's ﷺ supplication for children

'Ā'ishah says:

كان رسولُ الله يُؤتىٰ بالصبيانِ فيدعولهم ويبرّكُ عليهم...

---

[1] Sūrah Banī Isrā'īl 17:24.
[2] Sūrah al-Baqarah 2:128.

"The Prophet's ﷺ technique was to bring children near him and then he would pray for them and supplicate for their well-being."[1]

Prophet Ya'qūb ؑ seeks forgiveness for his sons

It is narrated from Imām Ṣādiq ؑ regarding the statement of Prophet Ya'qūb ؑ, who said to his sons:

قَالَ سَوْفَ أَسْتَغْفِرُ لَكُمْ رَبِّيٓ...

"He said: I shall (in future) plead with my Lord to forgive you…"[2]

"In fact, Ya'qūb ؑ delayed asking for forgiveness for his sons until the dawn of Friday night."

Imām Ṣādiq's prayer on behalf of his children

'Umar b. Yazid says:

كَانَ أَبُو عَبْدِ اللَّهِ ع يُصَلِّي عَنْ وَلَدِهِ كُلَّ لَيْلَةٍ رَكْعَتَيْنِ وَ عَنْ وَالِدَيْهِ فِي كُلِّ يَوْمٍ رَكْعَتَيْنِ قُلْتُ لَهُ جُعِلْتُ فِدَاكَ كَيْفَ صَارَ لِلْوَلَدِ اللَّيْلُ قَالَ لِأَنَّ الْفِرَاشَ لِلْوَلَدِ قَالَ وَ كَانَ يَقْرَأُ فِيهِمَا إِنَّا أَنْزَلْنَاهُ فِي لَيْلَةِ الْقَدْرِ- وَ إِنَّا أَعْطَيْنَاكَ الْكَوْثَرَ.

The program of Imām Ṣādiq ؑ was that every night he prayed two units on behalf of his children and two units every day on behalf of his father, and in those two units, he recited Sūrah Qadr and Sūrah Kawthar.[3]

Imām Zayn al-'Ābidīn's ؑ prayer for his children

Imām Zayn al-'Ābidīn ؑ supplicates for his children in *Sahīfa Sajjādiyyah*:

---

[1] *Kitāb al-'Ayāl*, vol. 1, p. 402.
[2] Sūrah Yūsuf 12:98.
[3] *Mustadrak al-Wasā'il*, vol. 6, p. 347; *Wasā'il al-Shī'ah*, vol. 2, p. 656.

O Lord, oblige me by sparing my children from death, by educating them for me and by blessing me with them.

My God, prolong their lives for me. Increase their terms of existence for me. Bring up those of tender years for me. Strengthen the weak ones for me. Heal their bodies, faith, and morals. Let them be safe in soul and body and in everything I am anxious about concerning them. Let their sustenance flow into my hand. Let them be virtuous, pious, able to see and hear, obedient unto You, and lovers and well-wishers of Your friends and hostile and implacable to all Your enemies. Amen!

O Lord, strengthen my arm with them and straighten with them my crookedness. Enlarge my number because of them. Adorn my society with them. Keep my memory alive by means of them. Make them take care of my affairs in my absence. Help me with them to satisfy my need. Let them love me, be kind to me, favourable, faithful, obedient, not disobedient, not wicked, nor adverse nor guilty. Help me in training them, educating them and in doing good to them. Grant me from Yourself male descendants among them. Let this be a benefit to me. Let them be my helpers in whatever I ask of You. Protect me and my offspring from the accursed Satan. For verily You created us, command us, put prohibitions upon us and encouraged us with the reward for doing what You ordered and threatened us with punishment for disobedience. You have made him our enemy who deceived us. You have given him dominion over some of us while over some of us You have not given him dominion. You have established him in our breasts and made him run through our blood vessels. He is not careless even if we are careless. He does not forget if we forget. He makes us feel secure from Your torment and threatens us with (the punishment of someone) other than You. If we intend some glaring sin, he encourages us in it. If we intend to do any good thing, he hinders us. He exposes irresistible appetites to us and raises doubts for us. If he makes promises to us, he lies and if he holds out hopes to us, he disappoints us. If You do not turn his cunning away from us, he shall mislead us. If You do not guard us from his corruption, he shall cause us to err. Therefore, O Lord, overthrow his authority from over us with Your Power till You completely restrain him from us owing to our diligent prayer to You so that we may pass out of the power of his cunning into the group of those defended by You. O Lord, grant me all my desires. Satisfy my needs. Do not refuse me Your answer whilst You have given surety for it to me. Do not keep off my prayer from You while You have required it of me. Favor me with all that will do me good in this world and the next, whatever I remember of it and whatever I have forgotten, expressed, concealed, revealed or withheld. Let me be (by my imploring You Alone) of the righteous, of those who are successful in applying to You, of those who are not deprived because of their trust in You, of those who benefitted by their bargains with You, of those who take refuge in Your Majesty, of those who have abundance of lawful sustenance conferred on them by Your boundless Kindness, Your Bounty and Generosity; of those who are exalted to honour from disgrace by You; of those who seek shelter from tyranny in Your Justice; of those who are safe from calamity with Your Grace; of those who are raised to prosperity from poverty by Your Endless Wealth. of those who are protected from sins, slips and error by fear of You; of those who have grace for goodness, virtue and righteousness owing to their obedience to You; of those having a barrier between them and sin because of Your Power; of those who renounce all sins; of those who dwell in Your neighbourhood...

O Lord, grant us all this with Your Grace and Mercy. Protect us from the torment of Hell. Favour all the Muslim men and women and true believers, male and female, with the like of what I have begged of You for myself and my offspring in the present world and the future...[1]

Three supplications are definitely fulfilled!

Imām Ṣādiq ﵇ says:

ثلاثُ دعواتٍ لا يُحجَبْنَ عن اللهِ ... دعاءُ الوالد لولدِه اذا بَرَّه، ودعوتُه عليه اذا عَقَّه...

ثَـلَاثُ دَعَوَاتٍ لَا يُحْجَبْنَ عَنِ اللَّهِ (تعَالَى): دُعَاءُ الْوَالِدِ لِوَلَدِهِ إِذَا بَرَّهُ، وَ دَعْوَتُهُ عَلَيْهِ إِذَا عَقَّهُ

"There are three prayers that are never deprived of Allāh's ﷻ grace, mercy and response...the prayer of a father for his child if he has done a good turn to his father and curse of a father if he has disobeyed his father..."[2]

---

[1] *Sahīfa Sajjādiyyah*, (translation by Fayḍ al-Islām) p. 168.
[2] *Safīnat al-Biḥār*, vol. 1, p. 458.

Increase in grades through parents' forgiveness

Abū al-Qāsim Kūfī narrates from the Holy Prophet ﷺ who said:

إِنَّ الْعَبْدَ لَيُرْفَعُ لَهُ دَرَجَةٌ فِي الْجَنَّةِ لاَ يَعْرِفُهَا مِنْ أَعْمَالِهِ فَيَقُولُ رَبِّ أَنَّى لِي هَذِهِ فَيَقُولُ بِاسْتِغْفَارِ وَالِدَيْكَ لَكَ مِنْ بَعْدِكَ

"A servant will be raised a level higher in heaven though he did not think it to be a result of his actions. So he asks the Lord ﷻ: O Lord! Why did I get this grade?

Allāh ﷻ says: Because of the forgiveness your parents sought for you after you."[1]

'Allamah Majlisī's supplication for his infant

Āghā Aḥmad (maternal grandson of the great teacher, Bahbahānī) in *Mirātul Aḥwāl* has quoted through some sources from Mullā Muḥammad Ṭaqī (Majlisī) who said: On certain nights after the Midnight Prayer and vigil, a condition arose in me about which I knew that if I pray in that situation, my prayer would definitely be answered. So, I was thinking what I should pray for and beseech from Allāh ﷻ when I heard Muḥammad Bāqir crying in the cradle. I said: O Allāh ﷻ, by the right of Muḥammad ﷺ and the Progeny of Muḥammad ﷺ – blessings of Allāh ﷻ be on them all ﷺ – make this son of mine a promoter of religion and disseminator of the laws of the best messenger and bless him with infinite opportunities of doing good...[2]

8. Patience in bereavement of a child

Another good characteristic of an exemplary parent is that in mourning for their lost child, even though he was dear and noble, they do not commit excess and do not say anything that angers Allāh ﷻ. This high moral attribute of the Prophet ﷺ, the Infallibles ﷺ and the

[1] *Mustadrak al-Wasā'il*, vol. 67, p. 439.
[2] *Mardān 'Ilm dar Maydān 'Amal*, p. 117.

great scholars has been bequeathed to us and it indicates their intellectual superiority and the scope of existence. Because they are more aware of the realities of the world and the nature of worldly life, which is full of trials, and their great spirit does not suffer much from heartbreaking events.[1]

The Holy Prophet ﷺ mourned his son, Ibrāhīm

When Ibrāhīm, the son of the Messenger of Allāh ﷺ was in the throes of death, His Eminence ﷺ said:

لَوْ لَا أَنَّ الْمَاضِيَ فَرَطُ الْبَاقِي وَ أَنَّ الْآخِرَ لَاحِقٌ بِالْأَوَّلِ لَحَزِنَّا عَلَيْكَ يَا إِبْرَاهِيمُ ثُمَّ دَمَعَتْ عَيْنُهُ وَ قَالَ ص تَدْمَعُ الْعَيْنُ وَ يَحْزَنُ الْقَلْبُ وَ لَا نَقُولُ إِلَّا مَا يَرْضَى الرَّبُّ وَ إِنَّا بِكَ يَا إِبْرَاهِيمُ لَمَحْزُونُونَ.

"Verily, the eyes shed tears and the heart is grieved, but we will not say anything except what is pleasing to our Lord ﷻ. We are saddened by your departure, O Ibrāhīm." [2]

Imām Bāqir ؑ in mourning for his son

Yūnus b. Ya'qūb has narrated from certain people that a group was present in the company of Imām Bāqir ؑ when one of his children was unwell.

On noticing that the Imām ؑ was sad and anxious, they said to each another: By Allāh ﷻ! We are afraid that if something happens to this child and he dies, it will affect the Imām ؑ very deeply. After some time, wails were heard from inside the house and Imām ؑ arose and went into the inner chambers. But contrary to expectations, he returned to us soon and he seemed normal.

---

[1] More on this can be found in Shaheed Thani, *Musakkin Al Fouad* "Soothing the heart of the bereaved" Published by Lantern Publications.

[2] *Tuḥaf al-'Uqūl*, p. 37.

We said: May our lives be sacrificed on you; we dreaded that if this child passes away, we will see you in a condition that would make us distraught forever.

Imām said: We prefer our loved ones to regain health, but if Allāh's command comes and he passes away, we submit to the divine will.[1]

Imām Ṣādiq mourned for Ismā'īl

لَمَّا حَضَرَتْ إِسْمَاعِيلَ بْنَ جَعْفَرٍ الصَّادِقِ ع الْوَفَاةُ نَظَرَ النَّاسُ إِلَى الصَّادِقِ ع جَزِعاً يَدْخُلُ مَرَّةً وَ يَخْرُجُ أُخْرَى وَ يَقُومُ مَرَّةً وَ يَقْعُدُ أُخْرَى فَلَمَّا تُوُفِّيَ إِسْمَاعِيلُ دَخَلَ الصَّادِقُ ع إِلَى بَيْتِهِ وَ لَبِسَ أَنْظَفَ ثِيَابِهِ وَ سَرَّحَ شَعْرَهُ وَ جَاءَ إِلَى مَجْلِسِهِ فَجَلَسَ سَاكِتاً عَنِ الْمُصِيبَةِ كَأَنْ لَمْ يُصَبْ بِمُصِيبَةٍ فَقِيلَ لَهُ فِي ذَلِكَ فَقَالَ إِنَّا أَهْلَ الْبَيْتِ نُطِيعُ اللَّهَ فِيمَا أَحَبَّ وَ نَسْأَلُهُ مَا نُحِبُّ وَ إِذَا فَعَلَ بِنَا مَا نُحِبُّ شَكَرْنَا وَ إِذَا فَعَلَ بِنَا مَا نَكْرَهُ رَضِينَا

When Ismā'īl, the son of Imām Ṣādiq was dying, Imām seemed to be impatient and anxious, as sometimes he went inside the house and sometimes came out. Sometimes he stood and sometimes sat down. But when Ismā'īl passed away, Imām went in and put on his cleanest clothes; shook his head and returned to his gathering and sat down in his place without mentioning anything about the calamity, as if nothing had happened. They asked: Why don't you talk about this incident? He said, "We are *Ahl al-Bayt*, who obey Allāh in what He likes, and we ask Him for what we like; if He grants it to us, we thank Allāh, and if He does to us something we don't like, we are satisfied with divine will."[2]

Imām Riḍā narrates from his father, Imām Mūsā that:

نُعِيَ إِلَى الصَّادِقِ ع إِسْمَاعِيلُ وَ هُوَ أَكْبَرُ أَوْلَادِهِ وَ هُوَ يُرِيدُ أَنْ يَأْكُلَ وَ قَدِ اجْتَمَعَ نُدَمَاؤُهُ فَتَبَسَّمَ ثُمَّ دَعَا بِطَعَامِهِ فَقَعَدَ مَعَ نُدَمَائِهِ وَ جَعَلَ يَأْكُلُ أَحْسَنَ مِنْ أَكْلِهِ سَائِرَ

---

[1] *al-Kāfī*, vol. 37 p. 226.
[2] *Majmu'ah Warrām*, p. 440.

الأَيَّامِ وَ يَحُثُّ نُدَمَاءَهُ وَ يَضَعُ بَيْنَ أَيْدِيهِمْ وَ يَعْجَبُونَ مِنْهُ لَا يَرَوْنَ لِلْحُزْنِ فِي وَجْهِهِ أَثَراً فَلَمَّا فَرَغَ قَالُوا يَا ابْنَ رَسُولِ اللَّهِ لَقَدْ رَأَيْنَا مِنْكَ عَجَباً أُصِبْتَ بِمِثْلِ هَذَا الِابْنِ وَ أَنْتَ كَمَا نَرَى فَقَالَ مَا لِي لَا أَكُونُ كَمَا تَرَوْنَ وَ قَدْ جَاءَنِي خَبَرُ أَصْدَقِ الصَّادِقِينَ أَنِّي مَيِّتٌ وَ إِيَّاكُمْ إِنَّ قَوْماً عَرَفُوا الْمَوْتَ فَلَمْ يُنْكِرُوا مَا يَخْطَفُهُ الْمَوْتُ مِنْهُمْ وَ سَلَّمُوا لِأَمْرِ خَالِقِهِمْ عَزَّ وَ جَلَّ.

When the news of Ismā'īl's death reached Imām Ṣādiq ؏, he was with his companions and ready to eat. The Imām smiled and asked for his food and started eating.

That day Imām Ṣādiq ؏ ate better than ever and also encouraged his companions to eat more and brought food for them. They were amazed by the fact that they did not see any trace of sadness in the Imām ؏. When they finished eating, they asked His Eminence ؏: Today we observed something strange! Though you faced such a calamity regarding a child, but you are the same as you were before? His Eminence said, "Why shouldn't I be like that when I have been told by the most truthful one that you and I also will die?" Then he said, "Verily, there are some people who have recognized death, have prepared themselves for it, do not deny the (existence) of one who has been taken away by death, and submit themselves to the will of Allāh ؏."[1]

All this impatience for a small calamity

It is narrated from Imām Ṣādiq ؏ that:

أَنَّهُ رَأَى رَجُلاً قَدِ اشْتَدَّ جَزَعُهُ عَلَى وَلَدِهِ فَقَالَ يَا هَذَا جَزِعْتَ لِلْمُصِيبَةِ الصُّغْرَى وَ غَفَلْتَ عَنِ الْمُصِيبَةِ الْكُبْرَى لَوْ كُنْتَ لِمَا صَارَ إِلَيْهِ وَلَدُكَ مُسْتَعِدّاً لَمَا اشْتَدَّ عَلَيْهِ جَزَعُكَ فَمُصَابُكَ بِتَرْكِكَ الِاسْتِعْدَادَ أَعْظَمُ مِنْ مُصَابِكَ بِوَلَدِكَ

---

[1] *Wasā'il al-Shī'ah*, vol. 27, p. 901.

He saw a man wailing over the death of his child. The Imām ﷺ said, "O the one, who is crying over a minor calamity and is neglecting the major one! Had you prepared yourself for the loss of your child, it would not have been so difficult for you. Thus, not being prepared is a calamity that is greater than the loss of your child."[1]

On the death of the son of Mu'adh b. Jabal the Noble Prophet of Islam ﷺ wrote to him:

From Muḥammad, the Messenger of Allāh ﷺ, to Mu'adh b. Jabal: Peace be on you. I thank Allāh ﷻ, except whom no one is worthy of praise - so to say - I have received the news of your grief for your son. Your son was one of Allāh's ﷻ pleasant gifts and loans that He deposited with you. He let you enjoy with him for a period then took him back at the fixed time. We are surely Allah's ﷻ and to Him we shall return. Your grief should never waste your rewards. If you only had known of the great rewards for this misfortune that befell you, you would have realized that the misfortune had been too short to meet the great rewards of Allāh ﷻ for people of submission – to Him – and steadfastness. You should know that grief will never return the dead or stop the fate. You should do well with consolation and work for obtaining the promised rewards. You should never grieve for what will unquestionably come to you, as well as all creatures. Peace and Allāh's ﷻ mercy and blessings be on you.[2]

'Alī b. Mahziyār says: A man wrote to Imām Jawād ﷺ and complained about the tragedy of losing his son and the severity of grief caused by it. Imām ﷺ wrote in reply:

أَما عَلِمتَ أَنَّ اللَّهَ عَزَّ وَ جَلَّ يَختارُ مِن مالِ المُؤمِنِ وَ مِن وُلدِهِ أَنفَسَهُ؛ لِيَأجُرَهُ عَلى ذلِكَ

"Don't you know that Allāh, the mighty, the sublime chooses the best from the wealth of the believer and his children (and takes from him) so that he will be rewarded for it?"[3]

---

[1] *Wasā'il al-Shī'ah*, vol. 2, p. 65.
[2] *Tuḥaf al-'Uqūl*, p. 85.
[3] *al-Kāfī*, vol. 3, p. 263.

It can be concluded from the traditional reports mentioned above that if parents face this great divine test and lose a child, they must not lose their mental balance and be impatient or hit upon the head, pull at the hair, and scratch the face - or worst of all - utter blasphemy and lose their divine reward.

The lives of the men of Allāh ﷻ

We have seen and heard the effect of this Muḥammadan *Sunnah* in the lives of many servants of Allāh ﷻ, scholars and elders that in such cases, there was no reaction from them except submission to divine providence.

I clearly remember that when the news of the passing of my brother (the late Shaykh Muḥammad ʿAlī Ṭabasī) was given to my late father - even though this 23-year-old young man was my father's hope for the future and the object of his attention and affection – and I was afraid that he would give up his life on this great calamity! But this man of Allāh ﷻ followed the path of the prophets, the infallible, the righteous, and the religious scholars; he did not say anything other than surrender to fate. On the contrary upon hearing the news of his sons death, he prostrated and thanked Allāh ﷻ for this great test and trial.

Impatience, before calamity

It may seem from these narrations that the Infallibles ﷺ were very impatient in this regard, especially if the illness became severe and the patient was dying. In that case they were constantly restless and agitated. But we should remember that it was only before the patient died and before divine fate was revealed to them.

The feelings of the parents when the child is sick are a natural reaction and empathy with the human being who is a part of their body and who is in great pain. On the other hand, part of this sadness is also because they have failed to protect Allāh's ﷻ trusts. But after providence dictates the death of the child, one should surrender to Allāh's ﷻ command and must not continue to be distraught:

ما نداریم از رضای حق گله　　　عار نیاد شیر را از سلسله

We do not have the right to complain against divine will.

The lion should not be ashamed of the chain.

The reaction of the Infallibles ﷺ was nothing but this, and after the passing of the child, the sadness and grief of those nobles dissipated.

A conversation between Qutaybah ʿAshī and Imām Ṣādiq ؑ

Qutaybah ʿAshī says: Once I went to the house of Imām Ṣādiq ؑ to visit his sick son. I saw the Imām very anxious and sad at home. I said: "May I be sacrificed on you. How is the child?" He said, "By Allāh ﷻ, his condition is same." Then he entered the house and came out after a little while with a happy face; and that sad and depressed look was no longer visible.

Qutaybah says: Because I saw this condition in the Imām ؑ, I thought that perhaps his child had recovered, so I once again asked him about his condition, and he said, "He has passed away." I said: I am sorry, when your child was alive, you were very depressed and sorrowful, but now that he has passed away, I don't see agitation and mental anguish in you?!

Imām ؑ said, "We are a family that is always restless and impatient before a calamity, but when Allāh's ﷻ command comes, we are content, and we submit to His decree."

Part Three

Good upbringing and training of children

Good upbringing and training of children

One of the most important issues in the life of every human being is the feeling of responsibility towards children and interest in their upbringing. It is considered to be one of the rights of the child over the parents.

This important fact is mentioned in countless traditional reports of the *Ahl al-Bayt*.

Imām Kāẓim says:

جَاءَ رَجُلٌ إِلَى النَّبِيِّ ص فَقَالَ يَا رَسُولَ اللَّهِ- مَا حَقُّ ابْنِي هَذَا قَالَ تُحَسِّنُ اسْمَهُ وَ أَدَبَهُ وَ ضَعْهُ مَوْضِعاً حَسَناً

A man brought his son to the Prophet and said: O Messenger of Allāh; what is the right of this child of mine upon me? The Prophet said, "Choose a good name for him; raise him well and place him in a good position."[1]

Some have said regarding the third phrase that it could imply choosing a good wife for a child. Before this also we mentioned other narrations regarding choosing a good name and good upbringing of children.

Providing good education

Imām Ṣādiq says:

وَ تَجِبُ لِلْوَلَدِ عَلَى وَالِدِهِ ثَلَاثُ خِصَالٍ اخْتِيَارُهُ لِوَالِدَتِهِ وَ تَحْسِينُ اسْمِهِ وَ الْمُبَالَغَةُ فِي تَأْدِيبِهِ

---

[1] *Wasā'il al-Shī'ah*, vol. 15.

"The child has three rights on his father: (1) That he must choose a good wet nurse for him (2) Give him a good name and (3) Endeavor much to give him a good education."¹

The Prophet ﷺ says:

$$لَأَنْ يُؤَدِّبَ أَحَدُكُمْ وَلَدَهُ خَيْرٌ لَهُ مِنْ أَنْ يَتَصَدَّقَ بِنِصْفِ صَاعٍ كُلَّ يَوْم$$

"Indeed, if you endeavour to educate your child properly, it will be better for you than giving half a measure (Ṣā') of grain in charity every day."²

Ayyūb b. Mūsā narrates from the Prophet ﷺ that he said:

$$مَا نَحَلَ وَالِدٌ وَلَداً نُحْلاً أَفْضَلَ مِنْ أَدَبٍ حَسَن$$

"There is no better gift from the father to his son than good manners and upbringing."³

'Alī, in his will to his son, Imām Ḥusain says:

$$وَ الْأَدَبُ خَيْرُ مِيرَاث$$

"Courtesy is the best inheritance (from father to son)."⁴

Role of education in human development

Amīr al Mu'minīn 'Alī narrates from the Prophet ﷺ, who said:

---

¹ *Biḥār al-'Anwār*, vol. 75, p. 236.
² *Makārim al-'Akhlāq*, p. 222; *Mustadrak al-Wasā'il*, vol. 15, p. 166; *Kitāb al-'Ayāl*, vol. 1, p. 501.
³ *Kitāb al-'Ayāl*, vol. 1, p. 498; *Kanz al-'Ummāl*, vol. 16, p. 456; *Mustadrak al-Wasā'il*, vol. 15, pp. 164-165.
⁴ *Tuḥaf al-'Uqūl*, p. 85.

يَعْرِفُ الْمُؤمِنُ مَنْزِلَتَه عِنْدَ رَبِّه بأَنْ يُرَبِّى وَلَداً لَه كافياً قَبْلَ الموتِ

"The dignity of a believer in the eyes of his Lord ﷻ depends on raising a child and making him needless before his death."[1]

Most suitable time for education

Childhood and adolescence is the best and most appropriate period for parents to make their children familiar with Islamic morals and customs, because during this time, the child only knows his parents and his family environment. So to speak, his ears and eyes are closed, and he only receives spiritual and intellectual nourishment under the cover of his personality. He records all the behaviours in himself and gradually reveals what he has seen in the long term. If the parents neglect their child's training during this period and are not actually a proper educational model for their children and are satisfied with only dry and empty things, the children will tend to have undesirable behaviours and attitudes without the influence of such recommendations; and if they face negative moral models outside the home, they will show more happiness and effectiveness.

The fertile field of the teenage soul

In his advice to his son, Imām Ḥasan Mujtabā ؑ, Amīr al Mu'minīn ؑ pointed out that the soul of the youth is very suitable for growth and perfection, and said:

وَ إنَّمَا قَلْبُ الْحَدَثِ كَالأَرْضِ الْخَالِيَةِ مَا أُلْقِيَ فِيهَا مِنْ شَيْءٍ قَبِلَتْهُ فَبَادَرْتُكَ بِالأَدَبِ قَبْلَ أَنْ يَقْسُوَ قَلْبُكَ وَ يَشْتَغِلَ لُبُّك

"Undoubtedly, the heart of a teenager is like fallow land ready to accept any seed that is thrown in it, so I hastened to educate you before your heart becomes hard and your mind is occupied with something else."[2]

---

[1] *Kanz al-'Ummāl*, vol. 16, p. 489.
[2] *Wasā'il al-Shī'ah*, vol. 15, p. 197; *Tuḥaf al-'Uqūl*, p. 67.

Imām Ṣādiq said, "Luqmān the Wise gave his son the following advice :

يَا بُنَيَ إِنْ تَأَدَّبْتَ صَغِيراً انْتَفَعْتَ بِهِ كَبِيراً وَ مَنْ عَنَى بِالْأَدَبِ اهْتَمَّ بِهِ وَ مَنِ اهْتَمَّ بِهِ تَكَلَّفَ عِلْمَهُ وَ مَنْ تَكَلَّفَ عِلْمَهُ اشْتَدَّ لَهُ طَلَبُهُ وَ مَنِ اشْتَدَّ لَهُ طَلَبُهُ أَدْرَكَ مَنْفَعَتَهُ فَاتَّخِذْهُ عَادَةً فَإِنَّكَ تَخْلُفُ فِي سَلَفِكَ وَ تَنْفَعُ بِهِ خَلْفَكَ وَ يَرْتَجِيكَ فِيهِ رَاغِبٌ وَ يَخْشَى صَوْلَتَكَ رَاهِبٌ وَ إِيَّاكَ وَ الْكَسَلَ عَنْهُ بِالطَّلَبِ لِغَيْرِهِ

My child! If you learnt politeness as a child, you would benefit from it when you grow up.

My child! Anyone who is looking for manners and knowledge, who prepares for it and who strives in its path and puts himself through suffering and hardship to learn good manners, will find great enthusiasm in the pursuit of politeness and knowledge. If it is so, he will find its benefits. So, O child! Make a habit of learning good manners and beware of laziness in this path and of ignoring politeness and looking for something else.[1]

Yes, politeness is the capital of life, whoever achieves it, has obtained a great treasure.

Seven years of continuous training

The tree of education grows up gradually and becomes verdant after a long time. It takes a long time for a mulberry leaf to turn into silk, but when it reaches that stage, the gem of its existence is perfected and becomes precious and desirable. Raising a child is also like this, and it requires patience, perseverance, attention, vigilance, and constant monitoring, but its fruit is so sweet and joyful that it makes the parents satisfied and happy despite all the efforts they put in and continue to make in this way.

Yūnus narrates from another person from Imām Ṣādiq, who said:

---

[1] *Biḥār al-'Anwār*, vol. 13, p. 419.

دَعِ ابْنَكَ يَلْعَبْ سَبْعَ سِنِينَ وَ الْزَمْهُ نَفْسَكَ سَبْعَ سِنِينَ فَإِنْ أَفْلَحَ وَ إِلَّا فَإِنَّهُ مَنْ لَا خَيْرَ فِيه

"Let your child play up to seven years; and keep him with you (for education and training) for another seven years; then if he succeeds (well and good); otherwise, there is no good in him."[1]

This narration is narrated in two other ways with some difference and in both the narrations the period for the child's playing is mentioned as six years. But in another narration narrated by the late Ṭabarsī, the period of childhood and adolescence is divided into three stages: the first six years being the playing period, the next six years is the training period and then seven years of continuous education. While according to the first narration, the child's continuous education begins at the age of seven. But according to the narration of the late Ṭabarsī, this period begins at the age of thirteen.

Benefits of politeness in childhood and adolescence

The benefits of politeness during childhood and adolescence are so clear and obvious that they do not require detailed discussion and examination, because most triumphs and successes and sometimes failures and disturbances of the adult period are rooted in the type of education or training during childhood and adolescence. The ancients were correct when they said that acquiring knowledge and manners and being educated during childhood leaves an imprint on the child akin to a beautiful engraving on a stone, which is indestructible.

Saʿdī says:

هر که در خردیش ادب نکنند　　در بزرگی فلاح از او برخاست

چوب تر را چنان که خواهي پیچ　　نشود خشک جز به آتش راست

[1] *Wasāʾil al-Shīʿah*, vol. 15, pp. 193 and 195.

Whoever is not disciplined when a child, Will not prosper when he becomes a man.

While a stick is green you can bend it as you want, When it is dry, fire alone can make it straight.

Luqmān also mentioned to his son as follows:

فَاتَّخِذْهُ عَادَةً فَإِنَّكَ تَخْلُفُ فِي سَلَفِكَ وَ تَنْفَعُ بِهِ خَلْفَكَ وَ يَرْتَجِيكَ فِيهِ رَاغِبٌ وَ يَخْشَى صَوْلَتَكَ رَاهِب

My child! Make education your permanent habit, because you are the successor of the past generations and a model for the future ones, who will benefit from your good manners. The eager ones hope for your politeness, and the fearful are afraid of your majesty.[1]

قَالَ سُفْيَانُ الثَّوْرِيُ دَخَلْتُ عَلَى الصَّادِقِ ع فَقُلْتُ لَهُ أَوْصِنِي بِوَصِيَّةٍ أَحْفَظُهَا مِنْ بَعْدِكَ قَالَ ع وَ تَحْفَظُ يَا سُفْيَانُ قُلْتُ أَجَلْ يَا ابْنَ بِنْتِ رَسُولِ اللَّهِ قَالَ ع يَا سُفْيَانُ لَا مُرُوَّةَ لِكَذُوبٍ وَ لَا رَاحَةَ لِحَسُودٍ وَ لَا إِخَاءَ لِمُلُوكٍ وَ لَا خُلَّةَ لِمُخْتَالٍ وَ لَا سُؤْدُدَ لِسَيِّئِ الْخُلُقِ ثُمَّ أَمْسَكَ ع فَقُلْتُ يَا ابْنَ بِنْتِ رَسُولِ اللَّهِ زِدْنِي فَقَالَ ع يَا سُفْيَانُ ثِقْ بِاللَّهِ تَكُنْ عَارِفاً وَ ارْضَ بِمَا قَسَمَهُ لَكَ تَكُنْ غَنِيّاً صَاحِبْ بِمِثْلِ مَا يُصَاحِبُونَكَ بِهِ تَزْدَدْ إِيمَاناً وَ لَا تُصَاحِبِ الْفَاجِرَ فَيُعَلِّمَكَ مِنْ فُجُورِهِ وَ شَاوِرْ فِي أَمْرِكَ الَّذِينَ يَخْشَوْنَ اللَّهَ عَزَّ وَ جَلَّ ثُمَّ أَمْسَكَ ع فَقُلْتُ يَا ابْنَ بِنْتِ رَسُولِ اللَّهِ زِدْنِي فَقَالَ ع يَا سُفْيَانُ مَنْ أَرَادَ عِزّاً بِلَا سُلْطَانٍ وَ كَثْرَةً بِلَا إِخْوَانٍ وَ هَيْبَةً بِلَا مَالٍ فَلْيَنْتَقِلْ مِنْ ذُلِّ مَعَاصِي اللَّهِ إِلَى عِزِّ طَاعَتِهِ ثُمَّ أَمْسَكَ ع فَقُلْتُ يَا ابْنَ بِنْتِ رَسُولِ اللَّهِ زِدْنِي فَقَالَ ع يَا سُفْيَانُ أَدَّبَنِي أَبِي ع بِثَلَاثٍ وَ نَهَانِي عَنْ ثَلَاثٍ فَأَمَّا اللَّوَاتِي أَدَّبَنِي بِهِنَّ فَإِنَّهُ قَالَ لِي يَا بُنَيَّ مَنْ يَصْحَبْ صَاحِبَ السَّوْءِ لَا يَسْلَمْ وَ مَنْ لَا يُقَيِّدْ أَلْفَاظَهُ يَنْدَمْ وَ مَنْ يَدْخُلْ مَدَاخِلَ السَّوْءِ يُتَّهَمْ قُلْتُ يَا ابْنَ بِنْتِ رَسُولِ اللَّهِ فَمَا الثَّلَاثُ اللَّوَاتِي نَهَاكَ عَنْهُنَّ قَالَ ع نَهَانِي أَنْ أُصَاحِبَ

---

[1] *Biḥār al-'Anwār*, vol. 13, p. 411.

$$\text{حَاسِدَ نِعْمَةٍ وَ شَامِتاً بِمُصِيبَةٍ أَوْ حَامِلَ نَمِيمَةٍ.}$$

Sufyān Thawrī says: I went to Imām Ṣādiq ؑ and said: Give me an advice that I will always remember after you. He said:

"O Sufyān! Will you really remember it?" I said: Yes, son of the daughter of the Messenger of Allāh ﷺ!

Imām ؑ said, "O Sufyān! There is no manliness in a liar and there is no ease for the envious. It is not possible for the rulers and the arrogant to be friends with anyone, and the hot-tempered will not find a leader." Then he fell silent. I said: O son of the daughter of the Messenger of Allāh ﷺ! Tell me more.

He said, "O Sufyān! Trust in Allāh ﷻ in order to become a wise person. Be satisfied with what He has decreed for you, and you will become wealthy. Associate with others in the same way they associate with you, and you will have more faith. Do not accompany the evildoers so that they do not teach you evil deeds. Seek the advice of those who fear Allāh the Glorified. Then Imām ؑ was silent again. I said: O son of the daughter of the Messenger of Allāh ﷺ! Give me more advice.

He said: O Sufyān! He who searches for honour without dependence on the ruler, and who wants to live alone and without a friend as a great crowd, and who wants to attain dignity without wealth he must get rid of the humiliation of sins and rebellion and return to the nobility of Allāh's ﷻ obedience. Then Imām ؑ fell silent and I said: O son of the daughter of the Messenger of Allāh ﷺ! Tell me more.

He said: O Sufyān! My father taught me three things and prohibited three. As for the three things that he taught me; he said: Dear son, whoever befriends an evil person will not be safe. Anyone who does not control his tongue will regret, and whoever is found in a bad place will be blamed.

I said: O son of the daughter of the Messenger of Allāh ﷺ, who are the three people he forbade? He said: My father warned me against associating with the envious, those who rejoice at others' misfortunes, and the talebearers.[1]

Encouraging children

One of the important measures that can be used to improve children's behaviour is encouragement.

Encouragement is one of the most important issues of Islamic training and the best methods of raising children. Children cherish praise and encouragement, and it is their natural inclination, which should be used in the best way to encourage them towards valuable activities.

The need for encouragement is constant, and it is a mistake to imagine that because children have grown up, they no longer need encouragement, but except for prophets, saints and Allāh's ﷻ chosen ones, all people in all stages of life need encouragement and praise.

Benefits of encouragement

1. Encouraging strengthens children's spirit and gives them a new energy so that they can pursue their favourite and good deeds with self-confidence and warmth and realize their importance more than before.

2. Encouraging children's inner talents develops them and makes them flourish and eliminates the grounds of hopelessness and pessimism in them.

3. Due to encouragement, the child learns to overcome problems and difficulties in order to pursue his desired goal, and continuation of encouragement leads to continuation of the child's growth activities.

4. Encouragement of children by parents, friends and teachers makes them look upon them with a positive and optimistic view and consider them as their friends and close buddies, and this has many advantages.

---

[1] *Tuḥaf al-'Uqūl*, p. 396.

5. Sometimes a wise and simple encouragement may change the path of a child's life and save him from evil and deviations.

6. Encouraging children to undertake positive activities and reward them after doing them will create motivation in them and establish a good relationship between them.

But children, who are not encouraged, often suffer from mental failure, and lose their self-confidence and consider themselves inferior and do not dare to do anything because there is no doubt that encouragement is a very pleasant act. But more important than encouragement is the type and manner of encouragement that parents should consider because it might have a negative impact also.

Good encouragement is not only verbal, but practical as well, and that it does not create originality and does not turn into amusement, but it is exactly used to create and strengthen positive behaviour. Children know well what they are encouraged for and what they should do in order to be encouraged. In the same way, good encouragement is that which is done in the presence of a crowd, not just in secret.

Encouragement of Allāh ﷻ

On various occasions in the Holy Qur'ān, Allāh ﷻ has encouraged and praised his righteous servants: the prophets, righteous men, the saints, and infallible leaders. For example, Prophet Ayyūb (a), for his patience and steadfastness in the face of suffering and said about him:

...إِنَّا وَجَدْنَٰهُ صَابِرًا ۚ نِّعْمَ ٱلْعَبْدُ ۖ إِنَّهُۥٓ أَوَّابٌ ﴿٤٤﴾

"Indeed We found him to be patient. What an excellent servant! Indeed he was a penitent [soul]."[1]

In this way, he introduced him as one of His best servants.

[1] Sūrah Sa'd 38:44.

Likewise, many verses have come about Prophet Muḥammad b. 'Abdullāh ﷺ in praise of his holy existence. For example, it is mentioned about his good manners that:

$$\text{وَإِنَّكَ لَعَلَىٰ خُلُقٍ عَظِيمٍ}$$

"and indeed you possess a great character..."[1]

Encouragement of the Prophet ﷺ

The Holy Prophet ﷺ praised Amīr al Mu'minīn ؏ many times in front of others. In the battle of 'Uhud, after 'Amr b. 'Abd Wudd was slain by 'Alī ؏, the Prophet ﷺ said:

$$\text{لَضَرْبَةُ عَلِيٍّ يَوْمَ الْخَنْدَقِ أَفْضَلُ مِنْ عِبَادَةِ الثَّقَلَيْنِ}$$

"The blow that 'Alī ؏ inflicted (on 'Amr) on the day of Khandaq is superior to the combined worship of human beings and *Jinn*."[2]

There is another praiseworthy statement about him and other infallible A'immah from the Messenger of Allāh ﷺ, which is beyond the scope of this discussion. But as regards the present discussion, there are many narrations that infallible leaders ؏ encouraged their children on various occasions. We mention a few examples below:

Encouragement of Ibrāhīm ؏

The late Qutub Rāwandī writes in *Lab al-Lubāb*:

أَنَّ إِبْرَاهِيمَ قَالَ لِإِسْمَاعِيلَ ع فِي حَالِ الذَّبْحِ ادْعُ أَنْتَ بِالْفَرَجِ لِأَنَّكَ أَنْتَ الْمُضْطَرُّ- أَمَنْ يُجِيبُ الْمُضْطَرَّ إِذَا دَعَاهُ فَلَمَّا رَأَى الْكَبْشَ خَرَجَ لِيَأْخُذَهُ فَلَمَّا رَجَعَ رَأَى يَدَيْ إِسْمَاعِيلَ مُطْلَقَتَيْنِ قَالَ وَ مَنْ أَطْلَقَكَ قَالَ رَجُلٌ مِنْ صِفَتِهِ كَذَا قَالَ هُوَ

---

[1] Sūrah Qalam 68:4.
[2] *Mustadrak al-Wasā'il*, vol. 5, p. 247 (cited by Qutub Rāwandī).

جَبْرَئِيلُ وَ هَلْ قَالَ لَكَ قَالَ نَعَمْ قَالَ لِي ادْعُ اللَّهَ فَدَعْوَتُكَ الْآنَ مُسْتَجَابَةٌ قَالَ إِبْرَاهِيمُ وَ أَيَّ شَيْءٍ دَعَوْتَ قَالَ قُلْتُ اللَّهُمَّ اغْفِرْ لِلْمُؤْمِنِينَ وَ الْمُؤْمِنَاتِ قَالَ يَا بُنَيَّ إِنَّكَ لَمُوَفَّقٌ

It is narrated that Ibrāhīm said to his son, Ismā'īl, while he was being slaughtered: "My son! Pray for ease in this matter as you are in real distress."

Suddenly his eyes fell on a ram, and he got up to take it, when he turned back he saw that Ismā'īl's hands (which were tied) were now untied. He asked: Who untied your hands?

He said: A man with this name and sign.

Ibrāhīm said: He was Jibra'īl! Did he tell you anything? Ismā'īl said: Yes, he told me: Call on Allāh as your prayer is being answered now.

Ibrāhīm asked: What did you pray and what did you say?

Ismā'īl said: I said: O Allāh! Send mercy and forgiveness on the faithful.

Ibrāhīm said: My son! You are a successful person.[1]

Encouragement and praise in the conduct of Ahl al-Bayt

After the above examples, we present some other instances from the life of these great models of humanity:

Imām Bāqir said:

مَرِضْتُ مَرَضاً شَدِيداً فَقَالَ لِي أَبِي ع مَا تَشْتَهِي فَقُلْتُ أَشْتَهِي أَنْ أَكُونَ مِمَّنْ لَا أَقْتَرِحُ عَلَى [اللَّهِ] رَبِّي سِوَى مَا يُدَبِّرُهُ لِي فَقَالَ لِي أَحْسَنْتَ ضَاهَيْتَ إِبْرَاهِيمَ الْخَلِيلَ ع حَيْثُ قَالَ لَهُ جَبْرَئِيلُ ع هَلْ مِنْ حَاجَةٍ فَقَالَ لَا أَقْتَرِحُ عَلَى رَبِّي بَلْ حَسْبِيَ اللَّهُ وَ نِعْمَ الْوَكِيلُ

My father, 'Alī b. al-Ḥusain said: I was extremely unwell. My father [Imām Ḥusain] said: My son; what do you want? I said: I want

---

[1] *Mustadrak al-Wasā'il*, vol. 5, p. 247 (cited by Qutub Rāwandī).

to be one who does not propose anything to Allāh 🌸 and does not ask for anything, even though Allāh 🌸 has arranged everything for me.

My father 🌸 said: Well done, for being like Ibrāhīm 🌸, the friend of the Beneficent Lord 🌸. Because when Jibra'īl 🌸 asked: Do you need anything? Ibrāhīm 🌸 replied: I do not ask Allāh 🌸 for anything, because He is the one, who is sufficient for me and He is the best caretaker.[1]

It is narrated from Imām Riḍā 🌸 that he said:

Once Imām Mūsā b. Ja'far 🌸 said something in the presence of his father (Imām Ṣādiq 🌸) that surprised and pleased the latter.

By way of appreciation and encouragement of his son, Imām 🌸 said:

يَا بُنَيَّ الْحَمْدُ لِلَّهِ الَّذِي جَعَلَكَ خَلَفاً مِنَ الْآبَاءِ وَ سُرُوراً مِنَ الْأَبْنَاءِ وَ عِوَضاً عَنِ الْأَصْدِقَاءِ

"O my son! Praise be to Allāh 🌸, who made you a successor of your forefathers, and a source of pleasure among my children, and in return for my lost friends.[2]

That is, my son! With this nobleness that you display, you are the best successor and heir of your father, and you are the best son and light of your father's eyes, and you are the best friend and confidant of your father instead of his friends.

دَخَلَ أَبُو حَنِيفَةَ عَلَى أَبِي عَبْدِ اللَّهِ ع فَقَالَ لَهُ إِنِّي رَأَيْتُ ابْنَكَ مُوسَى يُصَلِّي وَ النَّاسُ يَمُرُّونَ بَيْنَ يَدَيْهِ فَلَا يَنْهَاهُمْ وَ فِيهِ مَا فِيهِ فَقَالَ أَبُو عَبْدِ اللَّهِ ع ادْعُ لِي مُوسَى فَلَمَّا جَاءَهُ قَالَ يَا بُنَيَّ إِنَّ أَبَا حَنِيفَةَ يَذْكُرُ أَنَّكَ تُصَلِّي وَ النَّاسُ يَمُرُّونَ بَيْنَ يَدَيْكَ فَلَا تَنْهَاهُمْ قَالَ نَعَمْ يَا أَبَهْ إِنَّ الَّذِي كُنْتُ أُصَلِّي لَهُ كَانَ أَقْرَبَ إِلَيَّ مِنْهُمْ يَقُولُ اللَّهُ تَعَالَى

Muḥammad b. Muslim says: Once Abū Ḥanīfah came to Imām Ṣādiq 🌸 and said: I saw your son, Mūsā 🌸, who was praying while

---

[1] *Biḥār al-'Anwār*, vol. 46, p. 67.
[2] *Biḥār al-'Anwār*, vol. 48, p. 24 (from *'Uyūn Akhbār al-Riḍā*, vol. 2, p. 127).

people were passing in front of him and he did not push them away, and that was wrong on his part!

Imām Ṣādiq said, "Call Mūsā." When Mūsā arrived, his father said, "My son! Abū Ḥanīfah says: You were praying, and people were passing in front of you, and you did not forbid them?" He said, "Yes, father dear; but the one I was praying to was closer to me than those who passed in front of me. Allāh says:

$$...وَنَحْنُ أَقْرَبُ إِلَيْهِ مِنْ حَبْلِ ٱلْوَرِيدِ ۝$$

...And we are closer to him than his jugular vein."[1]

قَالَ فَضَمَّهُ أَبُو عَبْدِ اللَّهِ ع إِلَى نَفْسِهِ وَ قَالَ بِأَبِي أَنْتَ وَ أُمِّي

Muḥammad b. Muslim says: As soon as Imām Ṣādiq heard this answer from his son, he hugged him and pressed him to his bosom and said, "May my parents be sacrificed for you, O repository of secrets."[2]

كُنْتُ قَاعِداً فَمَرَّ أَبُو الْحَسَنِ مُوسَى ع وَ مَعَهُ بَهْمَةٌ قَالَ قُلْتُ يَا غُلَامُ مَا تَرَى مَا يَصْنَعُ أَبُوكَ يَأْمُرُنَا بِالشَّيْءِ ثُمَّ يَنْهَانَا عَنْهُ أَمَرَنَا أَنْ نَتَوَلَّى أَبَا الْخَطَّابِ ثُمَّ أَمَرَنَا أَنْ نَلْعَنَهُ وَ نَتَبَرَّأَ مِنْهُ فَقَالَ أَبُو الْحَسَنِ ع وَ هُوَ غُلَامٌ إِنَّ اللَّهَ خَلَقَ خَلْقاً لِلْإِيمَانِ لَا زَوَالَ لَهُ وَ خَلَقَ خَلْقاً لِلْكُفْرِ لَا زَوَالَ لَهُ وَ خَلَقَ خَلْقاً بَيْنَ ذَلِكَ أَعَارَهُ الْإِيمَانَ يُسَمَّوْنَ الْمُعَارِينَ إِذَا شَاءَ سَلَبَهُمْ وَ كَانَ أَبُو الْخَطَّابِ مِمَّنْ أُعِيرَ الْإِيمَانَ قَالَ فَدَخَلْتُ عَلَى أَبِي عَبْدِ اللَّهِ ع فَأَخْبَرْتُهُ مَا قُلْتُ لِأَبِي الْحَسَنِ ع وَ مَا قَالَ لِي فَقَالَ أَبُو عَبْدِ اللَّهِ ع إِنَّهُ نَبْعَةُ نُبُوَّةٍ.

'Īsā Shalqān says: Once I was sitting when Imām Mūsā b. Ja'far passed by and with him was a goat. I (the narrator) asked him, 'O young man, do you know what your father does? He commands us to do something and then he prohibits us to do the same. He commanded us to be friends with Abū al-Khaṭṭāb and then ordered us to condemn and disown him.' Imām Mūsā Kāẓim said – and he was only a young boy - 'Allāh has created a creature for belief that does not

---

[1] Sūrah Qāf 50 : 16.
[2] *Biḥār al-'Anwār*, vol. 48, p. 171; *Wasā'il al-Shī'ah*, vol. 3, p. 436.

vanish. He has created a creature for disbelief that does not vanish. He has created a creature in between and has deposited belief in them and they are called people with transient belief. When He wills, He removes belief from them and Abū al-Khaṭṭāb was one in whom belief was deposited temporarily.'

'Isā Shalqān says: After this conversation, I came to Imām Ṣādiq and informed him about this incident. After listening to this conversation, the Imām said about Imām Mūsā Kāẓim, "He is a bubbling spring of prophethood."[1]

Corporeal punishment of children

One of the important and complex issues of training that most parents have doubts about is how to deal with their children's misbehaviour, so that most of the time parents are confused how to react to their children's mistakes and misbehaviour and their rejection of advice and guidance.

If they remain silent in front of their ugly and unpleasant actions, the children will become proud of their mistakes and be emboldened; if they react and punish them, they may create other problems.

In this section, in the light of the words of the Infallibles, we will first point out the prohibition and permissibility of corporeal punishment, and then suggest the best solution in this regard, and in the end, we will examine the life of the Infallibles.

Instances when corporeal punishment of children is forbidden

In traditional reports, some instances are mentioned when you are not supposed to beat children.

Mention of these instances does not imply that it is allowed to beat them in other cases, but in general, the basic and general principle of Islam - which has a very important educational and corrective role - is positive encouragement and motivation in good deeds. Punishment,

---

[1] *Biḥār al-'Anwār*, vol. 48, p. 116 (quoted from *al-Kāfī*).

except in special cases - some of which will be mentioned - often has a negative effect, and if it is asked whether corporeal punishment should be abandoned in these cases; we would say yes, it is better to abandon it, and not to support it in any case.

1. One of the cases in which children should not be beaten is when pure and sacred names have been given to children. In the naming section of the children, we mentioned that the *Ahl al-Bayt* were very strict that the children with the names of the Holy Prophet and Lady Fāṭimah Zahrā and the Infallible A'immah should not be abused or physically punished.

2. A child should not be beaten for prayer before the age of ten. The Prophet said:

أَدِّبْ صِغَارَ أَهْلِ بَيْتِكَ بِلِسَانِكَ عَلَى الصَّلَاةِ وَ الطَّهُورِ فَإِذَا بَلَغُوا عَشْرَ سِنِينَ فَاضْرِبْ وَ لَا تُجَاوِزْ ثَلَاثًا

"Discipline the children of your household with your tongue on prayer and purification, so when they reach ten years of age, beat them, but do not exceed three hits."[1]

You may beat them for laziness and sloth in prayer, but do not exceed three strikes.

It is concluded from this tradition that before the age of ten, it is not permissible to hit a child for prayer. Of course, the age specified for this purpose is mentioned differently in the traditions (seven, eight, nine and thirteen years). Therefore, it is necessary to observe caution and avoid hitting as much as possible and use more suitable methods.

Instances when beating is justified

1. To prevent deviation

Imām Ṣādiq said about a child, who reaches the stage of youth and chooses Christianity - while one or both of his parents were

---

[1] *Majmu'ah Warrām*, p. 358.

Muslims - he said, "The youth is not left to his own devices, but he is to be physically punished to accept Islam."[1]

2. For education

The Messenger of Allāh ﷺ said in a part of his advice to the Amīr al Mu'minīn, 'Alī ؑ: "Do not hit (a child) more than three times for the sake of education and training."[2]

Also, as seen in these narrations, parents are allowed to resort to punishment only in special cases that are fateful for the child - and not for every action of the child that is not acceptable to the parents.

Limits of corporeal punishment

From past narrations, it became clear that hitting children in some cases - even for education and morals - is allowed; but we have to see what are the limits of corporeal punishment? How much and with what means can the parents punish the child? Are they allowed to use the stick or whip brutally to discipline them while in fact torturing them to injure their bodies?

Are the parents allowed to mete out corporeal punishment to children of any age?

Can they, whenever they are angry with their child's disobedience, fall madly on innocent lives and, in addition to cursing and bad mouthing, beat them up? Undoubtedly, the answer is negative, and such an idea that some ignorant parents have about the education and training of their children is utterly incorrect. The narrations received from the Prophet ﷺ and the Holy A'immah ؑ have fixed absolutely clear limits of punishment.

---

[1] *Wasā'il al-Shī'ah*, vol. 18, p. 546.
عَنْ أَبِي عَبْدِ اللَّهِ ع فِي الصَّبِيِّ إِذَا شَبَّ فَاخْتَارَ النَّصْرَانِيَّةَ وَ أَحَدُ أَبَوَيْهِ نَصْرَانِيٌّ أَوْ مُسْلِمَيْنِ قَالَ لَا يُتْرَكُ وَ لَكِنْ يُضْرَبُ عَلَى الْإِسْلَام

[2] *Majmu'ah Warrām*, p. 358.
وَ عَنْهُ ع لَا تَضْرِبَنَ أَدَباً فَوْقَ ثَلَاثٍ فَإِنَّكَ إِنْ فَعَلْتَ فَهُوَ قِصَاصٌ يَوْمَ الْقِيَامَة

Limitation of corporeal punishment

Permissible punishment has certain conditions and after considering them we can see that it is a wise principle and not a violent way to compensate for the inability of parents to educate and guide children. Corporeal punishment of children under the age of ten is not allowed, and the quantum is strictly limited, if it is more than that, or it leads to bruises or harms the child's organs it would be a sinful act...

1. Ḥammād b. ʿUthmān says: I asked Imām Ṣādiq regarding disciplining and beating of a child or a slave. He said, "Do not exceed five or six strikes and be gentle in this also."[1]

2. More than three strikes make you liable to pay the retributive penalty (*Qiṣāṣ*). One of the Prophet's commandments to ʿAlī was that he said, "Never give more than three strikes in disciplining, because if you do so, you will be liable for retaliation on the Judgment Day."[2]

3. ʿAlī said to the children who brought their writings to His Eminence — to choose the best among them. He said, "Tell your teacher that if he hits you more than three times, he will be retaliated against."[3]

Proof of blood money

Whenever it is not possible to discipline the child except through beating, although it is permissible - subject to necessary conditions -

---

[1] *Wasāʾil al-Shīʿah*, vol. 18, p. 581.

عَنْ حَمَّادِ بْنِ عُثْمَانَ قَالَ: قُلْتُ لِأَبِي عَبْدِ اللَّهِ ع فِي أَدَبِ الصَّبِيِّ وَ الْمَمْلُوكِ فَقَالَ خَمْسَةً أَوْ سِتَّةً وَ ارْفُقْ

[2] *Majmuʿah Warrām*, p. 358.

وَ عَنْهُ ع لَا تَضْرِبَنَّ أَدَباً فَوْقَ ثَلَاثٍ فَإِنَّكَ إِنْ فَعَلْتَ فَهُوَ قِصَاصٌ يَوْمَ الْقِيَامَةِ

[3] *Wasāʾil al-Shīʿah*, vol. 18, 582.

أَبْلِغُوا مُعَلِّمَكُمْ إِنْ ضَرَبَكُمْ فَوْقَ ثَلَاثِ ضَرَبَاتٍ فِي الْأَدَبِ اقْتُصَّ مِنْهُ

but the father should be aware of the fact that if the child gets red marks or is bruised or injured, or possibly if the father hits the child hard and he dies, although the father is not retaliated for this (this rule is only for the father), but he must surely pay the blood money, even if the child was hit with no other intention other than to discipline.[1]

The *fatwā* of Grand Āyatullāh Arākī is as follows:

Question: When a father beats his child with the intention of beating him, does he have to pay retaliation or not?

Answer: It is permissible to hit the child anywhere except his head, but he should not get bruised, and assuming it is permissible, the obligatory sentence does not conflict with the situational one, such as in a predicament...which does not conflict with the guarantee, so whenever it becomes red or black, the payment of retaliation is fixed.[2]

Reminder

1. Islamic traditions prescribe corporeal punishment only in cases that have an educational and directive aspect, and the parents are not allowed to punish whenever the child does not act according to their wishes or for the sake of their personal tastes or desires; because in that case the beating would no longer be considered disciplining but would only be a means to quell the anger of parents.

2. Parents are not allowed to beat children under the age of seven (and to exercise caution till the age of thirteen) to make them pray.

3. Maximum corporeal punishment for children is six strokes. Of course, a teacher has no right to hit more than three times.[3] If he strikes more, in addition to having committed an unlawful act, he also becomes liable for punishment.

---

[1] Ref.: *Sharī'ah al-Isāam*, vol. 4, p. 192, (This issue is a part of the Muslim jurisprudential principles. For more information refer to the section on *Diyāh* in books of Islamic jurisprudence, in which the extent of penalties for every part of the body are mentioned).

[2] *Tawḍiḥ al-Masā'il*, Section of verdicts, p. 571.

[3] Ayatullāh al-'Uẓmā al-Khū'ī says: This is about non-teachers, and as for it, it seems that it is not permissible to strike more than three times...*Mabānī Takmīlat al-Minhāj*, vol. 1, p. 341.

Although it is permissible for the father to hit six times, but if he exceeds this limit, he will be punished on Judgment Day, and divine chastisement is much more severe and painful than punishment at human hands in this world.

Methods of punishment

Punishment may be meted out in various ways and is not limited to beating; because showing bitterness is also a form of punishment; in the same way depriving children of some pleasant and attractive things is another punishment; but in corporeal punishment also, it is not meant to resort to harsh and barbaric ways, hitting with lashes, hoses, whips, etc. For example, regarding the means of punishing a woman by her husband, which is mentioned in the Qur'ān in the verse of:

...وَٱضْرِبُوهُنَّ...

"...and [as the last resort] beat them..."[1]

في المجمع عن الباقر عليه السلام أنه الضرب بالسواك

The late Ṭabarsī in *Majmaʿ al-Bayān* narrates from Imām Bāqir that it implies hitting with a toothbrush.[2]

Therefore, if the punishment of the wife by the husband is dealt with in this way, the special method of punishing the child is also known. It is recommended for the parents and teachers to:

First: Don't use punishment, especially corporeal punishment, as a general and primary method of dealing with children's mistakes.

Second: To control their nerves and emotions and if necessary, use punishment to prevent the child from deviation, not to vent their anger on the child.

Third: To be satisfied with the minimum punishment and not to exceed it.

---

[1] Sūrah an-Nisā' 4:34.
[2] *Tafsīr Ṣāfī*, vol. 1, p. 354, quoted by *Majmaʿ al-Bayān*.

Four: Not to use every means to punish the child, also not to hit the child's face and vulnerable places and avoid harsh actions and words.

Being furious is the best solution

The best solution that can be offered in this important and complex issue is from the training lessons of Islam and the *Ahl al-Bayt* ﷺ that even if at all there is a need to punish children, do not beat them. They are the buds of Paradise that have made life sweeter, in such cases, be angry at them, because this act has a significant effect on the child's feelings, and the child feels that if the father or mother is angry with him, it is as if all the doors are closed upon him. He has no choice but to give up his bad deeds, so he should give up his ugly deeds and ask for forgiveness from his parents or teacher, but it should not take too long, otherwise it will have other negative repercussions.

Imām Mūsā b. Ja'far ﷺ said to one of his companions who was fed up with his son and was complaining about him:

لَا تَضْرِبْهُ وَ اهْجُرْهُ وَلَا تُطِل

"Don't hit him, but be furious with him, but do not prolong it."[1]

Ahl al-Bayt's ﷺ method of punishment

But it was not the way of the *Ahl al-Bayt* ﷺ to physically punish their children, and I have not come across a case where they have done such a thing. Therefore, we have to see what the upbringing method of those nobles was like. Or that some of them had many children, but they never saw the need to physically punish children, and this issue is very important and instructive. Since we do not have proper knowledge of high Islamic training, we imagine that beating is the only way of training a child.

The Infallible A'immah ﷺ did not only treat children with kindness and gentleness; they also treated their slaves similarly. They

[1] *'Udat al-Dā'ī*, p. 79.

were also well-behaved and mild-mannered, and that too at a time when slaves were treated in the worst ways in the society. Those nobles never used violence with the slaves and never treated them with anything but gentleness.

Teaching to read and write

Another right that a child has over his father is to enjoy the blessing of reading and writing. In order to fulfill this duty, the father must either do it personally or fund his child's education.

In the narrations recorded in this context, reading and writing are mentioned as rights and obligations. The Noble Prophet of Islam ﷺ says:

$$\text{مِنْ حَقِ الْوَلَدِ عَلَى وَالِدِهِ ثَلَاثَةٌ يُحَسِّنُ اسْمَهُ وَ يُعَلِّمُهُ الْكِتَابَةَ وَ يُزَوِّجُهُ إِذَا بَلَغَ}$$

"There are three rights of a child over his father: (1) To give him a good name. (2) To teach him how to write. (3) To get him married when he reaches puberty."[1]

In other narrations, even this is not all; the fathers are also asked to persuade their children to study and acquire knowledge.

Amīr al Mu'minīn 'Alī ؑ said:

$$\text{مُرُوا أَوْلَادَكُمْ بِطَلَبِ الْعِلْمِ}$$

"Encourage your children to seek knowledge."[2]

Luqmān encouraged knowledge and wisdom

Imām Ṣādiq ؑ says:

---

[1] *Makārim al-'Akhlāq*, p. 220; *Wasā'il al-Shī'ah*, vol. 15, p. 200; *Mustadrak al-Wasā'il*, vol. 15, p. 161.
[2] *Kanz al-'Ummāl*, vol. 16, p. 584.

كَانَ فِيمَا وَعَظَ لُقْمَانُ ابْنَهُ أَنْ قَالَ لَهُ: يَا بُنَيَّ، اجْعَلْ فِي أَيَّامِكَ وَ لَيَالِيكَ وَ سَاعَاتِكَ نَصِيباً لَكَ فِي طَلَبِ الْعِلْمِ، فَإِنَّكَ لَنْ تَجِدَ لَكَ تَضْيِيعاً مِثْلَ تَرْكِهِ

"Luqmān advised his son, saying: O my son, fix in your days, nights and hours a share for seeking knowledge, because nothing you have lost is like the loss of knowledge."[1]

Once Imām Ḥasan Mujtabā called his children along with his brother's children and said:

إِنَّكُمْ صِغَارُ قَوْمٍ وَ يُوشِكُ أَنْ تَكُونُوا كِبَارَ قَوْمٍ آخَرِينَ فَتَعَلَّمُوا الْعِلْمَ فَمَنْ يَسْتَطِعْ مِنْكُمْ أَنْ يَحْفَظَهُ فَلْيَكْتُبْهُ وَ لْيَضَعْهُ فِي بَيْتِهِ

"You are the children of today's society and soon you will be the elders of tomorrow's society, so learn knowledge [and try to study] and those of you who do not have a strong memory [and cannot memorize the teacher's material in the classroom], note down the material and keep the texts at home [so that you can refer to them when necessary and take advantage of them]."[2]

Military training

Today's children and youths are the men of the future, and they must find the necessary training and preparation for the goals of the Islamic society. There is always the danger of military attack by enemies, and according to the Qur'ān:

...وَلَا يَزَالُونَ يُقَاتِلُونَكُمْ حَتَّىٰ يَرُدُّوكُمْ...

"And they will not cease fighting you until they turn you away from your religion..."[3]

---

[1] Biḥār al-'Anwār, vol. 13, p. 415.
[2] Biḥār al-'Anwār, vol. 1, p. 110.
[3] Sūrah al-Baqarah 2:217.

Therefore, the fathers and educators of the society have the duty to acquaint the children of the Islamic society with military and defence issues and teach them archery, self-defence, war and defensive tactics, and teach them to fight with modern weapons and combat and defence methods and train them with modern weapons and methods. Make them familiar with their uses and the tactics and tricks of the enemy.

In fact, a huge army 20 million strong will march forward and a huge and fearsome fighting force of Muslims will emerge ready to defend the borders of the Islamic world in any way.

It is also hinted in the narrations that you must teach your children use of defensive tools and methods so that the enemies of Allāh ﷻ are intimidated and never dare to attack the borders of an Islamic country. It is true that if the youth of a country are men of campaign, war and defence and are familiar with military issues, which enemy can use threats and aggression against it?

Swimming and archery are two important defensive skills that are emphasized in Islamic traditions. In addition to being a physical sport in general, swimming is a source of agility, vitality, and physical activity. It also plays an important role in water and land operations. Archery is one of the most basic issues of war and defence, and it is clear that war is nothing but the use of weapons against the enemy.

Once the Holy Prophet ﷺ said to Abū Rāfiʿ, who wanted to spend all his wealth in the way of Allāh ﷻ:

كيف بک يا أبا رافعٍ اذا افتَقرتَ. قال: أفلا أتقدّم فی ذلک؟ قال: بلی قال: مامالک؟ قال: أربعون ألفاً وهی لله. قال : لا. أعطِ بعضاً وأمسِک بعضاً وأصلح الی ولدِک. قال: أولهم علينا حقّ كما لنا عليهم ؟ قال: نعم. حقُّ الولد علی الوالد أن يُعَلِّمه كتابَ الله، والرمیَ والسِباحة

"Abū Rāfiʿ what will you do when you become poor?" Abū Rāfiʿ said: I said: Shouldn't we take precedence in charity (and send something for our Hereafter)?

The Prophet ﷺ said, "Yes, send it."

Then he (Prophet ﷺ) asked, "How much do you have?"

I said: Forty thousand; and I want to spend it all in the way of Allāh ﷻ.

The Prophet ﷺ said, "Don't! On the contrary spend a part of it in the way of Allāh ﷻ and keep another part for your children." Abū Rāfiʿ asked: Do they have a right on us just as we have a right on them?

The Prophet ﷺ said, "The right of the child over the father is that he should make him familiar with the Holy Qur'ān, and also teach him archery and swimming."[1]

Amīr al Mu'minīn ؑ narrates the following from the Prophet ﷺ.

عَلِّمُوا أَوْلَادَكُمُ السِّبَاحَةَ وَ الرِّمَايَةَ

"Teach your children swimming and archery."[2]

Also, Jābir has narrated from the Prophet ﷺ, who said:

عَلِّموا بينكم الرمىُ ، فإنّه نكاية العدوّ

"Teach your children archery, which is the act of suppressing the enemies and defeating them."[3]

From these narrations, we conclude as follows:

1. Learning swimming and archery are the rights that a son has on his father, although this issue is almost forgotten, and fathers do not attach much importance to it.

2. Swimming and archery are important defensive skills that are only mentioned as examples and special methods of defence. There are many skills and defensive and offensive methods and all necessary tools for it are considered.

---

[1] *Kanz al-ʿUmmāl*, 16, p. 444; *Ḥilyat al-Awliyā'*, Vol. 1, p. 184.

[2] *Wasā'il al-Shīʿah*, vol. 15, p. 194.

[3] *Kanz al-ʿUmmāl*, vol. 16, p. 443.

3. It can be concluded from Abū Rāfiʿ conversation with the Messenger of Allāh ﷺ that the father should use some of his funds to train his son in warfare and defence skills such as swimming and archery, so that he can grow sufficiently in this direction and be a good defender of Islam and Islamic country.

4. It is obvious that a society, whose teenagers are familiar with military training will strike fear into the hearts of the enemies and their evil intentions will be defeated. And the verse:

وَأَعِدُّواْ لَهُم مَّا ٱسْتَطَعْتُم مِّن قُوَّةٍ وَمِن رِّبَاطِ ٱلْخَيْلِ تُرْهِبُونَ بِهِۦ عَدُوَّ ٱللَّهِ وَعَدُوَّكُمْ...

"Prepare against them whatever you can of [military] power and war-horses, awing thereby the enemy of Allāh, and your enemy..."[1]

...will present a concrete example.

Teaching dinner etiquette

There are customs and traditions about eating that are a part of Islamic teachings and it is appropriate that we should be bound by them and make our children familiar with them. One of these is to wash our hands before sitting to eat, to squat while sitting, to begin with 'in the name of Allāh', to take small bites, to chew food thoroughly, not to look at anyone while eating, not to lift bread or food placed before anyone, not to overeat, to stop eating before you're full, etc. Now we present some traditions regarding dinner etiquettes:

Mentioning the name of Allāh ﷻ : Mismaʿ narrates from Imām Ṣādiq ؑ from the Prophet ﷺ who said:

مَا مِنْ رَجُلٍ يَجْمَعُ عِيَالَهُ وَ يَضَعُ مَائِدَةً بَيْنَ يَدَيْهِ وَ يُسَمِّي وَ يُسَمُّونَ فِي أَوَّلِ الطَّعَامِ وَ يَحْمَدُونَ اللَّهَ عَزَّ وَ جَلَّ فِي آخِرِهِ فَتَرْتَفِعُ الْمَائِدَةُ حَتَّى يُغْفَرَ لَهُم

[1] Sūrah al-'Anfāl 8:60.

"Allāh ﷻ forgives a family who come together, prepare the table of food, they all mention the name of Allāh ﷻ at the beginning of food and praise Allāh, most Majestic, most Glorious, at the end of food."[1]

Aṣbagh b. Nubātah says: Amīr al Mu'minīn, 'Alī ؑ said to his son, Imām Ḥasan Mujtabā ؑ:

أَ لَا أُعَلِّمُكَ أَرْبَعَ خِصَالٍ تَسْتَغْنِي بِهَا عَنِ الطِّبِّ قَالَ بَلَى قَالَ لَا تَجْلِسْ عَلَى الطَّعَامِ إِلَّا وَ أَنْتَ جَائِعٌ وَ لَا تَقُمْ عَنِ الطَّعَامِ إِلَّا وَ أَنْتَ تَشْتَهِيهِ وَ جَوِّدِ الْمَضْغَ وَ إِذَا نِمْتَ فَاعْرِضْ نَفْسَكَ عَلَى الْخَلَاءِ

"My son, should I not tell you about four things which if you act upon you will never need medicine or treatment?"

'Why not?' said Imām Ḥasan ؑ. 'Alī ؑ said, "Never sit to eat unless you are hungry and get up from the table before you are full; chew the food well and visit the washroom before going to bed."[2]

Avoiding overeating

Luqmān the Wise said to his son:

يا بنيّ إذا امتلائت المعدة نامت الفكرة و خرست الحكمة و قعدت الأعضاء عن العبادة

"O my son! When the stomach is full of food, the thought process falls asleep, the tongue of wisdom becomes dumb, and the parts of the body stop worshiping."[3]

Gargle

Imām Riḍā ؑ narrates the following from his father:

---

[1] *al-Kāfī*, vol. 6, p. 296; *Wasā'il al-Shī'ah*, vol. 16, p. 515, 585, and 586.
[2] *Majmu'ah Warrām*, p. 73.
[3] *Makārim al-'Akhlāq*, p. 153.

أَنَّ الْحُسَيْنَ بْنَ عَلِيٍّ ع قَالَ كَانَ أَمِيرُ الْمُؤْمِنِينَ ع يَأْمُرُنَا إِذَا تَخَلَّلْنَا أَنْ لَا نَشْرَبَ الْمَاءَ حَتَّى نَتَمَضْمَضَ ثَلَاثاً

Imām Ḥusain ﷺ said: My father, the leader of the believers, used to tell his mother: "Whenever we brush our teeth, we should not drink the water, unless we gargle three times first (swirl the water in the mouth and throw it away).[1]

[1] *Makārim al-'Akhlāq*, p. 157.

Part Four

The period of rebuilding the child's personality

The period of rebuilding the child's personality

Removing corruption and deviance

One of the most important and difficult moral duties of parents is to destroy the grounds of moral deviance and corruption in their children, because no fire is more scorching than moral corruption and perversion to disrupt or to destroy a healthy environment. Since there is corruption and deviance among everyone, and children are constantly on the verge of slipping and deviating due to lack of experience and ignorance, and due to having the special spirit of adolescence and youth. Parents, who are aware of them, should try to remove the obstacles to a healthy life and not allow the pure and untouched nature of their children to become morally decadent and be infected with social evils. For this purpose, in addition to being aware of various issues, especially the physical and mental problems and needs of children, they should also have good guiding and educational behaviour so that they are considered friends and comrades of children and teenagers and they do not feel any separation between their parents. Before any physical and mental damage is caused, the children should share their problems with their parents and try to solve them. It is natural that parents should not neglect to read educational and moral books and always be a few steps ahead of the current needs of their children and be the real support and refuge for the children in their lives.

Now, we shall point out some subtleties of Islamic teachings in the pursuit of the above goals:

A) Separating the sleeping place and taking permission to enter

A very delicate and important instructive issue that is sometimes neglected by families is the issue of children taking permission from their parents to enter their private chambers.

During childhood, a child spends time with his parents and feels that he has no limits for many things, and because there is a lot of intimacy and dependence between him and his parents, he wants to go to the room without permission and stay with them, but gradually he should be trained, and he must get used to it. Children should be made to sleep in their own room and ask permission to enter their parents' bedroom. It is obvious that this should be done gently, and parents should proceed with it by strengthening the sense of mental independence and self-esteem of children and training them, so that before they reach the age of puberty, they may realize the necessity of this matter.

This is a very important moral lesson, which if followed properly would assure that the children grow up pure and chaste. The Holy Qur'ān says:

يَٰٓأَيُّهَا ٱلَّذِينَ ءَامَنُواْ لِيَسۡتَـٔۡذِنكُمُ ٱلَّذِينَ مَلَكَتۡ أَيۡمَٰنُكُمۡ وَٱلَّذِينَ لَمۡ
يَبۡلُغُواْ ٱلۡحُلُمَ مِنكُمۡ ثَلَٰثَ مَرَّٰتٖۚ مِّن قَبۡلِ صَلَوٰةِ ٱلۡفَجۡرِ وَحِينَ تَضَعُونَ
ثِيَابَكُم مِّنَ ٱلظَّهِيرَةِ وَمِنۢ بَعۡدِ صَلَوٰةِ ٱلۡعِشَآءِۚ ثَلَٰثُ عَوۡرَٰتٖ لَّكُمۡۚ لَيۡسَ
عَلَيۡكُمۡ وَلَا عَلَيۡهِمۡ جُنَاحُۢ بَعۡدَهُنَّۚ طَوَّٰفُونَ عَلَيۡكُم بَعۡضُكُمۡ عَلَىٰ بَعۡضٖۚ
كَذَٰلِكَ يُبَيِّنُ ٱللَّهُ لَكُمُ ٱلۡأٓيَٰتِۗ وَٱللَّهُ عَلِيمٌ حَكِيمٞ ٥٨ وَإِذَا بَلَغَ ٱلۡأَطۡفَٰلُ
مِنكُمُ ٱلۡحُلُمَ فَلۡيَسۡتَـٔۡذِنُواْ كَمَا ٱسۡتَـٔۡذَنَ ٱلَّذِينَ مِن قَبۡلِهِمۡۚ كَذَٰلِكَ يُبَيِّنُ ٱللَّهُ
لَكُمۡ ءَايَٰتِهِۦۗ وَٱللَّهُ عَلِيمٌ حَكِيمٞ ٥٩

"O you who have faith! Let your permission be sought by your slaves and those of you who have not reached puberty three times: before the dawn prayer, and when you put off your garments at noon, and after the night prayer. These are three times of privacy for you. Apart from these, it is not sinful of you or them to frequent one another [freely]...When your children reach puberty, let them ask permission [at all times] just as those who asked permission before them. Thus does Allāh clarify His signs for you, and Allāh is all-knowing, all-wise."[1]

---

[1] Sūrah Nūr 24:58-59.

It is mentioned in *Tafsīr Namūneh* under the interpretation of this verse that:

This is a type of Islamic politeness, although unfortunately it is less observed today, and even though the Qur'ān has explicitly mentioned it in the above verses, it is rarely seen in the writings, speeches and rulings and this Islamic rule and its philosophy are not discussed clearly. For what reason has this definitive ruling of the Qur'ān been neglected?!

Although the apparent connotation of the verse is that it is an obligation to comply with this ruling, even if we consider it to be recommended, it should still be mentioned, and its details should be discussed.

Contrary to what some simplistic thinkers say, children do not understand these issues and servants are also ignorant of the same, it has been proven that children (as well as adults) are extremely sensitive to this issue, and sometimes the carelessness of parents and children's exposure to sights that they should not see has become the source of moral deviations and sometimes mental illnesses.[1]

From the captioned verse it can be concluded that the parents' bedroom should be separate from the children's; because getting permission to enter the parents' room has no other meaning than that they sleep in a separate room. Considering this as necessary will prevent sexual deviations that children may be infected with in the future.

Traditions in this regard are divided into several categories; The first category refers to the age of separation, the second category refers to the separation of boys' and girls' dormitories, and the third category refers to the separation of girls' sleeping places from each other. The fourth category has mentioned the separation between children who have reached the age of understanding and ladies.

First category

There are narrations that refer to the age of children, and some of them have mentioned the age of six and some the age of seven years, and the third category states the age of two years.

---

[1] Vol. 14, p. 545.

1. It is narrated that six-year-old children should be made to sleep separately.¹

2. When your children reach the age of seven, separate their beds from each other.²

3. Imām Ṣādiq narrates from his forefathers that: Separate the beds of ten-year-old children from ladies.³

Second category

The late Ṣadūq has narrated on the authority of ʿAbdullāh b. Maymūn on the authority of Imām Ṣādiq on the authority of his forefathers on the authority of the Prophet, who said:

الصَّبِيُّ وَ الصَّبِيُّ وَ الصَّبِيُّ وَ الصَّبِيَّةُ وَ الصَّبِيَّةُ وَ الصَّبِيَّةُ يُفَرَّقُ بَيْنَهُمْ فِي الْمَضَاجِعِ لِعَشْرِ سِنِينَ

"Boys and girls...separate their beds when they are ten years old."⁴

Third category

Separation between girls: Imām Jaʿfar Ṣādiq said:

الصبيّة والصبيّة... يُفَرَّقُ بَيْنَهُمَا فِي المضاجع لعشر سنين

"Separate the beds for girls more than ten years old."⁵

Fourth category

---

¹ *Wasāʾil al-Shīʿah*, vol. 15, p. 183.

رُوِيَ أَنَّهُ يُفَرَّقُ بَيْنَ الصِّبْيَانِ فِي الْمَضَاجِعِ لِسِتِّ سِنِينَ

² *Kanz al-ʿUmmāl*, vol. 16, p. 441.

إذا بلغ أولادكم سبع سنين فقو قوا بين مضاجعهم

³ *Wasāʾil al-Shīʿah*, vol. 15, p. 183; *Mustadrak al-Wasāʾil*, vol. 14, p. 228; *al-Kāfī*, vol.7, p.69.

رُوِيَ أَنَّهُ يُفَرَّقُ بَيْنَ الصِّبْيَانِ فِي الْمَضَاجِعِ لِسِتِّ سِنِينَ

⁴ *Wasāʾil al-Shīʿah*, vol. 15, p. 183; *Mustadrak al-Wasāʾil*, vol. 14, p. 228; *al-Kāfī*, vol. 7, p. 69.

⁵ *Wasāʾil al-Shīʿah*, vol. 15, 182; *Mustadrak al-Wasāʾil*, vol. 4, p. 288.

It is separation of children and women, and as mentioned in the narrations of the first category, the beds for ten-year-old children should be separated from women.

B) Destroying the context of disobeying parents

The Noble Prophet of Islam ﷺ said to 'Alī (as):

يَا عَلِيُّ لَعَنَ اللَّهُ وَالِدَيْنِ حَمَلَا وَلَدَهُمَا عَلَى عُقُوقِهِمَا يَا عَلِيُّ يَلْزَمُ الْوَالِدَيْنِ مِنْ عُقُوقِ وَلَدِهِمَا مَا يَلْزَمُ الْوَلَدَ لَهُمَا مِنْ عُقُوقِهِمَا

"O 'Alī (as)! May Allāh curse the parents who force their child to disobey. O 'Alī (as)! Just as a child becomes disobedient ('Āq) to his parents, parents will also be 'Āq of their children (if they do not comply with their duties)."[1]

At this point it is necessary to explain several issues:

First: *'Āq* is said to be a child who disobeys the command of his parents and treats them unkindly and misbehaves, thereby causing them discomfort and annoyance.

Second: Indifference to parents is one of the major sins, and if a disinclined person does not seek the satisfaction of his parents, he will undoubtedly have a bad fate on the Judgment Day.

Third: Contrary to the imagination of some people, who think that only children become *'Āq* of parents, this narration says that there are mutual rights and duties between children and parents, and both of them have duties towards each other, and if they fail to fulfill these duties, the children are considered as wrongdoers and so are the parents. So, just as *'Āq* of the parents is discussed, its converse is also true. Therefore, it is appropriate that honourable parents should be aware of their specific responsibilities and create mutual respect between themselves and their children so that the children naturally are also conscious of their duty and there is no room for disrespect to parents.

---

[1] *Wasā'il al-Shī'ah*, vol. 15, p. 123; *Biḥār al-'Anwār*, vol. 74, p. 58.

One of the causes leading to *'Āq* of parents is their excessive kindness and leniency, as a result of which the sanctity of parents is broken by the child, and the parents themselves cause their disrespect.

Imām Ḥasan 'Askarī ﷺ says:

جُرْأَةُ الْوَلَدِ عَلَى وَالِدِهِ فِي صِغَرِهِ تَدْعُو إِلَى الْعُقُوقِ فِي كِبَرِهِ

"The audacity of the child against the father in childhood will compel him to disobey his parents when he grows up."[1]

C) Abstaining from forbidden food

One of the things that undoubtedly play a major role in eliminating corruption and deviance of children is keeping children away from eating unlawful things.

In this context, we mention two points, which are mentioned in the traditions:

1. Sometimes the thing is basically unlawful, like liquor; therefore, giving it to the child is also unlawful; 'Ijlān says:

قُلْتُ لِأَبِي عَبْدِ اللَّهِ ع الْمَوْلُودُ يُولَدُ فَنَسْقِيهِ الْخَمْرَ فَقَالَ لَا مَنْ سَقَى مَوْلُوداً مُسْكِراً سَقَاهُ اللَّهُ مِنَ الْحَمِيمِ وَ إِنْ غُفِرَ لَه

I said to Imām Ṣādiq ﷺ: When a child is born, we pour liquor on him. He said, "Don't! Whoever gives a child something intoxicating, Allāh ﷻ will make him drink boiling water (of Hell), even though he (the child) would be forgiven."[2]

2. Sometimes the thing itself is not inherently unlawful, but for some reasons it is forbidden to consume it. For example, someone is invited to a feast and no one other than him is invited; in spite of that he takes his child with him without the host's permission. In this case since the host had not invited his son and if he didn't make necessary

[1] *Tuḥaf al-'Uqūl*, p. 520.
[2] *Wasā'il al-Shī'ah*, vol. 17, p. 247.

preparations, he might be harassed and may be disgraced in front of others. From this aspect such a course of action is not justified as it invites the displeasure of Allāh and His creation.

Sakūnī narrates from Imām Ṣādiq, who said:

إِذَا دُعِيَ أَحَدُكُمْ إِلَى طَعَامٍ فَلَا يَسْتَتْبِعَنَّ وَلَدَهُ فَإِنَّهُ إِنْ فَعَلَ أَكَلَ حَرَاماً وَ دَخَلَ غَاصِبا

"If one of you is invited to a meal (alone), he should never take his child with him, otherwise, if he does so, he has committed unlawful and has entered the host's house in a state of sin and disobedience."[1]

Connection between prohibited food and corruption

They have mentioned in the account of Qāḍī Sharīk b. ʿAbdullāh al-Nakhaʿī that he was well known for his devotion and piety. Once Mahdī the Abbaside Caliph invited him and asked him to accept one of three things:

1. Post of Judge 2. Be the teacher of the Caliph's children, or: 3. Attend the Caliph's banquet.

Initially Sharīk did not accept any of them, but with the insistence of the Caliph, since he imagined it to be a lesser evil, he accepted the third option as a precaution. The Caliph ordered the cook to prepare those forbidden foods that he knew well how effective they were in removing the spirit of piety.

When Sharīk ate from those foods, he also accepted other two options: post of judge as well as to tutor the children of the Caliph. Once it so happened that he had gone to collect his money transfer from the cashier, but the latter was a little late in disbursing. Sharīk said: Hurry up man, I am getting late! The money changer asked: Have you sold oil that you are so impatient? Sharīk said: What is oil worth?

---

[1] *Wasāʾil al-Shīʿah*, vol. 16, p. 493; *Makārim al-ʾAkhlāq*, p. 147.

For this money I have sold my religion, which is dearer than everything![1]

D) Creating a supportive environment

One of the ways to remove corruption and deviance in children is to strengthen positive moral aspects in their personality. Positive talents and valuable moral qualities should be revived in the life of children and by strengthening them, the paths of deviance and corruption should be blocked.

The Prophet ﷺ said:

رَحِمَ اللَّهُ مَنْ أَعَانَ وَلَدَهُ عَلَى بِرِّهِ

"May Allāh ﷻ have mercy on a father, who assists his child in goodness."[2]

He also said:

رَحِمَ اللَّهُ عَبْداً أَعَانَ وَلَدَهُ عَلَى بِرِّهِ بِالْإِحْسَانِ إِلَيْهِ وَ التَّأَلُّفِ لَهُ وَ تَعْلِيمِهِ وَ تَأْدِيبِه

"May Allāh ﷻ have mercy on a father, who helps his son in his good deeds, does good to him, and is kind and affectionate to him, and teaches him knowledge and good manners."[3]

Yūnus b. Rabāṭ narrates from Imām Ṣādiq ؑ from the Prophet ﷺ, who said:

رَحِمَ اللَّهُ مَنْ أَعَانَ وَلَدَهُ عَلَى بِرِّهِ قَالَ قُلْتُ كَيْفَ يُعِينُهُ عَلَى بِرِّهِ قَالَ يَقْبَلُ مَيْسُورَهُ وَ يَتَجَاوَزُ عَنْ مَعْسُورِهِ وَ لَا يُرْهِقُهُ وَ لَا يَخْرَقُ بِهِ

---

[1] *Mardān-i-'Ilm Dar Maydān-i-'Āmāl*, vol. 1, p. 411 quoted from *Rawzat al-Jannah*, vol. 4, p. 102.
[2] *Majmu'ah Warrām*, p. 369; *Mustadrak al-Wasā'il*, vol. 15, p. 168.
[3] *al-Ḥadīth*, vol. 3, p. 92.

"May Allāh ﷻ have mercy on the one, who helps his child in his good deeds."

The narrator asked: How to help your child to be good?

In response, His Eminence ﷺ said, "Accept what is within the child's ability and he does it, because it is hard for the child. Do not oppress him by imposing too much, and do not show harshness to him."[1]

Remind your children of the enormity of sin

It is not acceptable for any human being to be contaminated by crime and sin, especially if he has the position of a parent, or if in fact, he is a teacher of children and their mentor.

According to religious leaders, sin is a very serious matter, and it is the duty of the child's parents and educators to remind him of the graveness of sin and to tell him about its negative effects.

It is natural that until parents distance themselves from sin, they cannot have a beneficial effect on their children, because children are under the constant influence of the actions and behaviour of their parents and teachers, and they observe the words and actions of their parents, and they compare the two, and as a result they understand what they should do and what they should not. For example, whenever they hear an arrogant father or mother who themselves are infected with sin and deviance and yet continue to advise the children, they say to themselves: It is a joke! They are not serious! Because if such a thing is bad, why don't they refrain from it themselves?

An exemplary parent should make sin appear so ugly and abnormal in the eyes of their children that the children automatically distance themselves from it by understanding its bad effects and consequences.

It is obvious that when their words settle in the hearts of the children it would make them pure and chaste; because how can one prohibit something that one himself indulges in?

---

[1] *Wasā'il al-Shī'ah*, vol. 15, p. 19.

Of course, sometimes teenagers with the original nature, when they realize the ugliness of sin, despite the pollution of their parents, they refrain from committing sins, and even influence their parents.

In their lives, the Infallible A'immah ﷺ used their words and actions to teach their children piety and fear and reminded them of sin with its ugly face. Therefore, in the privacy of their life and influence, there was no mention of sin and deviance, because their presence was always bathed in effulgence; and sin and its bad effects were depicted in taste like a deadly poison and a destructive trap. Very few children and relatives of that respected personality would be ready for this deadly poison and the abyss of approaching destruction.

Now, we draw your attention to some brief moral lessons:

1. Luqmān the Wise, while advising his son, says:

يَا بُنَيَّ كَيْفَ تَسْكُنُ دَارَ مَنْ قَدْ أَسْخَطْتَهُ أَمْ كَيْفَ تُجَاوِرُ مَنْ قَدْ عَصَيْتَه

My child! How do you occupy the house of someone you have angered and how are you in the company of someone you have sinned against?[1]

Through a simple comparison, Luqmān has equated the world to be a house where Allāh ﷻ is the host and human beings are His guests. A sin in the presence of Allāh ﷻ, who is the owner of the house, does not befit a guest. It is far from fairness and masculinity for someone to attend a banquet and then argue with the host or commit ugly acts in his presence and displease him.

When the guest makes the host angry by committing a sin and being contaminated with ugliness, how can he continue to live in that house!

Yes, in this way, Luqmān stimulates his child's sense of conscience and intelligence to make him understand what a sin is and to make clear to him its enormity in the presence of the Lord ﷻ of the worlds.

2. Luqmān the Wise said to his son:

[1] Shaykh Mufīd, *al-Ikhtiṣāṣ*, p. 336.

يَا بُنَيَّ إِنَّهُ قَدْ أُحْصِيَ الْحَلَالُ الصَّغِيرُ فَكَيْفَ بِالْحَرَامِ الْكَثِيرِ

My child! When even minor lawful issues are accounted for, how could numerous forbidden ones be ignored?[1]

3. Imām Ṣādiq ﷺ says to his son, Imām Mūsā Kāẓim ﷺ:

وَمَن استَصغَرَ زَلّةَ نفسِهِ استعظَمَ زَلّةَ غيرِه، وَمَن استعظَمَ زَلّةَ نَفسِهِ استَصغَرَ زَلّةَ غيرِه

"Whoever considers his mistakes small, will find others' mistakes big, and whoever considers other people's mistakes small, will see his own mistakes big."[2]

So let us teach our children to regard their mistakes as serious so that they don't consider themselves superior to others and don't feel proud.

4. 'Alī ﷺ, in his will to his son, Imām Ḥusain ﷺ says:

وَ الْوَيْلُ لِمَنْ بُلِيَ بِحِرْمَانٍ وَ خِذْلَانٍ وَ عِصْيَانٍ فَاسْتَحْسَنَ لِنَفْسِهِ مَا يَكْرَهُهُ مِنْ غَيْرِهِ وَ أَزْرَى عَلَى النَّاسِ بِمِثْلِ مَا يَأْتِي

"Woe to him, who is afflicted with deprivation, failure and disobedience, and considers his acts good, which he considers a fault for others, and blames people for acts he himself does."[3]

5. Luqmān the Wise said to his son:

يَا بُنَيَّ لَا تَشْتِمِ النَّاسَ فَتَكُونَ أَنْتَ الَّذِي شَتَمْتَ أَبَوَيْكَ

My child! Don't abuse others lest they retaliate by abusing your parents.[4]

---

[1] Shaykh Mufīd, *al-Ikhtiṣāṣ*, p. 336.
[2] *Biḥār al-'Anwār*, vol. 75, p. 202.
[3] *Tuḥaf al-'Uqūl*, p. 87.
[4] *al-Ikhtiṣāṣ*, p. 336.

It means that a part of the good or bad behaviour of others is reaction to our own good or bad behaviour and attitude, and it is natural that if we are disrespectful towards others, they will also reciprocate. And one who mentions ugly and insulting words to others should expect to receive more ugly words.

6. Luqmān says to his son:

يَا بُنَيَّ لَا يُعْجِبْكَ إِحْسَانُكَ وَ لَا تَتَعَظَّمَنَّ بِعَمَلِكَ الصَّالِحِ فَتَهْلِك

My child! Don't be proud of the good deeds you do to others and don't let your good deeds appear big in your eyes lest you perish.[1]

7. Luqmān the Wise said to his son:

يَا بُنَيَّ اتَّعِظْ بِالنَّاسِ قَبْلَ أَنْ يَتَّعِظَ النَّاسُ بِك

My child! Take advice from people's fate before people take advice from your fate and you become a lesson for others.[2]

8. Also, Luqmān the Wise said to his son:

يَا بُنَيَّ انْهَ النَّفْسَ عَنْ هَوَاهَا فَإِنَّكَ إِنْ لَمْ تَنْهَ النَّفْسَ عَنْ هَوَاهَا لَمْ تَدْخُلِ الْجَنَّةَ وَ لَمْ تَرَهَا

My child, restrain yourself from lust and desires, because if you don't do that and you don't stop yourself from evil, neither you will enter Paradise nor (even) see it.[3]

9. 'Alī ﷺ, in his will to his son, Imām Ḥusain ﷺ says:

لَيسَ مَعَ قطيعة رَحِمٍ نماءُ

[1] *al-Ikhtiṣāṣ*, p. 336.
[2] *al-Ikhtiṣāṣ*, p. 331.
[3] *al-Ikhtiṣāṣ*, p. 334.

"Severing relations destroys the splendour of life."[1]

10. One of the advices of Luqmān the Wise to his son was:

يَا بُنَيَّ إِيَّاكَ وَ التَّجَبُّرَ وَ التَّكَبُّرَ وَ الْفَخْرَ فَتُجَاوِرَ إِبْلِيسَ فِي دَارِهِ يَا بُنَيَّ دَعْ عَنْكَ التَّجَبُّرَ وَ الْكِبْرَ وَ دَعْ عَنْكَ الْفَخْرَ وَ اعْلَمْ أَنَّكَ سَاكِنُ الْقُبُورِ

My child, don't be arrogant and boast to others as you will be with the devil in your house.[2]

My child: put aside the pursuit of superiority and priding over others and know that your final abode will be in the cemetery.[3]

11. He also says to his son:

يَا بُنَيَّ وَيْلٌ لِمَنْ تَجَبَّرَ وَ تَكَبَّرَ كَيْفَ يَتَعَظَّمُ مَنْ خُلِقَ مِنْ طِينٍ وَ إِلَى طِينٍ يَعُودُ ثُمَّ لَا يَدْرِي إِلَى مَا ذَا يَصِيرُ إِلَى الْجَنَّةِ فَقَدْ فَازَ أَوْ إِلَى النَّارِ فَقَدْ خَسِرَ خُسْرَاناً مُبِيناً وَ خَابَ

My child! Woe to the one who is arrogant and proud. How does he become arrogant when he was created from dust and returns to dust? Does he not know where he is going? Whether he will go to heaven where he will be saved or to the fire of Hell where he will see obvious loss, and despair and regret?[4]

12. 'Alī ؑ advised his son, Imām Ḥusain ؑ:

أَيْ بُنَيَّ كَمْ نَظْرَةٍ جَلَبَتْ حَسْرَةً

"My son! How often a (mere) look causes longing and regret."[5]

13. Imām Ṣādiq ؑ says: My father ؑ used to tell me:

---

[1] *Tuḥaf al-'Uqūl*, p. 85.
[2] It is an allusion to the fact that arrogance is the house of the devil, and it is not worthy for a person to live there.
[3] *al-Ikhtiṣāṣ*, p. 334.
[4] *al-Ikhtiṣāṣ*, p. 334.
[5] *Tuḥaf al-'Uqūl*, p. 85.

$$\text{مَنْ لَا يَمْلِكُ لِسَانَهُ يَنْدَم}$$

"Whoever does not control his tongue will regret it."¹

14. 'Alī ؏ said in his advice to his son, Imām Ḥusain ؏:

$$\text{وَ مَنْ عَلِمَ أَنَّ كَلَامَهُ مِنْ عَمَلِهِ قَلَّ كَلَامُهُ إِلَّا فِيمَا يَنْفَعُهُ}$$

"When a person knows that his words are also part of his actions, he speaks less and does not speak unless it is beneficial."²

15. 'Alī ؏, in his advice to his son, Imām Ḥusain ؏ says:

$$\text{وَ مَنْ حَفَرَ بِئْراً لِأَخِيهِ وَقَعَ فِيهَا}$$

"Whoever digs a hole for others falls into it himself."³

16. Imām Ḥusain ؏ says to his son, Imām Sajjad ؏:

$$\text{يا بُنَيَّ إِيَّاكَ وظُلمَ مَن لا يَجِدُ عَلَيكَ ناصِراً إِلَّا اللَّه}$$

"My child, beware of oppressing someone who has no helper, except Allāh the Almighty.⁴

17. Similarly, 'Alī ؏ said in his advice to his son, Imām Ḥusain ؏:

$$\text{وَ مَنْ هَتَكَ حِجَابَ غَيْرِهِ انْكَشَفَتْ عَوْرَاتُ بَيْتِه}$$

"Whoever exposes the secrets of others; the secrets and defects of his life will also be exposed."⁵

---

¹ *Biḥār al-'Anwār*, vol. 75, p. 90.
² *Tuḥaf al-'Uqūl*, p. 84.
³ *Tuḥaf al-'Uqūl*, p. 84.
⁴ *Biḥār al-'Anwār*, vol. 75, p. 118.
⁵ *Tuḥaf al-'Uqūl*, p. 84.

18. Luqmān the Wise said to his son:

يَا بُنَيَّ لَا تَأْكُلْ مَالَ الْيَتِيمِ فَتَفْتَضِحَ يَوْمَ الْقِيَامَةِ وَ تُكَلَّفَ أَنْ تَرُدَّهُ إِلَيْهِ

My child! Do not trespass on the property of an orphan, because you will be disgraced on the Judgment Day, and you will be forced to compensate to the orphan.[1]

Friends! Sin is so ugly that our leaders did not even think about it. Sin is the spark of Hellfire that may fall into one's personality.

Have you ever come across a sane person who thought of killing himself! Sin is filth, scandal, humiliation, and wastefulness. Some sins burn the root of a person's existence, some damage the Hereafter; and it is even possible that all good deeds of a person will be destroyed, and some may even cause disgrace in this world and disgrace in the Hereafter.

On the Judgment Day, the sinners will enter the gathering with a distinct face and mark, or blackness will cover their entire face and their animal nature will be revealed and they will appear in the form of animals! Can disgrace and torment get any worse?

Vaccinating the children

The third principle that is mentioned in the reconstruction of the child's personality is the issue of vaccinating the child's mind and brain. This important principle is also mentioned in the traditions, and also emphasized a lot in health care and treatment today. It is an important principle of disease prevention. Imām Kāẓim said:

الحمية رأس الدواء

"Prevention is the best cure."

The various vaccines that are injected into children today to prevent the occurrence of rabies etc. play an important role in preventing them from contracting it; and it is clear that preventing the

---

[1] al-Ikhtiṣāṣ, p. 335.

occurrence of diseases is much easier and more economical than medical treatments. Many moral education recommendations also have a preventive aspect, and as a vaccine works, they insure the child's thinking and brain from childhood against all kinds of deviations and corruptions. Take your time to answer children's religious questions or introduce them to Islamic teachings. If these teachings are passed on to children in a favourable and effective way, they will play an important role in preventing deviations and moral and ideological deviations from the very childhood. It will also fulfill and guarantee their mental and intellectual health.

A) Raising children on the love of Ahl al-Bayt ﷺ

There are many traditions in which the Prophet ﷺ has advised the parents to raise their children to love the family of the Messenger of Allāh ﷺ, especially ʿAlī b. Abi Ṭālib ؑ.

Imām ʿAlī ؑ narrates from the Prophet ﷺ, who said:

أدِّبوا أولادَكم على ثلاثِ خصال: حبِّ نبيِّكم، وحبِّ أهل بيته، وقراءة القرآنِ، فا نّ حَمَلة القرآنِ فى ظل اللهِ يومَ لاظِلَّ الاّ ظِلّه مع أنبيائه و أصفيائه

"Train your children on three traits: love for your Prophet ﷺ, love for his family, and reading the Qur'ān: because the bearers of the Qur'ān- on that day when there will be no shade, except the shade of Allāh ﷻ - will be in the shade of Allāh ﷻ with the Prophets ؑ and His chosen ones."[1]

Abū Zubayr Makkī narrates:

I saw Jābir b. ʿAbdullāh Anṣārī walking around the streets of the *Anṣār* areas and by their gatherings (in Madinah) leaning on his cane, and saying:

عَلِيٌّ خَيْرُ الْبَشَرِ فَمَنْ أَبَى فَقَدْ كَفَرَ يَا مَعْشَرَ الأَنْصَارِ أَدِّبوا أَوْلاَدَكُمْ عَلَى حُبِّ عَلِيٍّ

[1] *Kanz al-ʿUmmāl*, vol. 16, p. 456

ʿAlī is the best of mankind and whoever denies it is a disbeliever. Then he would say: O *Anṣār*! Raise your children on the love of ʿAlī b. Abi Ṭālib.[1]

The love of ʿAlī is the criterion of faith and disbelief: loving him is faith and hating him is disbelief. All this emphasis on the love of *Ahl al-Bayt*– which is mentioned in the traditions and some verses of Qur'ān– is because love and affection for everything and everyone has a great role and influence in life; and its effects and complications cannot be doubted.

For this reason, the enemies of Islam, especially Muʿawiyāh, the son of Abū Sufyān, tried very hard to destroy the love of ʿAlī in the hearts of the people, but affection for ʿAlī still exists and will remain so.

Deceiving ʿAlī's friends

The late Shaykh ʿAbbās Qomī writes in *Safīnat al-Biḥār*: "It is narrated that once Muʿawiyāh sent a gift of sweets to Abū al-'Aswad Du'alī (poet of *Ahl al-Bayt*) so that it may permeate his heart and he may give up on the affection of ʿAlī.

At the time, the young daughter (five or six years old) of Abū al-'Aswad put some of that sweet meat into her mouth.

Abū al-'Aswad said: O Daughter! Spit it out at once! It is poison! It is a trick that Muʿawiyāh sent to deceive us so that we stop loving ʿAlī and the *Ahl al-Bayt*.

Abū al-'Aswad's daughter said: May Allāh degrade and expose him! He wanted to deceive us with this sweet so that we give up on ʿAlī and his love! May the hands of the sender and its eater perish.

Then she spat out what she had placed in her mouth. After that she recited the following verses:

أَ بِالشَّهْدِ المُزَعْفَرِ يابن هندٍ   نَبِيعُ عليك أَحساباً ودينا

فلا واللهِ ؛ كَيفَ يَكونَ هذَا   ومولانا أميرُ المؤمنينا

---

[1] *al-'Amālī Ṣadūq*, p. 68.

O son of Hind! Did you imagine that by means of this sweet saffron sweet meat you will trick us into selling our religion and the honour of our ancestors to you? No, by Allāh ﷻ such a thing is not possible, as our Master is Amīr al Mu'minīn 'Alī ؑ.[1]

B) Arming the child against deviant thoughts

Another important advice of the *Ahl al-Bayt* ؑ is to speed up the teaching of traditions and Islamic sciences of *Ahl al-Bayt* ؑ to the children so that they have the necessary preparation at a young age to confront and confute deviant thoughts; and by acquiring the correct, clear, and deep understanding of Islamic knowledge they will never be influenced by such thoughts. Imām Ṣādiq ؑ said:

بَادِرُوا أَحْدَاثَكُمْ بِالْحَدِيثِ قَبْلَ أَنْ تَسْبِقَكُمْ إِلَيْهِمُ الْمُرْجِئَةُ

"Teach Islamic traditions to your young people and speed up this education before the misguided enemies overtake you and put their wrong thoughts in their minds and make them go astray."[2]

C) Discussing, inquiring, and justifying Islamic knowledge with children

Once, Amīr al Mu'minīn ؑ asked his two sons, Imām Ḥasan ؑ and Imām Ḥusain ؑ:

مَا بَيْنَ الْإِيمَانِ وَ الْيَقِينِ فَسَكَتَا فَقَالَ لِلْحَسَنِ ع أَجِبْ يَا أَبَا مُحَمَّدٍ قَالَ بَيْنَهُمَا شِبْرٌ قَالَ وَ كَيْفَ ذَاكَ قَالَ لِأَنَّ الْإِيمَانَ مَا سَمِعْنَاهُ بِآذَانِنَا وَ صَدَّقْنَاهُ بِقُلُوبِنَا وَ الْيَقِينُ مَا أَبْصَرْنَاهُ بِأَعْيُنِنَا وَ اسْتَدْلَلْنَا بِهِ عَلَى مَا غَابَ عَنَّا

---

[1] *Safīnat al-Biḥār*, vol. 1, p. 669.

[2] *Wasā'il al-Shī'ah*, vol. 12, p. 247, p. 15, p. 196, vol. 18, p. 62; *al-Kāfī*, vol. 6, p. 47; *Biḥār al-'Anwār*, vol. 2, p. 17 (with slight difference).

"What is the limit of faith and certainty?" But they chose to remain silent?

He said to Imām Ḥasan ﷺ, "Abū Muḥammad ﷺ! You answer."

Imām Ḥasan ﷺ said, "There is a gap of one span between faith and certainty."

'How?' 'Alī ﷺ asked.

Imām Ḥasan ﷺ replied, "Because faith is what we have heard through our ears and confirmed with our hearts, but certainty is what we have seen with our eyes and by means of it we can reason about the existence of things hidden from us."[1]

قَالَ عَلِيٌّ ع لِلْحَسَنِ ابْنِهِ ع فِي مَسَائِلِهِ الَّتِي سَأَلَهُ عَنْهَا يَا بُنَيَّ مَا السَّفَهُ فَقَالَ اتِّبَاعُ الدُّنَاةِ وَ مُصَاحَبَةُ الْغُوَاةِ

Among the issues that Amīr al Mu'minīn ﷺ asked his son, Imām Ḥasan ﷺ is that he asked, "My son! What is stupidity?"

Imām Ḥasan ﷺ replied, "Following the debased fellows and associating with the misguided."[2]

Also, 'Allāmah Majlisī narrates a detailed traditional report from *Ma'nī al-Akhbār*[3] that 'Alī ﷺ used to pose many questions to his sons, Imām Ḥasan ﷺ and Ḥusain ﷺ and their replies were wonderful. At the end of these questions and answers, the Imām turned to Ḥārith 'Āwar and said:

يَا حَارِثُ عَلِّمُوا هَذِهِ الْحِكَمَ أَوْلَادَكُمْ فَإِنَّهَا زِيَادَةٌ فِي الْعَقْلِ وَ الْحَزْمِ وَ الرَّأْيِ

"O Ḥārith, convey these wisdoms to your children, which will increase their intelligence and perception."[4]

---

[1] *Biḥār al-'Anwār*, vol. 70, p. 182.
[2] *Biḥār al-'Anwār*, vol. 75, p. 299.
[3] P. 401.
[4] *Biḥār al-'Anwār*, vol. 75, p. 102; *Tuḥaf al-'Uqūl*, p. 225.

Zayd's query and Imām Sajjād's reply

Zayd b. 'Alī says: I said to my father, Zayn al-'Ābidīn: Father! Tell me about my grandfather, the Messenger of Allāh, from the time when he was taken up to the heavens, and his Lord ordered him to perform fifty prayers. How he didn't want to ask Allāh to reduce them for his *Ummah* until Mūsā b. 'Imrān said: Ask Allāh for relief, because your nation cannot tolerate such a thing.

Imām said, "My son! The Prophet of Allāh was not someone who would retract after the command of his Lord and ask Him for something; and when Mūsā requested the Prophet and became the intercessor of the *Ummah* of the Holy Prophet, the Prophet did not reject such a request as well. Therefore, he asked the Lord of the Universe to reduce the number of prayers for his nation, and Allāh reduced the fifty prayers to five."

Zayd said: I said: O father! Why didn't he ask for a reduction again after the prayers were reduced? Imām said, "My son! The Prophet wanted to get a discount for his *Ummah* by counting the reward of those fifty prayers, because Allāh says:

مَن جَآءَ بِٱلْحَسَنَةِ فَلَهُۥ عَشْرُ أَمْثَالِهَا...

"Whoever brings virtue shall receive ten times its like..."[1]

Don't you see that when that Prophet returned to the earth, Jibra'īl descended to him and said: O Muḥammad! Your Lord greets you and says: These five prayers are instead of those fifty prayers."

مَا يُبَدَّلُ ٱلْقَوْلُ لَدَىَّ وَمَآ أَنَا۠ بِظَلَّٰمٍ لِّلْعَبِيدِ ﴿٢٩﴾

"The word [of judgment] is unalterable with Me, and I am not tyrannical to the servants."[2]

He says: then I asked, "O father! Did Allāh, the Exalted, not mention that He cannot be described in terms of space?" So he

[1] Sūrah al-An'ām 6:160.
[2] Sūrah Qāf 50:29.

responded, "Of course, exalted is Allāh ﷻ from that." Therefore, I asked, "Then what is the meaning of the statement of Mūsā ﷺ to the Messenger of Allāh ﷺ, "Go back to your Lord ﷻ?'" Thus, he ﷺ replied, The meaning of this is the same as the word of Ibrāhīm ﷺ:

...إِنِّي ذَاهِبٌ إِلَىٰ رَبِّي سَيَهْدِينِ ﴿٩٩﴾

"...Indeed I am going toward my Lord, who will guide me."[1]

Or like what Mūsā ﷺ said:

...وَعَجِلْتُ إِلَيْكَ رَبِّ لِتَرْضَىٰ ﴿٨٤﴾

"...and I hurried on to You, my Lord, that You may be pleased."[2]

And it implies the meaning of Allāh's ﷻ words that He ﷻ said:

فَفِرُّوٓاْ إِلَى ٱللَّهِۖ...

"So flee toward Allāh..."[3]

That is, return to His (Allāh's ﷻ) house and perform *Ḥajj*.

My son, the Ka'bah is the house of Allāh ﷻ, and whoever visits the house of Allāh ﷻ has undoubtedly gone to Allāh ﷻ. Likewise, Mosques are the houses of Allāh ﷻ, and whoever goes to them is as if he has gone to Allāh ﷻ, and as long as he is praying, he is standing in the presence of Allāh ﷻ. And those who have stood in *'Arafāh* are standing in front of Allāh ﷻ. Verily, for Allāh, the Blessed and Exalted, are places in His Heavens, whoever ascends to them ascends to Him.

Haven't you heard that Allāh ﷻ says:

تَعْرُجُ ٱلْمَلَٰٓئِكَةُ وَٱلرُّوحُ إِلَيْهِ...

"The angels and the Spirit ascend to Him..."[4]

And He ﷻ says:

---

[1] Sūrah al-Ṣāffāt 37:99.
[2] Sūrah ṬaḤā 20:84.
[3] Sūrah al-Dhāriyāt 51:50.
[4] Sūrah al-M'ārij 70:4.

...إِلَيْهِ يَصْعَدُ ٱلْكَلِمُ ٱلطَّيِّبُ...

"...To Him ascends the good word...[1]

It means that they are lifted up.[2]

Control of the friends

Two people named 'Uqbah and Ubayy were friends. They both liked each other very much. When any of them would return from a trip, he would organize a feast and invite the nobles and elders of his tribe.

Once, 'Uqbah, as usual, organized a feast and invited the elders of his tribe and his friends, and invited the Messenger of Allāh ﷺ as well.

The table was laid, and the food was served. The Prophet of Allāh ﷺ said: 'Uqbah! I will not eat at your place unless you bear witness to the oneness of Allāh ﷻ and accept my message (and become a *Muslim*). So 'Uqbah testified that there is no god besides Allāh ﷻ and that Muḥammad ﷺ is the Apostle of Allāh ﷻ; and he went on to become a *Muslim*, to tear the curtain of ignorance, polytheism and darkness and make himself fit to enter Paradise forever. When Ubayy, whose disbelief and polytheism had penetrated to the depths of his soul learnt of this he became very upset and said to 'Uqbah: You have deviated from your religion, 'Uqbah! His friend said: No, by God I did not. But a man came to me, who did not eat my food unless I testified to Allāh's ﷻ unity and his mission. I was ashamed that he was about to leave my place without eating, so I testified. 'Ubayy said: I will not be happy with you unless you stand before him and insult him. 'Uqbah did this and apostatized and joined the ranks of the polytheists and finally joined the ranks of the infidels in the Battle of Badr where he was killed at the hands of Amīr al Mu'minīn ؑ; and his friend was also killed in the Battle of 'Uḥud at the hands of the Muslims.[3] He was the one who

---

[1] Sūrah Fāṭir 35:10.
[2] al-*Tawḥīd al-Ṣadūq*, p. 176.
[3] *Tafsīr Namūnih*, vol. 15, pp. 68-69.

gave his heart to the evil temptations of unworthy friendship, and in the end, became liable to be sent to Hell.

The following verses were revealed about the debasement of these two fellows:

وَيَوْمَ يَعَضُّ ٱلظَّالِمُ عَلَىٰ يَدَيْهِ يَقُولُ يَـٰلَيْتَنِي ٱتَّخَذْتُ مَعَ ٱلرَّسُولِ سَبِيلًا ﴿٢٧﴾ يَـٰوَيْلَتَىٰ لَيْتَنِي لَمْ أَتَّخِذْ فُلَانًا خَلِيلًا ﴿٢٨﴾ لَّقَدْ أَضَلَّنِي عَنِ ٱلذِّكْرِ بَعْدَ إِذْ جَآءَنِي ۗ وَكَانَ ٱلشَّيْطَـٰنُ لِلْإِنسَـٰنِ خَذُولًا ﴿٢٩﴾

"A day when the wrongdoer will bite his hands, saying, 'I wish I had followed the Apostle's way! Woe to me! I wish I had not taken so and so as a friend! Certainly he led me astray from the Reminder after it had come to me, and Satan is a deserter of man."[1]

This true story and the verse of the Qur'ān in this regard show the importance and influence of a friend in the destiny of a person. Therefore, it is mentioned in the traditions that a person is attached to the religion and belief of his friend.

Undoubtedly, one of the factors that shape a person's personality, after his own will, is the role of friends, because most people, especially teenagers, take an important part of their thoughts and moral qualities from their friends and are influenced by their behaviour, speech, and morals.

And this is something that has been scientifically and experimentally proven. The influence of friends is sometimes to the extent that it can overcome the role and influence of parents, even if the child's family is full of virtue. Also, as mentioned in the Quranic verses and manifested in Persian literature, the son of Prophet Nūḥ ﷺ spent only a few mornings in the company of immoral friends, and he was cut off from the house of prophethood and joined the misguided.

پسر نوح با بدان بنشست　　خاندان نبوتش گمشد

Nūḥ's son had bad company　　His prophetic family was lost.[2]

[1] Sūrah al-Furqān 25:27-29.

[2] Persian couplet.

Friend: A perfect mirror

'Alī ﷺ said:

فَمَنِ اشْتَبَهَ عَلَيْكُمْ أَمْرُهُ وَ لَمْ تَعْرِفُوا دِينَهُ فَانْظُرُوا إِلَى خُلَطَائِهِ فَإِنْ كَانُوا أَهْلَ دِينِ اللَّهِ فَهُوَ عَلَى دِينِ اللَّهِ

"When the personal status of a person is not known and you are unaware of his religion and faith, look at his friends, if they are folks of divine faith and religion, he is also a follower of Allāh's ﷻ religion."[1]

Duty of parents regarding friends of their children

Considering that friendship is one of the most important needs of children and nothing else fills this need, the parents can play an effective role in this regard. For example, friendly or family or professional relationships of parents with certain people, the neighbourhood they choose to live in, the school they enrol their children in, and the places they go for recreation and so on...all of them have a huge impact in the formation of friendship of children and teenagers with certain people. In addition, the vigilance and attention of parents in the affairs of their children and the people with whom their children are in contact, and the compassionate and wise attitudes they show to their children in this regard will guide them on how to choose pure, committed, and hard-working friends and to avoid false friends, who would ruin their life:

1. Encouragement to choose a friend

Luqmān said to his son:

يَا بُنَيَّ اسْتَكْثِرْ مِنَ الْأَصْدِقَاءِ وَ لَا تَأْمَنْ مِنَ الْأَعْدَاءِ فَإِنَّ الْغِلَّ فِي صُدُورِهِمْ مِثْلُ الْمَاءِ

---

[1] *Biḥār al-'Anwār*, vol. 74, p. 197.

تَحْتَ الرَّمَادِ

My child! Increase the number of your friends and be safe from your enemies, because hatred is concealed in their breasts just as water remains hidden in the soil.[1]

2. First the research, then the selection

Imām Ḥasan Mujtabā ﷺ said to one of his children:

يَا بُنَيَّ لَا تُؤَاخِ أَحَداً حَتَّى تَعْرِفَ مَوَارِدَهُ وَ مَصَادِرَهُ فَإِذَا اسْتَنْبَطْتَ الْخِبْرَةَ وَ رَضِيتَ الْعِشْرَةَ فَآخِهِ عَلَى إِقَالَةِ الْعَثْرَةِ وَ الْمُوَاسَاةِ فِي الْعُسْرَةِ

"My son! Do not fraternize with someone, until you know where he goes and with what people he interacts, and when you are well aware of his circumstances and you like his company, fraternize with him until you stop him from deviation and help him in times of need."[2]

3. Maintaining relations with good friends

In the advice of Luqmān the Wise to his son, it is emphasized to establish relations with good friends, some of which are that he said to his son:

يَا بُنَيَّ الصَّاحِبُ الصَّالِحُ خَيْرٌ مِنَ الْوَحْدَةِ

My child! A good friend is better than being alone.[3]

He also said:

---

[1] *al-Ikhtiṣāṣ*, p. 333.
[2] *Tuḥaf al-'Uqūl*, p. 236.
[3] *al-Ikhtiṣāṣ*, p. 332.

يَا بُنَيَّ كُنْ عَبْداً لِلْأَخْيَارِ وَ لَا تَكُنْ وَلَداً لِلْأَشْرَا

My child! Be a servant of the good, not a child of the wicked.[1]

He also said:

يَا بُنَيَّ اتَّخِذْ أَلْفَ صَدِيقٍ وَ أَلْفٌ قَلِيلٌ وَ لَا تَتَّخِذْ عَدُوّاً وَاحِداً وَ الْوَاحِدُ كَثِيرٌ فَقَالَ أَمِيرُ الْمُؤْمِنِينَ

My child! Acquire a thousand friends for yourself and know that even a thousand friends are less, and do not make a single enemy, because one enemy is too many.

And that noble one said:

تَكَثَّرْ مِنَ الْإِخْوَانِ مَا اسْتَطَعْتَ إِنَّهُمْ   عِمَادٌ إِذَا مَا اسْتُنْجِدُوا وَ ظُهُورُ

وَ لَيْسَ كَثِيراً أَلْفُ خِلٍّ وَ صَاحِبٍ   وَ إِنَّ عَدُوّاً وَاحِداً لَكَثِيرُ

Make as many friends as you can. Friends are a person's support when seeking help. Know that a thousand friends are not many, but one enemy is too much for you.[2]

4. Avoid unsuitable friends

In the traditions, as much as they have ordered friendship and association with good and committed people, they have warned against friendship with unrighteous and unscrupulous people. We refer to some of these traditions:

Imām Ṣādiq said:

---

[1] *Biḥār al-'Anwār*, vol. 13, p. 416.
[2] *'Amālī al-Ṣadūq*, p. 597; *Biḥār al-'Anwār*, vol. 13, p. 414 and vol. 75, p. 90.

$$\text{قَالَ لِي يَا بُنَيَّ مَنْ يَصْحَبْ صَاحِبَ السَّوْءِ لَا يَسْلَم}$$

"My father said to me: My son! Whoever befriends an evil man will not find safety and peace."[1]

Luqmān said to his son:

$$\text{يَا بُنَيَّ الْوَحْدَةُ خَيْرٌ مِنْ صَاحِبِ السَّوْء}$$

My child! Loneliness is better than a bad companion.[2]

He also said:

$$\text{يَا بُنَيَّ نَقْلُ الْحِجَارَةِ وَ الْحَديدِ خَيْرٌ مِنْ قَرِينِ السَّوْءِ يَا بُنَيَّ إِنِّي نَقَلْتُ الْحِجَارَةَ وَ الْحَديدَ فَلَمْ أَجِدْ شَيْئاً أَثْقَلَ مِنْ قَرِينِ السَّوْء}$$

My child! Moving rocks and irons is better for me than a bad companion. My child! I have lifted rocks, but I have not found anything heavier than a bad friend.[3]

Forbidden friendships

A) Liar

Imām Sajjād said to one of his sons about not having a relationship with several groups:

$$\text{يَا بُنَيَّ انْظُرْ خَمْسَةً فَلَا تُصَاحِبْهُمْ وَ لَا تُحَادِثْهُمْ وَ لَا تُرَافِقْهُمْ فِي طَرِيقٍ فَقُلْتُ يَا أَبَهْ مَنْ هُمْ قَالَ إِيَّاكَ وَ مُصَاحَبَةَ الْكَذَّابِ فَإِنَّهُ بِمَنْزِلَةِ السَّرَابِ يُقَرِّبُ لَكَ الْبَعِيدَ وَ يُبَاعِدُ}$$

---

[1] *al-Ikhtiṣāṣ*, p. 332.
[2] *al-Ikhtiṣāṣ*, p. 333.
[3] *al-Ikhtiṣāṣ*, p. 333.

لَكَ الْقَرِيبَ

"My child, keep the five categories in mind and do not take them as a companion for talking or walking!"

He said: Who are they, father?

Imām ﷺ said, "Don't be friends with a liar. He will be like a mirage. He will trick you. When a thing is far, he will say it is near; and when it is at hand, he will say that it is very far.[1]

B) Transgressor

Imām Sajjād ﷺ said (in continuation of the previous narration):

وَ إِيَّاكَ وَ مُصَاحَبَةَ الْفَاسِقِ، فَإِنَّهُ بَائِعُكَ بِأُكْلَةٍ أَوْ أَقَلَّ مِنْ ذلِك

"Don't make a transgressor and sinner your friend, because he might sell you for a low price."[2]

Luqmān said to his son:

يَا بُنَيَّ إِيَّاكَ وَ مُصَاحَبَةَ الْفُسَّاقِ هُمْ كَالْكِلَابِ إِنْ وَجَدُوا عِنْدَكَ شَيْئاً أَكَلُوهُ وَ إِلَّا ذَمُّوكَ وَ فَضَحُوكَ وَ إِنَّمَا حُبُّهُمْ بَيْنَهُمْ سَاعَة

My child! Don't associate with evildoers, because they are like dogs, if they find something near you, they will eat it, and if they don't get anything, they will criticize and scandalize you again and again.[3]

He also said:

يَا بُنَيَّ مُعَادَاةُ الْمُؤْمِنِينَ خَيْرٌ مِنْ مُصَادَقَةِ الْفَاسِقِ يَا بُنَيَّ الْمُؤْمِنُ تَظْلِمُهُ وَ لَا يَظْلِمُكَ

---

[1] *Tuḥaf al-'Uqūl*, p. 286; *al-Kāfī*, vol. 2, p. 376, tr. 7.
[2] *Tuḥaf al-'Uqūl*, p. 286.
[3] *al-Ikhtiṣāṣ*, p. 333.

وَ تَطْلُبُ عَلَيْهِ فَيَرْضَى عَنْكَ وَ الْفَاسِقُ لَا يُرَاقِبُ اللَّهَ فَكَيْفَ يُرَاقِبُكَ

My child! Enmity with a believer is better than friendship with a transgressor. My son! If you oppress a believer, he will not oppress you. Sometimes you do something against him, he will forgive you and be satisfied, but the transgressor does not respect Allāh's ﷻ rights, how can he respect your rights?[1]

A transgressor is someone, who has deviated from the right path and completely disregards the laws and rulings of *Sharī'ah*. He is the one who ignores Allāh's ﷻ orders and rights, and of course he will easily ignore people's rights.

An immoral person is mean and depraved. He is only looking for his own interests in the presence of others, if the interest is in friendship, he will make a friend, and when another interest comes, he will sacrifice the previous friendship. For this reason, the friendship of the wicked is always dubious and he cannot be trusted.

The immoral person has become audacious, shameless, and disregarding of human modesty due to his arrogance and shame. And a shameless person indulges in every vile and despicable act to satisfy his desires. He tries to put a show of the character of the pure people and attributes his qualities to them. Therefore, he thinks that everyone is vain and profit-seeking and does not know Allāh ﷻ and the Prophet, because he finds himself like that.

The immoral person is rude and indecent, and in anger, he unleashes his tongue to utter all kinds of swearing and slander.

This feature is such that he harms himself and infects his friends and neighbours. Accordingly, one should avoid the friendship of such reckless and rebellious people.

C) Miser

Imām Sajjād عليه السلام said to one of his children:

---

[1] *al-Ikhtiṣāṣ*, p. 333.

$$\text{وَ إِيَّاكَ وَ مُصَاحَبَةَ الْبَخِيلِ فَإِنَّهُ يَخْذُلُكَ فِي مَالِهِ أَحْوَجَ مَا تَكُونُ إِلَيْهِ}$$

"Don't be friends with a miser, because he will abandon you when you desperately need his financial help."¹

D) Stupid

Imām Sajjād ؏ said:

$$\text{وَ إِيَّاكَ وَ مُصَاحَبَةَ الْأَحْمَقِ فَإِنَّهُ يُرِيدُ أَنْ يَنْفَعَكَ فَيَضُرَّكَ}$$

"Do not associate with a fool, because it is possible that with all good intentions, he might bring harm to you with his foolish actions."²

(E) One who breaks off relations

He also said:

$$\text{وَ إِيَّاكَ وَ مُصَاحَبَةَ الْقَاطِعِ لِرَحِمِهِ فَإِنِّي وَجَدْتُهُ مَلْعُوناً فِي كِتَابِ اللَّهِ عَزَّ وَ جَلَّ فِي ثَلَاثَةِ مَوَاضِعَ قَالَ اللَّهُ عَزَّ وَ جَلَّ}$$

"You must avoid the company of the one who has cut off relations with the kin as I have found such a person to be cursed in three places in the Book of Allāh ﷻ:

$$\text{فَهَلْ عَسَيْتُمْ إِن تَوَلَّيْتُمْ أَن تُفْسِدُوا۟ فِى ٱلْأَرْضِ وَتُقَطِّعُوٓا۟ أَرْحَامَكُمْ ۝ أُو۟لَٰٓئِكَ ٱلَّذِينَ لَعَنَهُمُ ٱللَّهُ فَأَصَمَّهُمْ وَأَعْمَىٰٓ أَبْصَٰرَهُمْ ۝}$$

"May it not be that if you were to wield authority you would cause corruption in the land and ill-treat your blood relations? They are the ones whom Allāh has cursed, so He made them deaf, and blinded their sight."³

---

¹ *Tuḥaf al-ʿUqūl*, p. 286.
² *Tuḥaf al-ʿUqūl*, p. 286.
³ Sūrah Muḥammad 47:22-23.

وقال:

And He said:

وَٱلَّذِينَ يَنقُضُونَ عَهْدَ ٱللَّهِ مِنۢ بَعْدِ مِيثَٰقِهِۦ وَيَقْطَعُونَ مَآ أَمَرَ ٱللَّهُ بِهِۦٓ أَن يُوصَلَ وَيُفْسِدُونَ فِى ٱلْأَرْضِ أُو۟لَٰٓئِكَ لَهُمُ ٱللَّعْنَةُ وَلَهُمْ سُوٓءُ ٱلدَّارِ ﴿٢٥﴾

"But as for those who break Allāh's compact after having pledged it solemnly, and sever what Allāh has commanded to be joined, and cause corruption in the earth —it is such on whom the curse will lie, and for them will be the ills of the [ultimate] abode."[1]

وقال فى البقرة:

And He ﷻ said in Sūrah al-Baqarah:

ٱلَّذِينَ يَنقُضُونَ عَهْدَ ٱللَّهِ مِنۢ بَعْدِ مِيثَٰقِهِۦ وَيَقْطَعُونَ مَآ أَمَرَ ٱللَّهُ بِهِۦٓ أَن يُوصَلَ وَيُفْسِدُونَ فِى ٱلْأَرْضِ ۚ أُو۟لَٰٓئِكَ هُمُ ٱلْخَٰسِرُونَ ﴿٢٧﴾

"those who break the covenant made with Allāh after having pledged it solemnly, and sever what Allāh has commanded to be joined, and cause corruption on the earth— it is they who are the losers."[2][3]

F) Profligate

Imām Ṣādiq (a) said the following in a will to his son, Imām Kāẓim (a):

يَا بُنَيَّ إِذَا زُرْتَ فَزُرِ الْأَخْيَارَ وَ لَا تَزُرِ الْفُجَّارَ فَإِنَّهُمْ صَخْرَةٌ لَا يَنْفَجِرُ مَاؤُهَا وَ شَجَرَةٌ

[1] Sūrah Ra'd 13:25.
[2] Sūrah al-Baqarah 2:27.
[3] *al-Kāfī*, Vol. 2, p. 376, tr. 7; *Biḥār al-'Anwār*, vol. 75, tr. 7.

$$\text{لَا يَخْضَرُّ وَرَقُهَا وَ أَرْضٍ لَا يَظْهَرُ عُشْبُهَا}$$

"O my son, if you want to meet someone, visit the good people and never visit evil fellows, because they are like a stone from which water never flows, and a tree whose leaves do not turn green, and a land whose vegetation does not appear."[1]

G) Foul language

Luqmān the Wise said to his son:

$$\text{يَا بُنَيَّ لَا يَغُرَّنَّكَ خَبِيثُ اللِّسَانِ فَإِنَّهُ يُخْتَمُ عَلَى قَلْبِهِ وَ تَتَكَلَّمُ جَوَارِحُهُ وَ تَشْهَدُ عَلَيْهِ}$$

O my child! Never let a foul-mouthed (person) deceive you, because (due to disobedience and rebellion) his heart would be sealed, and his limbs will speak up and testify against him.[2]

H) Ignorant

Amīr al Mu'minīn said to his son, Imām Ḥasan:

$$\text{صُحْبَةُ الْجَاهِلِ شُؤْم}$$

"The company of an ignorant person is unblessed."[3]

I) Contemptible

Similarly, Imām ʿAlī said to Imām Ḥusain:

$$\text{وَمَنْ خَالَطَ الْأَنْذَالَ، حُقِّر}$$

"Whoever associates with lowly people will be degraded."[4]

J) Evil

Imām Jawād said:

---

[1] *Biḥār al-'Anwār*, vol. 75, p. 202.
[2] *al-Ikhtiṣāṣ*, p. 336.
[3] *Biḥār al-'Anwār*, vol. 74, p. 208.
[4] *Tuḥaf al-'Uqūl*, p. 84.

إِيَّاكَ وَ مُصَاحَبَةَ الشَّرِيرِ، فَإِنَّهُ كَالسَّيْفِ الْمَسْلُولِ، يَحْسُنُ مَنْظَرُهُ وَ يَقْبُحُ أَثَرُه

"Don't form friendship and establish relationship with an evil fellow, because he is like a wielded sword that is beautiful to see, but its effect is terrible."[1]

[1] *Biḥār al-'Anwār*, vol. 74, p. 198.

Part Five

Nurturing faith and religion

Nurturing faith and religion

A) Children's relationship with Allāh ﷻ

What is mentioned in the Islamic traditions - especially in the *Treatise of Rights* of Imām Sajjād (a) - as one of the great responsibilities of parents is the issue of introducing the child to Allāh ﷻ, the Creator of the world. Parents should familiarize their children with Allāh's ﷻ attributes and His blessings in a simple and understandable language, inspired by the school of *Ahl al-Bayt* (a).

It is obvious that a child's familiarity with Allāh ﷻ from childhood has a great impact on his personality and gives direction to his future life.

Imām Sajjād (a) said about the duty of a father:

وأنَّكَ مَسؤولٌ عَمَّا ولَّيتَهُ مِن حُسْنِ الأدَبِ، والدَّلالة على رَبِّه

"You have a responsibility to take care of your child, to educate him well and to make him know his Lord ﷻ."[1]

Knowing Allāh ﷻ

'Alī (a) said to his son, Imām Ḥasan Mujtabā (a):

وَ اعْلَمْ يَا بُنَيَ أَنَّهُ لَوْ كَانَ لِرَبِّكَ شَرِيكٌ لَأَتَتْكَ رُسُلُهُ وَ لَرَأَيْتَ آثَارَ مُلْكِهِ وَ سُلْطَانِهِ وَ لَعَرَفْتَ صِفَتَه

My child! Know that if there was another god, his ambassadors and messengers would certainly have arrived, and you would

[1] *Makārim al-'Akhlāq*, p. 421.

have seen the effects of his rule[1]

وَ فِعَالَهُ وَ لَكِنَّهُ إِلَهٌ وَاحِدٌ كَمَا وَصَفَ نَفْسَهُ لَا يُضَادُّهُ فِي ذَلِكَ أَحَدٌ وَ لَا يُحَاجُّهُ وَ أَنَّهُ خَالِقُ كُلِّ شَيْءٍ وَ أَنَّهُ أَجَلُّ مِنْ أَنْ يُثْبِتَ لِرُبُوبِيَّتِهِ بِالْإِحَاطَةِ قَلْبٌ أَوْ بَصَرٌ وَ إِذَا أَنْتَ عَرَفْتَ ذَلِكَ فَافْعَلْ كَمَا يَنْبَغِي لِمِثْلِكَ فِي صِغَرِ خَطَرِكَ وَ قِلَّةِ مَقْدُرَتِكَ وَ عِظَمِ حَاجَتِكَ إِلَيْهِ أَنْ يَفْعَلَ مِثْلَهُ فِي طَلَبِ طَاعَتِهِ وَ الرَّهْبَةِ لَهُ وَ الشَّفَقَةِ مِنْ سُخْطِهِ فَإِنَّهُ لَمْ يَأْمُرْكَ إِلَّا بِحَسَنٍ وَ لَمْ يَنْهَكَ إِلَّا عَنْ قَبِيحٍ

and power, and you would know his characteristics and acts; but He (Allāh ﷻ) is the only deity, as He has praised himself. He has no opposition and no one to argue with Him.

He is the Creator of everything. He is too great to have His divinity proved by the encompassing heart or eye. When you have understood this, you should do what is done by him who is like you by way of his low position, his lack of authority, his increasing incapability, and his great need of his Lord ﷻ for seeking His obedience, fearing His chastisement, and apprehending His anger, because He does not command you save for virtue and does not refrain you save from evil.[2]

Pondering on the signs of Allāh ﷻ

Imām ʿAlī (a) said in his will to his son, Imām Ḥasan (a):

ولا عِبادَةَ كالتَفكُّرِ في صَنْعَةِ اللّه عز و جل

"There is no worship like pondering on the creations of Allāh, the mighty, the sublime."[3]

Luqmān the Wise said to his son:

---

[1] *Wasāʾil al-Shīʿah*, vol. 18, p. 129.
[2] *Tuḥaf al-ʿUqūl*, p. 70.
[3] *Biḥār al-ʾAnwār*, vol. 74, p. 402.

يَا بُنَيَّ اتَّقِ النَّظَرَ إِلَى مَا لَا تَمْلِكُهُ وَ أَطِلِ التَّفَكُّرَ فِي مَلَكُوتِ السَّمَاوَاتِ وَ الْأَرْضِ وَ الْجِبَالِ وَ مَا خَلَقَ اللَّهُ فَكَفَى بِهَذَا وَاعِظاً لِقَلْبِك

My child…think a lot about the kingdom of the heavens, the earth, the mountains, and everything that Allāh has created, because pondering on the world is the best advisor for your heart.[1]

Ascribing partners to Allāh ﷻ

It is stated in the Holy Qur'ān:

وَإِذْ قَالَ لُقْمَٰنُ لِٱبْنِهِۦ وَهُوَ يَعِظُهُۥ يَٰبُنَيَّ لَا تُشْرِكْ بِٱللَّهِ ۖ إِنَّ ٱلشِّرْكَ لَظُلْمٌ عَظِيمٌ ﴿١٣﴾

"When Luqmān said to his son, as he advised him: 'O my son! Do not ascribe any partners to Allāh. Polytheism is indeed a great injustice.'"[2]

Under the interpretation of this verse, it is mentioned in *Tafsīr Namūneh* as follows:

Wisdom of Luqmān demands that before everything else he goes to the most basic ideological issue and that is the issue of monotheism in all fields and dimensions, because every destructive and anti-God movement originates from polytheism, worldliness, status-seeking, lust, and the like, each of which is considered a branch of polytheism, just as the basis of all correct and constructive movements is monotheism. Attachment to Allāh ﷻ and to obey His commands implies cutting off from all other than Him and breaking all the idols at His threshold. It is noteworthy that Luqmān the Wise mentions the reason for rejecting polytheism: that polytheism is a great injustice, that too with an interpretation that from several aspects includes emphasis.

Now what injustice is greater than this, which has been done against Allāh, to be equated to worthless creatures and regarding those

[1] *al-Ikhtiṣāṣ*, p. 336.
[2] Sūrah Luqmān 31:13.

they lead astray, and oppress them with their criminal acts, and themselves turn the glory of Allāh's ﷻ honour and worship into the bottom of the valley of humiliation of the worship of other than Him.[1]

Relationship with Allāh ﷻ

Imām 'Alī ؑ said to his son, Imām Ḥasan ؑ:

وَأی سببٍ أوثِق من سَبَبٍ بَيْنَکِ وَبَيْنَ الله جلّ جلالُه اِن أخَذْتَ بِه

"Which means is stronger and more reliable than the relationship you have with the Almighty - if you remain attached to it?"[2]

Remember Allāh ﷻ everywhere

Amīr al Mu'minīn ؑ in his will at the time of his martyrdom and said:

يا بُنَىَّ وَ كُنْ لِلَّهِ ذَاكِراً عَلَى كُلِّ حَال

"My child! Remember Allāh ﷻ at all times."[3]

Luqmān the Wise said to his son:

يا بُنَىَّ أقِلَّ الْكَلامَ واذكُرِ اللهَ عزّوجلّ فى كُلّ مَكانٍ؛ فَاِنّه قد أنذَرک وَحَذَّرَک وَبَصَّرَک وَعَلَّمَک

يَا بُنَيَّ أَقِلَ الْكَلاَمَ وَ اذْكُرِ اللَّهَ عَزَّ وَ جَلَّ فِي كُلِّ مَكَانٍ فَإِنَّهُ قَدْ أَنْذَرَكَ وَ حَذَّرَكَ وَ

[1] *Tafsīr Namūneh*, Vol. 17, p. 38.
[2] *Biḥār al-'Anwār*, vol. 74, p. 199.
[3] *Biḥār al-'Anwār*, vol. 93, p. 152.

بَصَّرَكَ وَ عَلَّمَكَ

My son! Speak softly and remember Allāh ﷻ everywhere, because He has guided you, warned you and made you seeing and aware.[1]

Amīr al Mu'minīn ؑ said to Imām Ḥasan ؑ:

وأُوصِيكَ بِتَقْوَى اللَّهِ في سِرِّ أَمْرِكَ وعَلانِيَّتِه

"I advise you to fear Allāh ﷻ in your actions, whether done in secret or openly."[2]

Awza'ī narrates from Yaḥyā that Sulaymān said to his son:

يا بُنَيَّ، عَلَيْكَ بِخَشيةِ اللهِ؛ فَإِنَّها غَلَبَتْ كُلَّ شَيْءٍ

My child! Be constantly afraid of Almighty Allāh because the fear and awe of the Almighty encompasses everything.[3]

Creating a state of fear and hope

Likewise, Amīr al Mu'minīn ؑ said to his son, Imām Ḥasan ؑ:

يا بُنىَّ ، خِفِ اللهَ خوفاً تَرى اِنَّکَ لو أَتَيتَه بِحَسَناتِ أَهْلِ الأرضِ لَمْ يَقبَلها منکَ وَارجُ الله رَجاءٍ أنَّک أتيَته بسيّئاتِ أهلِ الأعضِ غَفَرَ ها لک

"My child, fear Allāh ﷻ in such a way that even if you bring all the good deeds of the people of the earth to His presence, He will not accept from you, and hope in Allāh ﷻ in such a way that even if you bring all the sins of the people of the earth to Him, He will forgive them all."[4]

---

[1] *al-Ikhtiṣāṣ*, p. 331.
[2] *Majmu'ah Warrām*, p.378.
[3] *Ḥilyat al-Awliyā'*, vol. 3, p. 71.
[4] *Majmu'ah Warrām*, p.37; *Biḥār al-'Anwār*, vol. 70, p. 394.

Ḥārith or his father Mughīrah asked Imām Ṣādiq ؑ: What was Luqmān's will to his son? He said:

كَانَ فِيهَا الْأَعَاجِيبُ وَ كَانَ أَعْجَبَ مَا كَانَ فِيهَا أَنْ قَالَ لِابْنِهِ خَفِ اللَّهَ عَزَّ وَ جَلَّ خِيفَةً لَوْ جِئْتَهُ بِبِرِّ الثَّقَلَيْنِ لَعَذَّبَكَ وَ ارْجُ اللَّهَ رَجَاءً لَوْ جِئْتَهُ بِذُنُوبِ الثَّقَلَيْنِ لَرَحِمَكَ ثُمَّ قَالَ أَبُو عَبْدِ اللَّهِ ع كَانَ أَبِي يَقُولُ إِنَّهُ لَيْسَ مِنْ عَبْدٍ مُؤْمِنٍ إِلَّا [وَ] فِي قَلْبِهِ نُورَانِ نُورُ خِيفَةٍ وَ نُورُ رَجَاءٍ لَوْ وُزِنَ هَذَا لَمْ يَزِدْ عَلَى هَذَا وَ لَوْ وُزِنَ هَذَا لَمْ يَزِدْ عَلَى هَذَا

"It contained amazing things and the most amazing one was what he said to his son: My son, be pious before Allāh, the Majestic, the Glorious, such that even if you come into His presence with the good deeds of all men and *Jinn*, you will still fear His punishment. On the other hand, your hope in Him must be so great that even if you come into His presence with all the sins of all men and *Jinn*, you will still be hopeful for His kindness and mercy. Then Imām ؑ said, 'My father ؑ has said, "There is no believing servant of Allāh ﷻ without the presence of two lights in his heart. There is the light of hope and the light of fear. They are such that on weighing, no one exceeds the other in any way (in lightness or heaviness).[1]

Luqmān said to his son, Nāmān:

يَا بُنَيَّ لَوْ شُقَّ جَوْفُ الْمُؤْمِنِ لَوُجِدَ عَلَى قَلْبِهِ سَطْرَانِ مِنْ نُورٍ لَوْ وُزِنَا لَمْ يَرْجَحْ أَحَدُهُمَا عَلَى الْآخَرِ مِثْقَالَ حَبَّةٍ مِنْ خَرْدَلٍ أَحَدُهُمَا الرَّجَاءُ وَ الْآخَرُ الْخَوْفُ

My child, if the heart of a believer finds a light, they will see two lines of light written in it, and if they weigh both of them, neither one will be heavier than the other even as much as a mustard seed, one of those two lines is hope and the other is fear.[2]

He also said:

يَا بُنَيَّ كُنْ ذَا قَلْبَيْنِ قَلْبٍ تَخَافُ بِاللَّهِ خَوْفاً لَا يُخَالِطُهُ تَفْرِيطٌ وَ قَلْبٍ تَرْجُو بِهِ اللَّهَ

[1] *al-Kāfī*, vol. 2, p. 67; *Biḥār al-'Anwār*, vol. 70, p. 352; *'Amālī al-Ṣadūq*, p. 597.
[2] *'Udat al-Dā'ī*, p. 28.

رَجَاءً لَا يُخَالِطُهُ تَغْرِير

O my son, have two hearts, a heart with which you fear Allāh ﷻ: a fear that is not mixed with shortcomings and laziness, and a heart with which you hope in Allāh ﷻ; a hope that is not mixed with negligence and deception.[1]

Among the precious advice of Luqmān is that he said:

يَا بُنَيَّ خَفِ اللَّهَ مَخَافَةً لَا تَيْأَسُ مِنْ رَحْمَتِهِ وَ ارْجُهُ رَجَاءً لَا تَأْمَنُ مِنْ مَكْرِهِ

My child! Fear Allāh ﷻ so much that you will not despair of His mercy and hope in Him so much that you will not be safe from His strategy.[2]

The interesting point in these few narrations is that children and teenagers should be brought up with their own spirit and these two conditions should take form in their existence so that they will not despair of Allāh's ﷻ mercy due to sin and slight slip, and they don't imagine that now Allāh ﷻ will not forgive them. On the other hand, they will not be under the impression that if they do a few good deeds, then every wrong they do will be forgiven. Under the pretext that Allāh ﷻ is Merciful and Forgiving, they should not dare to commit more sins: on the contrary they should always remain between hope and fear and not deviate from the line of moderation and not fall into excess.

Fruits of the tree of religious cognition (Ma'rifat)

The seeker is the finder

Luqmān said to his son:

يَا بُنَيَّ مَنْ ذَا الَّذِي عَبَدَ اللَّهَ فَخَذَلَهُ وَ مَنْ ذَا الَّذِي ابْتَغَاهُ فَلَمْ يَجِدْهُ يَا بُنَيَّ وَ مَنْ ذَا الَّذِي ذَكَرَهُ فَلَمْ يَذْكُرْهُ وَ مَنْ ذَا الَّذِي تَوَكَّلَ عَلَى اللَّهِ فَوَكَلَهُ إِلَى غَيْرِهِ وَ مَنْ ذَا الَّذِي تَضَرَّعَ إِلَيْهِ جَلَّ ذِكْرُهُ فَلَمْ يَرْحَمْه

---

[1] *Majmu'ah Warrām*, p.37.
[2] *al-Ikhtiṣāṣ*, p. 334.

My child! Who worshiped Allāh ﷻ and Allāh ﷻ deprived him of his help and care!

And who searched for Allāh ﷻ and did not find Him! My child! Who remembered Allāh ﷻ, but Allāh ﷻ did not remember him!

And who trusted in Allāh ﷻ and Allāh ﷻ left him to someone else! And who cried and supplicated to him and Allāh ﷻ did not make him a subject of His grace and mercy![1]

The Holy Prophet ﷺ said: One of Luqmān's advice to his son was:

يَا بُنَيَّ مَنْ ذَا الَّذِي ابْتَغَى اللَّهَ فَلَمْ يَجِدْهُ وَ مَنْ ذَا الَّذِي لَجَأَ إِلَى اللَّهِ فَلَمْ يُدَافِعْ عَنْهُ أَمْ مَنْ ذَا الَّذِي تَوَكَّلَ عَلَى اللَّهِ فَلَمْ يَكْفِهِ

"Who searched for Allāh ﷻ and did not find Him! And who sought refuge in Allāh ﷻ and Allāh ﷻ did not support him! Who trusted in Allāh ﷻ and Allāh ﷻ did not make him needless!"[2]

Good expectation from Allāh ﷻ

Luqmān said:

My child! Call upon Allāh ﷻ then ask the people: Has anyone called upon Allāh ﷻ and He did not answer them? Or has he asked Allāh ﷻ for something that He has withheld?

My child! Trust in the Allāh Almighty, then ask people: Has there been anyone who trusted in Allāh ﷻ and He did not solve their problems?

My child! Have good faith in Allāh ﷻ, then ask the people: Whoever had good faith in Allāh ﷻ and Allāh ﷻ did not have good faith in him?

My child! Whoever seeks Allāh's ﷻ pleasure makes himself angry, and whoever does not control himself and does not anger it, he will

---

[1] *al-Ikhtiṣāṣ*, p. 333.

[2] *Biḥār al-'Anwār*, vol. 13, p. 433.

not please Allāh ﷻ, and whoever does not suppress his anger, would make the enemy happy.[1]

Know Allāh ﷻ by these attributes

It is mentioned in the will of Amīr al Mu'minīn ؑ to his son, Imām Ḥasan ؑ as follows:

"(My child!) Know that He Who owns the treasuries of the heavens, and the earth has permitted you to pray to Him and has promised you acceptance of the prayer. He has commanded you to beg from Him in order that He may give you and to seek His mercy in order that He may have mercy on you. He has not placed anything between you and Him that may veil Him from you. He has not required you to get a mediator for you to reach Him, and if you err, He has not prevented you from repentance. He does not hasten with punishment. He does not taunt you for repenting, nor does He humiliate you when you are deserving humiliation. He has not been harsh in accepting repentance. He does not severely question you about your sins. He does not disappoint you of His mercy. Rather He regards abstention from sin as a virtue. He counts your one sin as one while He counts your one virtue as ten. He has opened for you the door of repentance. Therefore, whenever you call Him, He hears your call, and whenever you whisper to Him He knows the whispers. You place before Him your needs, unveil yourself before Him, complain to Him of your worries, beseech Him to remove your troubles, seek His help in your affairs and ask from the treasuries of His mercy that which no one else has power to give…[2]

B) Teaching religion and Islamic laws

Correct and appropriate religious awareness should play an important role in their future destiny: because the foundation of a person is his thought and culture, and if this thought and culture is based on documented and justified religious awareness, life will have a

---

[1] *Biḥār al-'Anwār*, vol. 13, p. 432.
[2] *Tuḥaf al-'Uqūl*, p. 73; *Biḥār al-'Anwār*, vol. 74, p. 205.

religious significance. Therefore, teaching religious issues and rulings to children is very important in enlightening their minds and creating interest in religious affairs and stability in religion.

Once the Holy Prophet ﷺ saw some children and said:

ويل لأطفالِ آخِرَ الزمانِ من آبائهم . فقيل: يا رَسولَ الله مِن آبائهم المشركينَ؟ فقال: لاَ من آبائهم الْمومِنينَ لا يُعَلِّمُونَهُمْ شَيئاً مِن الفرائضِ، وَاذا تَعلَّموا أولادَهم مَنَعوهم ورَجوا عنهم بعَرَضٍ يَسير مِن الدنيا فَأنا منهم بَرِىءٌ وهُم مِنّى بُراءٌ

"Woe upon the children of the last age at the hands of their fathers! It was said: Messenger of Allāh ﷺ, from their polytheist fathers? He said, "No, from their *Muslim* fathers, who do not teach them anything about religious duties, and if their children want to educate themselves about religious matters, they prevent them from doing so, and they only want their children to gain a little wealth from the world. I declare immunity from such fathers, and they also have nothing to do with me."[1]

In any case, we should not underestimate the importance of religious education, lest we make our children, who were created for heaven, away from the path of heaven by neglecting religious matters.

Let's take a little courage and, based on the instructions received from the Prophet ﷺ and the Infallible A'immah ﷺ, introduce our dear children to religious issues so that they can be self-made and become a good example for others in the future.

From the moment the child begins to speak, his learning period starts and according to the Infallibles ﷺ, the development of the child takes place in stages and his training and education also has stages.

The statement of 'there is no god, except Allāh ﷻ

Ibn 'Abbās narrates from the Prophet ﷺ as follows:

---

[1] *Mustadrak al-Wasā'il*, vol. 15, p. 164, quoted from *Ja'mī al-Akhbār*.

اِفتَحوا على صِبيانكم أوّلَ كَلِمَة لا اله الاّ الله...

"The first word you put on your children's tongue should be: [لَا إِلَٰهَ إِلَّا اللَّهُ] There is no god but Allāh ﷻ."[1]

Also, Ibn 'Umar narrated from the Prophet ﷺ that he said:

اِذا أفصَحوا أولادُكُم فَعَلّموهم لا اله الاّ الله...

"When your children open their tongues, teach them: [لَا إِلَٰهَ إِلَّا اللَّهُ] There is no god but Allāh ﷻ."[2]

'Ā'ishah narrates from the noble Prophet of Islam ﷺ, who said:

من رَبّىٰ صغيراً حَتّى يقولَ لا اله الاّ الله لَم يَحاسِبه اللهُ

Whoever raises a child until he says: [لَا إِلَٰهَ إِلَّا اللَّهُ] 'There is no god, but Allāh', Allāh ﷻ will not hold him accountable on Judgment Day.[3]

'Abdullāh b. Faḍālah says: I heard from Imām Bāqir ﷺ and Imām Ṣādiq ﷺ that they said:

When a child reaches 3 years of age, teach him seven times to recite [لَا إِلَٰهَ إِلَّا اللَّهُ]. Then leave him at that till he is 3 years, 7 months, and 20 days old; then train him to say [مُحَمَّدٌ رَسُولُ اللَّهِ]. Then leave him at that till he completes 4 years, then teach him seven times to say [صَلَّى اللَّهُ عَلَى مُحَمَّدٍ وَ آلِهِ]. Then leave him at that till he reaches the age of 5 years; then see if he can distinguish between the right and the left hand.

---

[1] *Kanz al-'Ummāl*, vol. 16, p. 441.
[2] *Kanz al-'Ummāl*, p. 440.
[3] *Kanz al-'Ummāl*, p. 456.

When he knows the difference, make him face *Qiblah* and tell him to do *Sajdah*, continue this till he is 6 years of age. Then he should be told to pray and taught *Rukūʿ* and *Sajdah*. When he completes 7 years, then he should be asked to wash his face and hands, and then told to pray. This will continue till he reaches the age of 9 years, when he should be taught proper ritual ablution for prayer and proper *Ṣalāh*. When he learns proper *Wuḍū* and *Ṣalāh*, Allāh ﷻ forgives the sins of his parents.[1]

Patience and perseverance

Sometimes children create problems for parents and teachers according to their age, however the latter should not get angry at once, but treat children with patience and gentleness in order to overcome their behavioural problems, Imām Ṣādiq عليه السلام said:

إِنَّ رَسُولَ اللَّهِ ص كَانَ فِي الصَّلَاةِ وَ إِلَى جَانِبِهِ الْحُسَيْنُ بْنُ عَلِيٍّ- فَكَبَّرَ رَسُولُ اللَّهِ ص فَلَمْ يُحِرِ الْحُسَيْنُ ع بِالتَّكْبِيرِ ثُمَّ كَبَّرَ رَسُولُ اللَّهِ ص فَلَمْ يُحِرِ الْحُسَيْنُ التَّكْبِيرَ فَلَمْ يَزَلْ رَسُولُ اللَّهِ ص يُكَبِّرُ وَ يُعَالِجُ الْحُسَيْنُ ع التَّكْبِيرَ فَلَمْ يُحِرْ حَتَّى أَكْمَلَ سَبْعَ تَكْبِيرَاتٍ فَأَحَارَ الْحُسَيْنُ ع التَّكْبِيرَ فِي السَّابِعَةِ فَقَالَ أَبُو عَبْدِ اللَّهِ ع فَصَارَتْ سُنَّةً

Once, the Holy Prophet ﷺ was praying and Imām Ḥusain عليه السلام (who had not started speaking as yet) was standing next to him.

The Prophet ﷺ said *Takbīrat al-Iḥrām* to start the prayer. Imām Ḥusain عليه السلام also tried to say *Allāhu Akbar*, but he was unable to. The Prophet ﷺ said *Takbīr* again, and the Imām عليه السلام tried to say *Allāhu Akbar*, but he could not. The Prophet ﷺ continued to repeat *Takbīrat al-Iḥrām* so that Ḥusain عليه السلام may also recite it. But its pronunciation was difficult for him until the Prophet ﷺ repeated *Allāhu Akbar* seven times. When he said the seventh *Takbīr*, Imām Ḥusain's عليه السلام tongue also opened and he recited *Takbīrat al-Iḥrām* correctly.

Imām Ṣādiq عليه السلام said: This is why the seven *Takbīr* became *Sunnah*.[2]

---

[1] *'Amālī al-Ṣadūq*, p. 351; *Wasā'il al-Shīʿah*, vol. 15, p. 193.
[2] *Wasā'il al-Shīʿah*, vol. 4, pp. 140 and 721.

C) Practical training in Islamic laws

After teaching a summary of Islamic teachings in simple language, children should be gradually familiarized with *Sharīʻah* rules and issues. That is, we should show them concretely how to follow the rules so that they don't have doubts in the way of learning the rules. For example, let us consider ablution.

In this regard, at the beginning, the child should be taught the correct way to perform ablution, then we do it practically and ask him to observe carefully, and sometimes we should also watch the child perform ablution.

Obviously, the educational aspect of the practical and visual method is much more effective and attractive than only verbal instruction.

Mirzā Nūrī narrates from *Fiqh al-Riḍā*:

Once, Amīr al Mu'minīn ﷺ was with Muḥammad b. Hanafiyyah; he said, "Muḥammad, bring water for me to perform ablution for the *Ṣalāh*." When Ibn. Hanafiyyah brought the vessel of water, he placed his hand in it reciting:

بِسْمِ اللَّهِ وَ الْحَمْدُ لِلَّهِ الَّذِي جَعَلَ الْمَاءَ طَهُوراً وَ لَمْ يَجْعَلْهُ نَجِساً

In the name of Allāh ﷻ, and praise be to Allāh ﷻ who made the water pure and did not make it impure.

Then he washed himself after evacuation and recited:

اللَّهُمَّ حَصِّنْ فَرْجِي وَ أَعِفَّهُ وَ اسْتُرْ عَوْرَتِي وَ حَرِّمْنِي عَلَى النَّارِ

O Allāh ﷻ, make my privies chaste and cover my shame and prohibit for me the fire of Hell.

Then he rinsed his mouth and recited:

اللَّهُمَّ لَقِّنِّي حُجَّتِي يَوْمَ أَلْقَاكَ وَ أَطْلِقْ لِسَانِي بِذِكْرِكَ

O Allāh ﷻ, give me my argument on the day I meet You, and make my tongue mention Your remembrance.

Then he put water in his mouth reciting:

اللَّهُمَّ لَا تُحَرِّمْ عَلَيَّ رِيحَ الْجَنَّةِ وَ اجْعَلْنِي مِمَّنْ يَشَمُّ رِيحَهَا وَ رَوْحَهَا وَ طِيبَهَا

O Allāh ﷻ, do not deprive me of the breeze of Paradise, and make me among those who smell its fragrance, its spirit, and its goodness.

Then he washed his face and recited:

اللَّهُمَّ بَيِّضْ وَجْهِي يَوْمَ تَسْوَدُّ فِيهِ الْوُجُوهُ وَ لَا تُسَوِّدْ وَجْهِي يَوْمَ تَبْيَضُّ فِيهِ الْوُجُوهُ

O Allāh ﷻ, whiten my face on the day when You will blacken existence, and do not darken my face on the day when faces will be whitened.

Then he washed his right hand reciting:

اللَّهُمَّ أَعْطِنِي كِتَابِي بِيَمِينِي وَ الْخُلْدَ فِي الْجِنَانِ بِيَسَارِي وَ حَاسِبْنِي حِساباً يَسِيراً

O Allāh ﷻ, give me my scroll of deeds in my right hand, and to abide forever in Paradise with left, and take my easy reckoning.

Then he washed his left hand, reciting:

اللَّهُمَّ لَا تُعْطِنِي كِتَابِي بِشِمَالِي وَ لَا تَجْعَلْهَا مَغْلُولَةً إِلَى عُنُقِي وَ أَعُوذُ بِكَ مِنْ مُقَطَّعَاتِ النِّيرَانِ

O Allāh ﷻ, do not give me my scroll of deeds in my left hand, and do not chain it to my neck, and I seek refuge in You from the cuts of fire.

Then he wiped his head reciting:

O Allāh ﷻ, cover me with Your mercy and Your blessings and Your forgiveness.

Then he wiped his feet reciting:

اللَّهُمَّ ثَبِّتْ قَدَمَيَّ عَلَى الصِّرَاطِ [ثَبِّتْنِي عَلَى الصِّرَاطِ] يَوْمَ تَزِلُّ فِيهِ الْأَقْدَامُ وَ اجْعَلْ سَعْيِي فِيمَا يُرْضِيكَ عَنِّي

O Allāh ﷻ, make me firm-footed on the Ṣirāṭ on the day when feet would stumble and make my endeavor to be in what pleases You, O the most merciful of the merciful ones.

Then he turned towards Muḥammad b. Hanafiyyah and said, "O Muḥammad! One who performs ablution like me and recites these supplications, the Almighty Allāh will create an angel for every drop of water used and these angels will continue to glorify Allāh ﷻ till the Day of Judgment and their reward will go to that person."[1]

D) Encouraging children for worship and good deeds

Another duty of Muslim parents is to encourage children to worship and to do good deeds. There are two ways to encourage: The first way is for parents to encourage their children to worship. It means that the hearts of their loved ones should be prepared and attracted to spiritual and devotional situations; and the desire and interest of the parents in religious affairs and acts of worship is the best practical incentive for children to these activities.

When children and teenagers observe that their parents are sensitive and serious about religious matters and show great importance to worship, and they rush towards worship with enthusiasm and actively participate in religious occasions and religious ceremonies, they automatically also feel interest and joy in these activities and are attracted to supplications and prayers.

The second way is verbal encouragement: the role of speech along with the role of action is effective and important. Speech itself is a part of action; verbal endeavour is also important in its own place, and the educational effect of encouraging and attractive words and wise advice of parents to children in stimulating and encouraging them to perform acts of worship is clear to all.

---

[1] *Mustadrak al-Wasā'il*, vol. 1, p. 308; *Thawāb al-'Amāl*, p. 16.

Striving in obedience to Allāh ﷻ

Amīr al Mu'minīn ؑ says to his son, Muḥammad b. Hanafiyyah:

يَا بُنَيَّ إِذَا قَوِيتَ فَاقْوَ عَلَى طَاعَةِ اللَّهِ وَ إِنْ ضَعُفْتَ فَاضْعُفْ عَنْ مَعْصِيَةِ اللَّهِ

"My child, if you want to become strong and powerful, become strong in endurance and worship of Allāh ﷻ, and if you feel weakness, become weak and powerless in disobeying Allāh ﷻ."[1]

Ḥammād Laḥḥām narrates from Imām Ṣādiq ؑ from his father, who said:

يَا بُنَيَّ إِنَّكَ إِنْ خَالَفْتَنِي فِي الْعَمَلِ لَمْ تَنْزِلْ غَداً مَعِي فِي الْمَنْزِلِ ثُمَّ قَالَ إِنَّ اللَّهَ عَزَّ وَ جَلَّ لَيُوَلِّيَنَّ قَوْماً قَوْماً يُخَالِفُونَهُمْ فِي أَعْمَالِهِمْ يَنْزِلُونَ مَعَهُمْ يَوْمَ الْقِيَامَةِ كَلَّا وَ رَبِّ الْكَعْبَةِ

"My child, if you oppose me, you will not be with me (on the Judgment Day)." Then he said, "How is it acceptable that Allāh ﷻ, the Mighty, the Sublime should keep a people who oppose Him in their actions to be with Him in the same place? No, I swear by the Lord of the Ka'bah that such a thing is not possible."[2]

Unexpected effort

Sa'd b. Abī Khalaf narrates that Imām Kāẓim ؑ advised one of his children:

يَا بُنَيَّ عَلَيْكَ بِالْجِدِّ لَا تُخْرِجَنَّ نَفْسَكَ مِنْ حَدِّ التَّقْصِيرِ فِي عِبَادَةِ اللَّهِ عَزَّ وَ جَلَّ وَ طَاعَتِهِ فَإِنَّ اللَّهَ لَا يُعْبَدُ حَقَّ عِبَادَتِهِ

"My child, be diligent and industrious. Never consider yourself blameless in worshiping and obeying Allāh ﷻ, because Allāh ﷻ is not worshiped as He deserves to be worshiped."[3]

---

[1] *Makārim al-'Akhlāq*, p. 218.
[2] *Majmu'ah Warrām*, p. 376.
[3] *al-Kāfī*, vol. 2, p. 72; *Tuḥaf al-'Uqūl*, p. 432.

Provision of the journey

Luqmān the Wise says to his son:

يَا بُنَيَّ إِيَّاكَ أَنْ تَخْرُجَ مِنَ الدُّنْيَا فَقِيراً وَ تَدَعَ أَمْرَكَ وَ أَمْوَالَكَ عِنْدَ غَيْرِكَ قَيِّماً فَتُصَيِّرَهُ أَمِيراً

My child, don't leave this world empty-handed, while you hand over your achievements and the custody of your property to someone else and make him the controller of your affairs.[1]

Luqmān the Wise says to his son:

يَا بُنَيِّ بَادِرْ بِعَمَلِكَ قَبْلَ أَنْ يَحْضُرَ أَجَلُكَ وَ قَبْلَ أَنْ تَسِيرَ الْجِبَالُ سَيْراً وَ تُجْمَعَ الشَّمْسُ وَ الْقَمَر

My child! Hasten to do good deeds before your death and before the mountains move and the sun and the moon come together.[2]

Avoid laziness

Imām Mūsā b. Jaʿfar ﵇ used to say this to some of his children:

وَ إِيَّاكَ وَ الضَّجَرَ وَ الْكَسَلَ فَإِنَّهُمَا يَمْنَعَانِ حَظَّكَ مِنَ الدُّنْيَا وَ الْآخِرَة

"Avoid boredom and laziness as these two things will deprive you of this world and the Hereafter."[3]

---

[1] *al-Ikhtiṣāṣ*, p. 332.
[2] *al-Ikhtiṣāṣ*, p. 332.
[3] *Tuḥaf al-ʿUqūl*, p. 433.

Spiritual poverty

Jābir b. ʿAbdullāh narrated the following from the Holy Prophet of Islam ﷺ:

قَالَتْ أُمُّ سُلَيْمَانَ بْنِ دَاوُدَ لِسُلَيْمَانَ يَا بُنَيَّ إِيَّاكَ وَ كَثْرَةَ النَّوْمِ بِاللَّيْلِ فَإِنَّ كَثْرَةَ النَّوْمِ بِاللَّيْلِ تَدَعُ الرَّجُلَ فَقِيراً يَوْمَ الْقِيَامَة

"Prophet Sulaymān's ﷺ mother said to him: My son! Avoid sleeping too much at night, because too much sleep at night makes one poor and needy on the Judgment Day."[1]

Arrogance in sin

ʿAlī ﷺ said to his son, Imām Ḥusain ﷺ:

أَيْ بُنَيَّ الْعَجَبُ مِمَّنْ يَخَافُ الْعِقَابَ فَلَمْ يَكُفَّ وَ رَجَا الثَّوَابَ فَلَمْ يَتُبْ وَ يَعْمَلْ

"My child! It is surprising for someone to be afraid of punishment, but not to stop sinning, who has hope of reward, but does not repent and does not act."[2]

Avoiding haughtiness and dereliction in worship

Another responsibility of parents after encouraging their children to worship and perform righteous deeds is to prevent them from selfishness and excess in worship, because either of these two causes harm.

Luqmān the Wise used to say to his son:

يَا بُنَيَّ لَا يُعْجِبْكَ إِحْسَانُكَ وَ لَا تَتَعَظَّمَنَّ بِعَمَلِكَ الصَّالِحِ فَتَهْلِك

[1] *'Amālī al-Ṣadūq*, p. 207.
[2] *Tuḥaf al-ʿUqūl*, p. 84.

My child, don't be proud of good deeds and consider them great, because you will perish.[1]

Fajī' 'Aqīlī says:

حَدَّثَنِي الْحَسَنُ بْنُ عَلِيِّ بْنِ أَبِي طَالِبٍ ع قَالَ: لَمَّا حَضَرَتْ وَالِدِيَ الْوَفَاةُ أَقْبَلَ يُوصِي إِلَى أَنْ قَالَ قَالَ ع وَ اقْتَصِدْ فِي عِبَادَتِكَ وَ عَلَيْكَ فِيهَا بِالْأَمْرِ الدَّائِمِ الَّذِي تُطِيقُهُ الْخَبَرَ

Imām Ḥasan ؑ said to me: When my father ؑ was in his last moments, he started making a will and said:

"Be moderate in worship and do what you can always do and what is in your power (not what you have the patience and ability to do)."[2]

If Allāh ﷻ loves a person...

Abū Baṣīr has narrated from Imām Ṣādiq ؑ, who said:

مرّ أبى ومعه فى الطواف وأنا حَدَثٌ قَقد اجتهدتُ فى العبادَة، قرآنى وأنا انصابُ عَرَقاً، فقال لى يا جعفرُ يا بُنَيَّ انّ اللهَ اذا أَحَبَّ عبداً أُدخلَه الجنّة وَرَضى عَنه باليسير.

"(When I performed Ḥajj with my father) I was doing Ṭawāf with him while I was young. (In one of the rounds) I was busy praying and sweating when my father passed by and noticed me; he said: Ja'far, my son; if Allāh ﷻ loves a servant, He takes him to Paradise and is satisfied with him with only a little worship."[3]

Likewise, Imām Ṣādiq ؑ said:

اجتهدتُ فى العِبادَة وأنا شابٌّ، فقال لى أبى: يا بُنَيَّ، دونَ ما أراك تصنعَه، فَاِنَّ

---

[1] al-Ikhtiṣāṣ, p. 336.
[2] Mustadrak al-Wasā'il, vol. 1, p. 130.
[3] Majmu'ah Warrām, p. 386.

اللهِ اذا أَحَبَّ عبداً رضى مِنه بِاليسير

"When I was very young, my father told me: My son (don't tire yourself too much) you can do less than this; it is a fact that if Allāh ﷻ loves a servant, He will be satisfied with his little worship."[1]

Fulfilling the duties

Imām Ṣādiq ؑ narrates from Luqmān the Wise, who said to his son:

وصُم صَوماً يَقطَعُ شَهْوتك ولا تَصُم صوماً يَمنعُكَ من الصَّلاة فاِنَّ الصَّلاة أَحَبُّ اَلَى اللهِ من الصيامِ

You must observe the fast in such a way that it should eradicate your lust, not that it should prevent you from Prayer, because Allāh ﷻ loves Prayer more than fasting.[2]

E) Preaching and good advice

One of the comprehensive principles that all difficult societies need is the issue of preaching and advice. It means urging and recommending each other to do good deeds. Preaching and advice is not specific to a particular category or group. It is a universal duty. At the same time, people should be engaged in self-improvement and purification of their souls and their actions, and they have a duty to influence others as well, as there is no one who is needless preaching. It is obvious that if this principle is followed well, many deviations and corruptions will disappear from the society.

Of course, the sermonizing should be gentle, honest, and sincere and not rude and arrogant, which will have the opposite effect.

---

[1] *Majmu'ah Warrām*, p. 386.
[2] *Mustadrak al-Wasā'il*, vol. 3, p. 43.

The Holy Qur'ān says:

يَٰٓأَيُّهَا ٱلَّذِينَ ءَامَنُوا۟ قُوٓا۟ أَنفُسَكُمْ وَأَهْلِيكُمْ نَارًا وَقُودُهَا ٱلنَّاسُ وَٱلْحِجَارَةُ عَلَيْهَا مَلَٰٓئِكَةٌ غِلَاظٌ شِدَادٌ لَّا يَعْصُونَ ٱللَّهَ مَآ أَمَرَهُمْ وَيَفْعَلُونَ مَا يُؤْمَرُونَ ۝٦

"O you who have faith! Save yourselves and your families from a Fire whose fuel is people and stones, over which are [assigned] angels, severe and mighty, who do not disobey whatever Allāh has commanded them, and carry out what they are commanded."[1]

This verse is absolutely clear that the believers have the duty to keep themselves, their families, and children away from the fire of Hell and to constantly fulfill their religious and moral duty by giving moral advice and reminding them of the divine verses.

Commentators have narrated many traditions from Shī'ah and Sunnī in the interpretation this verse.

The late Kolaynī has narrated through his chains of narrators from 'Abd al-'Alā'', retainer of Āl Sām from Imām Ṣādiq ﷺ that he said:

لَمَّا نَزَلَتْ هَذِهِ الْآيَةُ- يا أَيُّهَا الَّذِينَ آمَنُوا قُوا أَنْفُسَكُمْ وَ أَهْلِيكُمْ ناراً جَلَسَ رَجُلٌ مِنَ الْمُسْلِمِينَ يَبْكِي وَ قَالَ أَنَا عَجَزْتُ عَنْ نَفْسِي كُلِّفْتُ أَهْلِي فَقَالَ رَسُولُ اللَّهِ ص حَسْبُكَ أَنْ تَأْمُرَهُمْ بِمَا تَأْمُرُ بِهِ نَفْسَكَ وَ تَنْهَاهُمْ عَمَّا تَنْهَى عَنْهُ نَفْسَكَ

When the verse:

يَٰٓأَيُّهَا ٱلَّذِينَ ءَامَنُوا۟ قُوٓا۟ أَنفُسَكُمْ وَأَهْلِيكُمْ نَارًا...

"O you who believe, save yourselves and your families from a fire..."[2]

---

[1] Sūrah al-Taḥrīm 66:6.
[2] Sūrah al-Taḥrīm 66:6.

... was revealed, a believer sat down and cried saying: I am helpless to save myself; I have also become responsible for my family!

The Messenger of Allāh ﷺ said, "It is enough for you to just command them what you order yourself and forbid what you restrain yourself from."[1]

In the same way, it is mentioned in another narration:

Someone asked the Messenger of Allāh ﷺ: How can I protect my family (from sin)? He said, "Command them what Allāh ﷻ has ordered and forbid what He has forbidden. So, if they obey you, you will have restrained them, and if they disobeyed, you have performed your duty."[2]

What is the implication of 'save yourself'?

Under the exegesis of the verse:

يَٰٓأَيُّهَا ٱلَّذِينَ ءَامَنُوا۟ قُوٓا۟ أَنفُسَكُمْ وَأَهْلِيكُمْ نَارًا...

"O you who believe! save yourselves and your families from a fire..."

'Allāmah Ṭabāṭabāī has narrated from *Tafsīr Durr al-Manthūr* that Imām 'Alī ؑ said:

علّموا أنفسكم و أهليكم الخير و أدّبوهم

"Make yourself and your family form the habit of doing good deeds and educate them and teach them good behaviour."[3]

F) Connection with the afterlife

Children and teenagers have a pure divine nature. Therefore, they do not lie unless they have learnt it from their parents. Children try to

---

[1] *al-Mīzān*, vol. 28, p. 341.
[2] *Nūr al-Thaqlayn*, vol. 5, p. 372; *al-Mīzān*, vol. 28, p. 341.
[3] *al-Mīzān*, vol. 28, p. 341.

help their friends; they are inclined to good and avoid evil. This nature is inspired by the Creator, who has taught them to distinguish ugliness from beauty. Even though they have not acquired formal knowledge and education and may not even gone to school, they understand that telling the truth is good and cheating is bad, keeping trust is good and betrayal is bad, helping others is good and cruelty is bad.

Allāh ﷻ has inspired the knowledge of good and bad to their pure nature:

فَأَلْهَمَهَا فُجُورَهَا وَتَقْوَىٰهَا ﴿٨﴾

"And inspired it with [discernment between] its virtues and vices."[1]

We should think how this divine pure nature can be inculcated in our children and remain untainted and be their guide in the ups and downs life of the future and how to guide them to attach themselves to the lives of truthful and righteous people and those who seek Allāh ﷻ and how we can connect them with the lives of the truthful and the righteous and those who seek Allāh ﷻ and get rid of the devils of darkness and the ugly-natured satans?

Following the teachings of the Prophets ﷺ and true leaders, let us introduce our beloved children to resurrection and eternal life. Tell them about the end of the world and put them on the path of the realities of life and its lofty goals. Parents are also responsible for raising their children and providing for their livelihood, maintenance, and social needs. Most importantly, they are responsible for the spiritual and cultural training of their wards and to familiarize their children with divine teachings and the way of human life and the world of existence towards Allāh ﷻ and resurrection, which are also vital religious and human issues.

Acquainting children with eternal life and especially the beautiful scenes of heaven and its gardens and fountains saves them from intellectual stagnation and limited horizons.

The mention of Resurrection is also a strong and powerful motivator that guides young people towards human values, but also harnesses and enlightens their talent for improvement and

---

[1] Sūrah al-Shams 91:8.

development of worldly and Hereafter life, because they convey the belief that they have to account for their good or bad deeds in the next world. They also learn that they should not be a burden on others in the world. Under the shadow of resurrection, they would live a free, independent and a dignified life and use their ability to live honourably by using the blessings of Allāh ﷻ. It will also provide happiness in the Hereafter.

Yes, young people, who have the knowledge of the Hereafter in their life are different from those who were raised far from the teachings of the prophets and without belief in the afterlife. Belief in the eternal afterlife creates a surge of divine responsibility and the love to serve in the way of Allāh ﷻ, to have the heavenly promises fulfilled. It is in the light of belief in resurrection that the spirit of virtue, righteousness and abandoning vainglory and debauchery becomes a permanent character of a person. The memory of the Hereafter and its issues do not occupy any heart except that you remove the impurities, dirt and intellectual and practical darkness from it. In this way, life becomes purposeful and meaningful. By relying on these life-creating beliefs, young people can have a strong personality full of hope and self-confidence to be constructive and benevolent, and come out of the glitter of life and the accidents and troubles of the times in a healthy, successful, and prosperous way and be safe from all erosive and harmful things, and the ups and downs of life may not harm his honour and steadfastness.

Luqmān the Wise tells his son:

يَا بُنَيَّ تَعَلَّمْتَ بِسَبْعَةِ آلَافٍ مِنَ الْحِكْمَةِ فَاحْفَظْ مِنْهَا أَرْبَعَةً وَ مُرَّ مَعِي إِلَى الْجَنَّةِ أَحْكِمْ سَفِينَتَكَ فَإِنَّ بَحْرَكَ عَمِيقٌ وَ خَفِّفْ حَمْلَكَ فَإِنَّ الْعَقَبَةَ كَئُودٌ وَ أَكْثِرِ الزَّادَ فَإِنَّ السَّفَرَ بَعِيدٌ وَ أَخْلِصِ الْعَمَلَ فَإِنَّ النَّاقِدَ بَصِير

My child! I have learned seven thousand wisdoms, and you should memorize a few of them so that you can come to Paradise with me: 1. Steady your ship because your sea is very deep 2. Carry your burden lightly; you will face a difficult strait ahead 3. Have a lot of luggage with you, because you have a long journey ahead of you 4. And make your actions pure, because the one who evaluates your actions is All-knowing and All-seeing.[1]

The Infallible ﷺ are concerned about the Hereafter.

There are many narrations from the Infallible ﷺ that they used to make their children familiar with the Hereafter and preach about it. As examples, we mention a few narrations:

The abode of the Hereafter is near

Imām Ṣādiq ﷺ said: Luqmān the Wise said to his son:

أَنَا مُنْذُ سَقَطْتُ إِلَى الدُّنْيَا اسْتَدْبَرْتُ وَ اسْتَقْبَلْتُ الْآخِرَةَ فَدَارٌ أَنْتَ إِلَيْهَا تَسِيرُ أَقْرَبُ مِنْ دَارٍ أَنْتَ مِنْهَا مُتَبَاعِدٌ

Since I opened my eyes into the world, I turned my back on it and turned to the Hereafter, so the abode you are moving to is closer to you than the house you have turned your back to and are moving away from.[2]

Sleep and resurrection

Luqmān the Wise used to say to his son:

يَا بُنَيَّ كَيْفَ يَنَامُ ابْنُ آدَمَ وَ الْمَوْتُ يَطْلُبُهُ وَ كَيْفَ يَغْفُلُ وَ لَا يُغْفَلُ عَنْه

My child! How does man fall asleep while death is chasing him, and how he is oblivious and unaware while they are not oblivious of him?[3]

He also said to his son:

يَا بُنَيَّ كَمَا تَنَامُ كَذَلِكَ تَمُوتُ وَ كَمَا تَسْتَيْقِظُ كَذَلِكَ تُبْعَث

---

[1] *al-Ikhtiṣāṣ*, p. 337.
[2] *Biḥār al-'Anwār*, vol. 13, p. 418 & 411; *al-Ikhtiṣāṣ*, p. 337; *Majmu'ah Warrām*, p. 98 and 421 (with slight difference).
[3] *al-Ikhtiṣāṣ*, p. 334.

My child! As you sleep, you will die and as you wake up, you will be alive on the Judgment Day.[1]

Imām Bāqir said: Luqmān advised his son:

يَا بُنَيَّ إِنْ تَكُ فِي شَكٍّ مِنَ الْمَوْتِ فَارْفَعْ عَنْ نَفْسِكَ النَّوْمَ وَ لَنْ تَسْتَطِيعَ ذَلِكَ وَ إِنْ كُنْتَ فِي شَكٍّ مِنَ الْبَعْثِ فَارْفَعْ عَنْ نَفْسِكَ الِانْتِبَاهَ وَ لَنْ تَسْتَطِيعَ ذَلِكَ فَإِنَّكَ إِذَا فَكَّرْتَ فِي هَذَا عَلِمْتَ أَنَّ نَفْسَكَ بِيَدِ غَيْرِكَ وَ إِنَّمَا النَّوْمُ بِمَنْزِلَةِ الْمَوْتِ وَ إِنَّمَا الْيَقَظَةُ بَعْدَ النَّوْمِ بِمَنْزِلَةِ الْبَعْثِ بَعْدَ الْمَوْتِ

My child! If you have doubts about death, then avoid sleep! You are not able to do that and if you have doubt about Resurrection and Judgment Day prevent yourself from waking up from your sleep, while you can never do such a thing. And if you think about these issues, you will know that your life is in someone else's hands and your sleep is like death and waking up after sleep is like coming back to life after death.[2]

Reduce your desires

Imām 'Alī willed to his son, Imām Ḥasan:

يَا بُنَيَّ قَصِّرِ الْأَمَلَ وَ اذْكُرِ الْمَوْتَ وَ ازْهَدْ فِي الدُّنْيَا فَإِنَّكَ رَهِينُ مَوْتٍ وَ غَرَضُ بَلَاءٍ وَ طَرِيحُ سُقْمٍ

"My child! Reduce your desires and remember death and adopt piety and devoutness in the world, because you are a hostage of death and the target of troubles and diseases."[3]

Remembering death scenes

Luqmān said to his son:

يَا بُنَيَّ إِنَّكَ مُدْرَجٌ فِي أَكْفَانِكَ وَ مَحَلِّ قَبْرِكَ وَ مُعَايِنٌ عَمَلَكَ كُلَّهُ

---

[1] *Majmu'ah Warrām*, p. 57.
[2] *Biḥār al-'Anwār*, vol. 13, p. 417.
[3] *Majmu'ah Warrām*, p. 378.

My child! Without a doubt, you will be wrapped in your shroud and occupy a place in your grave and you will see all your deeds.[1]

The edifying effect of remembering resurrection in the life of young people.

1. The smallness of the world

'Alī, in his will to his son, Imām Ḥasan Mujtabā says:

وَأكْثِر مِن ذِكر الآخِرَة وما فيها مِنَ النِعم وَالْعذابِ الأليم، فانّ ذلك يُزَهّدُكَ فى الدنيا ويُصَغّرُها عندك

"Remember often the Hereafter and what it has from numerous blessings and painful punishment; as it would make you pious and devout in the world and make the world lowly and insignificant in your view."[2]

2. Contentment

Imām 'Alī, in a will to his son, Imām Ḥusain says:

ومَن أكْثرَ ذِكْرَ المَوْتِ رضِيَ مِنَ الدُّنيا باليَسير

"Anyone who remembers death often will be satisfied and content with a little bit of the world."[3]

3. Preparation for death

Also, 'Alī, in a will to his son, Imām Ḥasan Mujtabā says:

يا بُنَيَّ أكْثِر مِنْ ذِكْرِ المَوْتِ، وذِكرِ ما تَهْجُمُ عَلَيْهِ، وتُفْضِي بَعْدَ المَوْتِ إلَيْهِ، واجعلْه أمامَكَ حَيْثُ تَراه، حَتَّى يأتيك وقد أخذْتَ مِنه حِذْرَك، وشَدَدْتَ لَهُ أزْرَك، ولا يأتيك

---

[1] al-Ikhtiṣāṣ, p. 336.
[2] Biḥār al-'Anwār, vol. 74, p. 205.
[3] Tuḥaf al-'Uqūl, p. 84.

بَغْتَةً فَيَبْهَرَكَ، ولا يأْخُذَكَ على غِرَّتِكَ

"My son! Remember death often and remember what you would suddenly find yourself in and after death you would be drawn towards it. Keep death in front of you until it reaches you and you are safe from it and keep yourself firm in front of it, lest it surprise and confuse you and take away your dignity."[1]

4. Taking the provisions of the Hereafter

A young man, who gradually gets to know about the world of the afterlife from the age of puberty due to the guidance and wise teachings of his parents, realizes that worldly blessings are not permanent. Therefore, he strives for the eternal path ahead of him. He takes provisions for himself and on this basis, adjusts his future life, because he realizes that future happiness lies in his actions in the world. So, he tries to gather enough provision for the long road and the difficult passes of the future, and as much as he can, he prepares himself and adopts patience in every way.

Imām Ṣādiq said: Luqmān advised his son as follows:

My son: people before you collected for their children, but their collections never remained, neither those remained for whom the collections were made. You are only a servant for hire. You are ordered to perform a deed and receive payment for it. Do your deed and receive payment. Do not be like the sheep who, finds a green pasture and keeps eating until fatness kills it. Take the world as a bridge to cross a river and leave it when you are on the other side. Never return to it until the end of time. Destroy it and never repair it; you are not ordered to build it.

Bear in mind that tomorrow you will be questioned before Allāh, the Most Majestic, the Most Holy about four things. (1) You will be asked about your youth, how you spent it (2) about your life span, how you finished it (3) and about your wealth, how you earned it and (4) how you spent it.

---

[1] *Biḥār al-'Anwār*, vol. 74, p. 205.

Wake up for these questions and prepare the answers. Do not regret for what you have missed of worldly things. The little worldly things do not last very long and most of the worldly things are not without misfortune. Be cautious, work hard in your affairs; remove the curtain before you. Get involved in the lawful matters of your Lord, renew repentance in your heart, work hard when you are free and before you are targeted (by the angel of death) for dying and judgment is issued that separates you from your goal.[1]

In a letter he wrote to his son, Imām Ḥasan Mujtabā ﷺ, Amīr al Mu'minīn ﷺ says:

"Remember my son, that before you is a long and arduous journey (life). The journey is not only very long, exhausting, and onerous, but the route is mostly through dismal, dreary and deserted regions where you will be sadly in need of refreshing, renovating and enlivening aids and helps; and you cannot dispense with such provisions as to keep you going and to maintain you till the end of the journey - the Day of Judgment. But remember not to overload yourself (do not entrust yourself with so many obligations and duties that you cannot honourably fulfill them or with such luxurious life as to be wicked and vicious), because if this load is more than what you can conveniently bear then your journey will be very painful and tiresome. If you find around you such poor, needy, and destitute people who are willing to carry your load for you as far as the Day of Judgment then consider this to be a boon; engage them and pass your burden on to them. (Distribute your wealth amongst the poor, destitute and the needy, help others to the best of your ability and be kind and sympathetic to human beings). Thus, relieve yourself from heavy responsibility and liability of submitting an account on the Day of Judgment of how you have made use of His Bounties (of health, wealth, power and position) and thus you may arrive at the end of the journey, light and fresh, have enough provision for you there (reward of having done your duty to man and Allāh ﷻ in this world). Have as many weight-carriers as you can (help as many as you can) so that you may not miss them when you very badly need them (when your sins of commission and omission will be balanced against your good deeds you must have

---

[1] *al-Kāfī*, Vol. 2, p. 134; *Majmu'ah Warrām*, p. 391; *Biḥār al-'Anwār*, vol.13, p. 426.

enough good deeds to turn the scale in your favour). Remember that all you give out in charity and good venues are like loans which will be paid back to you. Therefore, when you are wealthy and powerful, make use of your wealth and power in such a way that you get all that back on the Day of Judgment, when you will be poor and helpless. Be it known to you, my son: that your passage runs through an appallingly dreadful valley (death or grave) and it is an extremely trying and arduous journey. Here a man with light weight is far better than an over-burdened person and one who can travel fast will pass through it quickly than the one whose encumbering forces make him proceed slowly. You shall have to pass through this valley. The only way out of it is either in Paradise or in Hell. Therefore, it is wise to send your things there beforehand so that they (good deeds) reach there before you. Prearrange for the place of your stay before you reach there because after death there is no repentance and no possibility of coming back to this world to undo the wrong done by you."[1]

G) Giving importance to children's prayers

One of the main duties of parents is to attach great importance to the prayer of their children and to familiarize them with its importance from childhood and to teach them that prayer is the remembrance of Allāh ﷻ and life without the remembrance of Allāh ﷻ is dark. Prayer is man's support; man without support is afraid and anxious. Prayer is an expression of servitude and gratitude to Allāh, the Beneficent and the Merciful. Prayer is a person's insurance against slipping and falling. The praying community is immune from many corruptions and fraud. The prayer is a source of peace for the anxious and tired, and it is a source of inner purity and clarity of the mind. Prayer is the light of the eyes of the Holy Prophet ﷺ and the advice of all the prophets and successors. Prayer removes the feeling of loneliness. Prayer is the call of human nature and the ascension of a believer. Prayer is speaking directly to the Creator. Prayer is like a clear and transparent river that washes away spiritual and mental pollution and gives purity and light to the heart. Prayer is the key to heaven. Prayer is a great struggle against the enemies of man. For this reason,

[1] *Nahj al-Balagha*, letter 31.

more than ever, Satan comes to man during prayer and tries to make the mind of the person who prays forget Allāh ﷻ and focus on daily affairs, problems and needs.

My son! Become steadfast in prayer

The Holy Qur'ānhas emphasized this important and fateful matter in many verses, and Luqmān the Wise also advised his son that:

يَٰبُنَيَّ أَقِمِ ٱلصَّلَوٰةَ وَأۡمُرۡ بِٱلۡمَعۡرُوفِ وَٱنۡهَ عَنِ ٱلۡمُنكَرِ وَٱصۡبِرۡ عَلَىٰ مَآ أَصَابَكَۖ إِنَّ ذَٰلِكَ مِنۡ عَزۡمِ ٱلۡأُمُورِ ﴿١٧﴾

"O my son! Maintain the prayer and bid what is right and forbid what is wrong and be patient through whatever may visit you. That is indeed the steadiest of courses."[1]

Āyatullāh Makārim Shirāzī writes under the interpretation of the captioned verse:

[Luqmān] "After consolidating the foundations of the origin and resurrection, which is the basis of all school of beliefs, addressed the most important actions, that is, the matter of prayer, and says: My son! Pray, because prayer is the most important link with the Creator ﷻ. Prayer protects your heart, purifies your soul, and illuminates your life. It removes the traces of sin from your soul; it makes the light of faith shine in the abode of your heart and prevents you from immorality and denial."[2]

Therefore, it is up to the parents to familiarize their children with this important divine duty from childhood and to vaccinate and insure them against future perils, so that they remain safe from deviation and corruption.

When Ibrāhīm ﷺ along with his son, laid the foundation of the house of Allāh ﷻ and finished the work, he raised his hands to the sky and asked Allāh:

---

[1] Sūrah Luqmān 31:17.
[2] *Tafsīr Namūnih*, vol. 17, p. 52.

$$\rbrace\text{رَبِّ ٱجْعَلْنِي مُقِيمَ ٱلصَّلَوٰةِ وَمِن ذُرِّيَّتِي} \ldots$$

"My Lord! Make me a maintainer of the prayer, and my descendants [too]..."[1]

Pillar of religion

Amīr al Mu'minīn, 'Alī ☬, in his last will, instructs his children as follows:

$$\text{وَ اللَّهَ اللَّهَ فِي الصَّلَاةِ، فَإِنَّهَا خَيْرُ الْعَمَلِ وَ إِنَّهَا عَمُودُ دِينِكُمْ}$$

"By Allāh ☬, as for the Prayer: It is the best act and pillar of your religion."[2]

Luqmān the Wise advised his son as follows:

$$\text{يَا بُنَيَّ أَقِمِ الصَّلَاةَ فَإِنَّ مَثَلَ الصَّلَاةِ فِي دِينِ اللَّهِ كَمَثَلِ عَمُودِ الْفُسْطَاطِ فَإِنَّ الْعَمُودَ إِذَا اسْتَقَامَ نَفَعَتِ الْأَطْنَابُ وَ الْأَوْتَادُ وَ الظِّلَالُ وَ إِنْ لَمْ يَسْتَقِمْ لَمْ يَنْفَعْ وَتِدٌ وَ لَا طُنُبٌ وَ لَا ظِلَالٌ}$$

My child, establish the Prayer, because the simile of prayer in Allāh's ☬ religion is like the centre pole of a tent. If the pole stands, the tent will also stand, and the tent pegs and nails will be useful, but if the tent pole is not fixed, you will not benefit from the pegs, nails, and shade.[3]

Advice of Imām Ṣādiq ☬ at the time of his passing

Abū Baṣīr has narrated on the authority of Imām Kāẓim ☬ that: My father said while he was in his last moments:

---

[1] Sūrah Ibrāhīm 14:40.
[2] *Tuḥaf al-'Uqūl*, p. 195.
[3] *Biḥār al-'Anwār*, vol. 13, p. 435.

يَا بُنَيَّ إِنَّهُ لَا يَنَالُ شَفَاعَتَنَا مَنِ اسْتَخَفَّ بِالصَّلَاةِ

"My son! Surely our intercession shall never reach to those who take their Prayer lightly."[1]

Abū Baṣīr says the following about the loyal companions of Imām Ṣādiq ﷺ:

After the martyrdom of Imām Ṣādiq ﷺ, I went to the Imām's ﷺ house to offer condolences and met with Umm Ḥamīdah. As soon as she saw me, she cried, and I also started crying.

Umm Ḥamīdah said: O Abu Muḥammad! Had you seen Imām Ṣādiq ﷺ in his last moments, you would have seen something strange! Imām ﷺ opened his eyes at that time and said: Call everyone who is related to me! So, we gathered all his relatives on the order of His Eminence ﷺ.

Imām ﷺ once again opened his eyes and looked at the crowd and said: "Know that our intercession will not reach the one who takes the Prayer lightly."[2]

This was the advice of the Imām of the pious, Imām Ṣādiq ﷺ to his relatives in the last moments of his blessed life; to those who were under the impression that only their kinship with Imām ﷺ would lead to their salvation and eternal happiness, and that they would benefit from his intercession in every way, even if they are negligent and lazy in Prayer!

Such was the conduct of all the A'immah ﷺ and the Prophets ﷺ, who used to urge regarding this divine duty a lot.

Imām Riḍā ﷺ was surprised by the child leaving the prayer

Ḥasan b. Qarūn says: I asked Imām Riḍā ﷺ...A man forces his child to pray because sometimes he does not pray for a day or two.

---

[1] *Wasā'il al-Shī'ah*, vol. 17, p. 262.

[2] *Maḥāsin al-Barqī*, p. 80.

Imām ﷺ asked, "How old is he (his child)?" Eight years, I replied.

Imām ﷺ said, "Glory be to Allāh ﷻ! Does he miss the Prayer totally!?"

I said: If he prays, he feels uncomfortable. Imām ﷺ said, "He should pray in any way he can and not leave it at all."[1]

Prayer at the earliest hour

Imām 'Alī ﷺ advised his son, Imām Ḥasan Mujtabā ﷺ:

أُوصيک يا بُنَّى ، بالصَّلاة عند وَقتِها

"My child: I advise you to pray at the earliest hour."[2]

The late Mirzā Nūrī writes in *Mustadrak*:

Imām Sajjad ﷺ used to persuade the children who were with him to pray Ẓuhr and 'Asr, and Maghrib and 'Ishā prayers together. Someone objected to His Eminence ﷺ about it, but he said, "This practice is easier and better for them, and it would lead them to take precedence in Prayer; and they would never miss it due to sleep or other activities." Imām ﷺ did not order children to do anything other than to pray the obligatory prayer and he said, "If they have the strength and energy to perform the obligatory prayers, do not deprive them of it."[3]

Ibn Qadāḥ narrated that Imām Ṣādiq ﷺ said:

إِنَّا نَأْمُرُ الصِّبْيَانَ أَنْ يَجْمَعُوا بَيْنَ الصَّلَاتَيْنِ الْأُولَى وَ الْعَصْرِ وَ بَيْنَ الْمَغْرِبِ وَ الْعِشَاءِ الْآخِرَةِ مَا دَامُوا عَلَى وُضُوءٍ قَبْلَ أَنْ يَشْتَغِلُوا

[1] *Wasā'il al-Shī'ah*, vol. 3, p. 13.
[2] *Biḥār al-'Anwār*, vol. 75, p. 458.
[3] *Mustadrak al-Wasā'il*, vol. 15, p. 160, v. 3, p. 19; *al-Kāfī*, vol. 2, p. 409; *Wasā'il al-Shī'ah*, vol. 3, p. 14 and 16 (with some difference).

"We instruct our children to perform the Ẓuhr Prayer with 'Asr and the Maghrib Prayer with 'Ishā, as long as they are having valid ablution (*Wuḍū*) and are not busy with anything else."[1]

Perhaps it can be concluded from these narrations that such was the way of all the Infallibles ﷺ with their children.

H) Preparing the children for prayer and fasting

Childhood is the best and most appropriate time to make an impression on the intellect, thoughts, and spirit. It is because of this preparation and acceptance that the enemy invests in children at this age to transform their thought patterns and behavioural characteristics with careful planning.

From a religious point of view, the seed of a person's religious and spiritual identity is planted in childhood, and with the passage of time, as the child grows older, its leaves, fruits, and roots become more stable. Family routines are inherited: if there is an interest in prayer and worship in school and educational environments, the tendency of young people to these matters will double. Because he sees his teacher, mentor and classmates as well as his parents in Allāh's ﷻ service, and at home with his father and at school, he stands behind his mentor in prayer, and in this way he builds a strong fortress of faith.

Yes, as the Qur'ān says:

...إِنَّ ٱلصَّلَوٰةَ تَنْهَىٰ عَنِ ٱلْفَحْشَآءِ وَٱلْمُنكَرِ...

"Surely prayer keeps (one) away from indecency and evil..."[2]

If your child is inclined to prayer from childhood and turns to Allāh ﷻ, the prediction of the Qur'ān about him will come true a hundred percent and you will gift righteous person to the society; because righteous deeds, prayer, worship, and the messages of the Qur'ān will resonate in the child's heart, and divine light will rule over him.

---

[1] *Wasā'il al-Shī'ah*, vol. 15, p. 183.

[2] Sūrah al-'Ankabūt 29:45.

Many traditions (around thirty) have been narrated from the Infallibles ﷺ to urge the children to pray, but there is a difference in the traditions about the age at which children should be made to pray. The age mentioned for this purpose is 6 to 13 years, which can be concluded from the sum of all the narrations and summaries. Parents have the duty to make the child pray before they reach puberty through various training methods. Suppose the children are negligent and careless in praying, the parents can even punish them (reasonably).

Boys should be trained to pray beginning at the age of seven years and till fifteen years of age which is the age of puberty for boys, while age of puberty is nine years for girls. It cannot be precisely determined at what age a child should be made to pray - even if punishment is needed - but it seems that the age of seven is implied, as most traditions confirm and indicate this.

Practice of the Infallibles ﷺ regarding prayer of children

The method of the A'immah ﷺ was that they used to persuade their children to pray from the age of five, but they themselves said that it is not necessary to force your children to pray at the age of five but encourage them to pray at the age of seven.

Ḥalabī has narrated from Imām Ṣādiq ؑ from his father as follows:

إِنَّا نَأْمُرُ صِبْيَانَنَا بِالصَّلَاةِ إِذَا كَانُوا بَنِي خَمْسِ سِنِينَ فَمُرُوا صِبْيَانَكُمْ بِالصَّلَاةِ إِذَا كَانُوا بَنِي سَبْعِ سِنِينَ

"We command our children to pray at the age of five, but you make your child to pray at the age of seven."[1]

[1] *Wasā'il al-Shī'ah*, vol. 15, p. 183.

From training to punishment

There are many narrations regarding training for prayer, ordering to recite it and punishing children for prayer, which are divided into three categories:

A) Teaching the prayer

Teaching children to pray is one of the primary duties of fathers.

Sabrah narrates from the Prophet ﷺ:

عَلِّمُوا الصبيَّ الصَّلاة، ابنَ سَبْعِ سِنينَ، وَاضْرِبُوه عَلَيها ابنَ عشرِ سنين

"Teach the children to pray at the age of seven and punish them (in case of laziness) for prayer at the age of ten."[1]

B) Order to pray

The second stage after teaching prayer is the stage of forcing children to pray. At this stage, several ages have been proposed, from six to ten; and we mention some of them:

The Holy Prophet ﷺ said:

إذا عَرَفَ الغُلامُ يَمْينَه مِن شِمالِه، فَمُروه بِا لصَّلاة

"If the boy differentiates between his right and left hands, order him to pray."[2]

The Prophet ﷺ also said:

مُرُوا صِبْيَانَكُمْ بِالصَّلَاةِ إِذَا كَانُوا أَبْنَاءَ عَشْرِ سِنِين

"Teach your children to pray at the age of six."[3]

---

[1] *Kanz al-'Ummāl*, vol. 16, p. 440.
[2] *Kanz al-'Ummāl*, vol. 16, p. 440.
[3] *Mustadrak al-Wasā'il*, vol. 3, p. 19.

Imām Ṣādiq said:

$$\text{مُرُوا صِبيانَكُمْ بِالصَّلاةِ اِذا بَلَغُوا سَبْعَ سِنينَ}$$

"Make your children pray when they are seven years old."¹

'Alī says:

$$\text{عَلِّمُوا صِبْيَانَكُمُ الصَّلَاةَ وَ خُذُوهُمْ بِهَا إِذَا بَلَغُوا ثَمَانِيَ سِنِينَ}$$

"Teach your children to pray and make them pray at the age of eight."²

Imām Ṣādiq says:

$$\text{مُرُوا صِبيانكم بِالصَّلاةِ اذا كانُوا أبناءَ عَشرَ سِنينَ}$$

"Instruct your children to pray at the age of ten."³

C) Punishment for not praying

The last stage that can be seen in the traditions about prayer is the issue of punishing the child for laziness in the matter of prayer, which was mentioned in more than these narrations.

Of course, since these traditions refer to the stages of making children pray - which starts with language training and finally leads to practical punishment - parents must pay attention that at a young age they should only be taught through encouragement, gentleness, and affection to pray and we must not be hard on them so that they suddenly stop praying and become disgusted with it. But as they get older, the parents should adopt a somewhat imperious tone and generally scold their children for being shortcoming in prayer -

---

¹ *Mustadrak al-Wasā'il*, vol. 15, p. 160, and vol. 14, p. 288; *Wasā'il al-Shī'ah*, vol. 13, p. 12 and 15, p. 182 and 183; *Kanz al-'Ummāl* Vol. 16, p. 440 and p. 442; *al-Kāfī*, vol. 4, p. 124.
² *Tuḥaf al-'Uqūl*, p. 110.
³ *Mustadrak al-Wasā'il*, vol. 3, p. 19.

especially at the age of less than 13 years, they should act with more caution and foresight and not consider punishment first. But it should be the last resort, and they should make sure that there are better and more effective ways to gain more awareness through study books on training. And discussions with the children and consulting with the teachers and those who are knowledgeable about education and so on, so that they understand the proper thinking and opinion.

Asking divine help can also play a significant role in this.

I) Giving importance to children's fasting

In Islamic traditions, there are many orders for fasting, such as it has been said that in the month of *Ramaḍān*, if a child has the strength to fast, encourage him to fast, and if he is overcome by hunger in the middle of the day, let him break his fast, because fasting in the month of *Ramaḍān* is a shield from fire and we must protect our children from the burning fire of Hell.

'Alī, in his advice to Imām Ḥasan Mujtabā says:

اللَّهَ اللَّهَ فِي صِيَامِ شَهْرِ رَمَضَانَ فَإِنَّ صِيَامَهُ جُنَّةٌ مِنَ النَّارِ

"I adjure you by Allāh regarding fasting in the month of *Ramaḍān*, because fasting in this month is a shield from the fire of Hell."[1]

'Allāmah Majlisī narrates from *al-'Amālī* of Shaykh Ṭūsī that Masma'i says:

Whenever the month of *Ramaḍān* arrived, I heard the voice of Imām Ṣādiq ordering his children to give importance to the month of *Ramaḍān* and he said, "So hasten with yourself, because during this month your sustenance will be distributed and the moments of everyone's death will be determined.

---

[1] *Tuḥaf al-'Uqūl*, p. 195.

Also, in this month, they write you as the guests of Allāh ﷻ; and in this month there is a night in which a deed is equal to the deeds of a thousand months."[1]

Muʿawiyāh b. Wahab says: I asked Imām Ṣādiq ؑ: At what age should we force our children to fast? Imām ؑ said:

مَا بَيْنَهُ وَ بَيْنَ خَمْسَ عَشْرَةَ سَنَةً وَ أَرْبَعَ عَشْرَةَ سَنَةً فَإِنْ هُوَ صَامَ قَبْلَ ذَلِكَ فَدَعْهُ وَ لَقَدْ صَامَ ابْنِي فُلَانٌ قَبْلَ ذَلِكَ فَتَرَكْتُهُ

"Between fourteen and fifteen years of age; if he fasts before that let him do and don't prevent him. One of my children fasted before reaching this age, and I let him and did not prevent him."[2]

Ḥalabī narrated from Imām Ṣādiq ؑ that he said:

"We encourage our children to fast at the age of seven, as much as they have the patience and ability to do so, even though they are thirsty and hungry until the middle of the day or more than that; and they break their fast (and this command to fast is because) they may get into the habit and ability to fast. So, make your children to fast from the age of nine and fast as much as they can, and if they are overcome by thirst, they may break the fast."[3]

J) Teaching the Qur'ān

Qur'ān is the last heavenly scripture that contains all the laws of guidance and felicity for humans. Qur'ān is a wide table of heavenly food and a treasure of divine truths and secrets. The Qur'ān is the spring of the treasured hearts and refreshment for the depressed and stagnant thoughts. The Qur'ān is the healing of the hearts and the divine rope, and whoever remains attached to it, will be saved, and whoever abandons it will perish.

---

[1] *Biḥār al-'Anwār*, vol. 96, p. 375, p. 63.
[2] *al-Kāfī*, vol. 4, p. 125.
[3] *al-Kāfī*, vol. 3, p. 409.

The Qur'ān is the guide of the worlds and the guarantor of happiness for its followers, the recitation of the Qur'ān is the key to the connection with Allāh ﷻ, and meditating on its verses is the cause of the awakening of the hearts and the enlightenment of the brains.

Imām Riḍā ؑ says:

"The Qur'ān is Allāh's ﷻ strong rope, it is a means of reassurance and His straight path, it is a path that leads to Paradise and it is the cause of salvation from the fire of Hell. The Qur'ān does not wear out by the passage of time, and discussions about it do not make it deficient, because it is not confined to a specific time period..."[1]

Therefore, the Messenger of Allāh ﷺ was very much concerned about the Qur'ān and his personality was a manifestation of the teachings of the Qur'ān. The Infallible A'immah ؑ in addition to caring for the Qur'ān themselves, encouraged and advised their children to read, memorize, and learn the Qur'ān and act upon it.

Amīr al Mu'minīn ؑ recommended the Qur'ān to his son, Imām Ḥasan ؑ as follows:

وَ اللَّهَ اللَّهَ فِي الْقُرْآنِ، لَا يَسْبِقُكُمْ إِلَى الْعَمَلِ بِهِ غَيْرُكُمْ.

"Be careful regarding the Qur'ān, lest others take precedence over you in understanding the Qur'ān."[2]

The teaching of this divine book is one of the rights of Muslim children, which the fathers must fulfill and familiarize them with, which means that they either teach them the Qur'ān themselves or get them a teacher. The Messenger of Allāh ﷺ said:

حَقُّ الْوَلَدِ عَلَى وَالِدِهِ إِذَا كَانَ ذَكَراً أَنْ يَسْتَفْرِهَ أُمَّهُ وَ يَسْتَحْسِنَ اسْمَهُ وَ يُعَلِّمَهُ كِتَابَ اللَّهِ

[1] *Biḥār al-'Anwār*, vol. 92, p. 14.

[2] *Tuḥaf al-'Uqūl*, p. 194.

"It is the right of a child over his father that he should give him a good name...and teach him the Qur'ān."[1]

Imām Ṣādiq ﷺ said:

عَلِّمُوا أَوْلَادَكُمْ (يس) فَإِنَّهَا رَيْحَانَةُ الْقُرْآن

"Teach your children Sūrah YāSīn, because this Sūrah is the blossom (garden) of the Qur'ān."[2]

The Prophet ﷺ said:

حَقُ الْوَلَدِ عَلى وَالِدِهِ إِذَا كَانَ ... أُنْثى... وَ يُعَلِّمَهَا سُورَةَ النُّور

"It is the right of a girl child upon her father that he should teach her Sūrah al-Nūr."[3]

Imām 'Alī's ﷺ advice to memorize the Qur'ān

Abū 'Umar Naḥwī says:

جاءَ غالب اِلى علىّ بنِ أبى طالب عليه السلام بِالفَرزدق بعد الجمل بالبصرة فقال: انّ ابنى هذا من شعراء مُضر فاسمع منه، قال:((علمه القرآن)) فكان ذلک فى نفس الفرزدق فقيد نفسه فى وقتٍ وآلى أن لا يحلَّ قيده حتّى يحفظ القرآن

Once, Ghālib along with his son, Farazdaq (the poet) came to 'Alī ﷺ in Baṣrah after the Battle of Jamal. He said: My son is a poet of the Muḍar tribe; listen to his compositions.

'Alī ﷺ said, "Teach him the Qur'ān." These words so much affected Farazdaq that at an appropriate time, he tied his feet and

---

[1] *Kanz al-'Ummāl*, vol. 16, p. 417.
[2] *al-'Amālī Shaykh Ṭūsī*, vol. 2, p. 290; *Mustadrak al-Wasā'il*, vol. 4, p. 325.
[3] *Wasā'il al-Shī'ah*, vol. 15, p. 199.

promised himself that he would not untie them until he memorized the Qur'ān.[1]

Ibn Abī al-Ḥadīd says: Farazdaq did not untie his feet till he had memorized the Qur'ān.[2]

The reward of learning the Qur'ān on the Judgment Day

There are many narrations from the Noble Prophet ﷺ and *Ahl al-Bayt* (a) that Allāh ﷻ has special honours for parents on the Judgment Day for teaching the Qur'ān to their children, among which are the following:

A) Crowning of the parents by Allāh

Muʿadh said: I heard the Messenger of Allāh ﷺ say:

مَا مِنْ رَجُلٍ عَلَّمَ وَلَدَهُ الْقُرْآنَ- إِلَّا تَوَّجَ اللَّهُ أَبَوَيْهِ يَوْمَ الْقِيَامَةِ تَاجَ الْمُلْكِ وَ كُسِيَا حُلَّتَيْنِ لَمْ يَرَ النَّاسُ مِثْلَهُمَا

"No one teaches his child the Qur'ān, except that Allāh ﷻ grants the child's parents the crown of rulership on the Judgment Day and covers them with two robes of Paradise the like of which is never seen before."[3]

B) Heavenly garments

Imām Ṣādiq (a) said:

وَ مَنْ عَلَّمَهُ الْقُرْآنَ دُعِيَ الْأَبَوَانِ فَكُسِيَا حُلَّتَيْنِ يُضِيءُ مِنْ نُورِهِمَا وُجُوهُ أَهْلِ الْجَنَّةِ

"Parents who teach their children the Qur'ān, on the Day of Judgment, they would be called and dressed in two robes of Paradise,

---

[1] *Qāmūs al-Rijāl*, vol. 7, p. 307.
[2] *Qāmūs al-Rijāl*, vol. 7, p. 307.
[3] *Wasā'il al-Shīʿah*, vol. 4, p. 825.

due to the effulgence of which the faces of the folks of Paradise would be lit up bright."[1]

C) Amazing reward

ʿĀʾishah narrates from the Messenger of Allāh ﷺ who said:

مَنْ عَلَّمَ وَلداً لَه القُرآنَ قَلَّدَه اللهُ عَزَّوجَلَّ يومَ القيامة بِقلادَة يَعجَبُ مِنه الأوَّلُون والآخِرونَ

"On Judgment Day, Allāh ﷻ will grant a necklace to whoever that teaches his child the Qurʾān; such that it will amaze all the creatures."[2]

D) Happiness and joy in the afterlife

Imām Ṣādiq عليه السلام said:

تَعَلَّمُوا الْقُرْآنَ فَإِنَّهُ يَأْتِي يَوْمَ الْقِيَامَةِ صَاحِبَهُ فِي صُورَةِ شَابٍّ جَمِيلٍ شَاحِبِ اللَّوْنِ فَيَقُولُ لَهُ الْقُرْآنُ أَنَا الَّذِي كُنْتُ أَسْهَرْتُ لَيْلَكَ وَ أَظْمَأْتُ هَوَاجِرَكَ وَ أَجْفَفْتُ رِيقَكَ وَ أَسَلْتُ دَمْعَتَكَ أَئُولُ مَعَكَ حَيْثُمَا أُلْتَ وَ كُلُّ تَاجِرٍ مِنْ وَرَاءِ تِجَارَتِهِ وَ أَنَا الْيَوْمَ لَكَ مِنْ وَرَاءِ تِجَارَةِ كُلِّ تَاجِرٍ وَ سَيَأْتِيكَ كَرَامَةٌ مِنَ اللَّهِ عَزَّ وَ جَلَّ فَأَبْشِرْ فَيُؤْتَى بِتَاجٍ فَيُوضَعُ عَلَى رَأْسِهِ وَ يُعْطَى الْأَمَانَ بِيَمِينِهِ وَ الْخُلْدَ فِي الْجِنَانِ بِيَسَارِهِ وَ يُكْسَى حُلَّتَيْنِ ثُمَّ يُقَالُ لَهُ اقْرَأْ وَ ارْقَهْ فَكُلَّمَا قَرَأَ آيَةً صَعِدَ دَرَجَةً وَ يُكْسَى أَبَوَاهُ حُلَّتَيْنِ إِنْ كَانَا مُؤْمِنَيْنِ ثُمَّ يُقَالُ لَهُمَا هَذَا لِمَا عَلَّمْتُمَاهُ الْقُرْآنَ.

"Learn the Holy Qurʾān as on the Judgment Day the Holy Qurʾān will come in the form of a handsome and fair complexion youth to one of its readers and say: I am the Qurʾān for which you kept awake so often and endured thirst during the heat of midday, dried up your mouth and let your tears flow. I will be with you whenever you will go. Every trader is after his trade. Today I look after the trade of everyone

---

[1] *ʿUdat al-Dāʿī*, p. 79; *Wasāʾil al-Shīʿah*, vol. 15, p. 194.
[2] *Kanz al-ʿUmmāl*, vol. 1, p. 478.

who had a deal with me. Honor will come to you from Allāh, the Most Majestic, the Most Holy, as good news for you. The man will receive a crown and peace will be placed on his right hand and eternal life in Paradise in his left hand and he will be dressed in two robes of paradise, then he will be told, 'Read and climb.' For each verse that he will read, he will climb up one degree and his parents, if they are of the believers, will each receive two robes of Paradise and they will be told that this is for your teaching the Holy Qur'ān to your child."[1]

E) Heaviness of the Scroll of deeds and passing over the Ṣirāṭ Bridge

The Messenger of Allāh ﷺ said:

مَنْ عَلَّمَ وَلَدَهُ الْقُرْآنَ ... وَ يَثْقُلُ مِيزَانُهُ وَ يُجَاوَزُ بِهِ عَلَى الصِّرَاطِ كَالْبَرْقِ الْخَاطِفِ وَ لَمْ يُفَارِقْهُ الْقُرْآنُ حَتَّى يَنْزِلَ بِهِ مِنَ الْكَرَامَةِ أَفْضَلَ مَا يَتَمَنَّى

"Whoever teaches his child the Qur'ān...(the same Qur'ān) will make his scroll of deeds heavy (on Judgment Day) and make him cross the *Ṣirāṭ* Bridge like a bolt of lightning; and it will not separate from him until he gets the best things he wished for from Allāh."[2]

F) Delayed chastisement

Shaykh Ṣadūq says:

وَ رُوِيَ وَ إِنَّ اللَّهَ تَبَارَكَ وَ تَعَالَى لَيُرِيدُ عَذَابَ أَهْلِ الْأَرْضِ جَمِيعاً حَتَّى لَا يُحَاشِيَ مِنْهُمْ أَحَداً فَإِذَا نَظَرَ إِلَى الشِّيبِ نَاقِلِي أَقْدَامِهِمْ إِلَى الصَّلَوَاتِ وَ الْوِلْدَانِ يَتَعَلَّمُونَ الْقُرْآنَ رَحِمَهُمُ اللَّهُ فَأَخَّرَ ذَلِكَ عَنْهُم

It is narrated that Allāh, the Mighty and the Blessed decides to punish all the people of the earth without exception (because of their sins) but when He looks at the senior citizens walking towards the

[1] *al-Kāfī*, vol. 2, p. 441.
[2] *Mustadrak al-Wasā'il*, vol. 1, p. 290.

Masjids, and observes the youth busy teaching the Qur'ān, He has mercy on them and postpones their torment.[1]

G) The reward of ten thousand Ḥajj and 'Umrah

The Holy Prophet ﷺ said:

مَنْ عَلَّمَ وَلَدَه الْقُرآنَ فَكَأنّما حَجَّ الْبَيتَ عَشَرَة آلاف حجّة، وَاعْتَمَرَ عَشَرَة آلاف عُمرَة، وَاَعْتَق عَشَرَة آلافِ رَقَبة مِنْ وَلْدِ اِسْماعيلَ. وَغزا عَشَرَة آلاف غزْوَة، وَأطْعَم عَزَرَة آلاف مِسْكِيْنٍ مُسلِمٍ جائعٍ، وَكَأنَّما كَسا عَشَرَة آلاف عارٍ مُسْلِمٍ، وَيُكتَبُ لَه بِكُلِّ حَرْفٍ عَشْرُ حَسَناتٍ، وَيَمْحُو اللهُ عَنْه عَشْرَ سَيِّئاتٍ، وَيَكُونُ مَعَه فى قَبْرِه حتّى يُبْعَثَ...

"Whoever teaches his child the Qur'ān is like one who visited the House of Allāh ﷻ ten thousand times, performed *'Umrah* ten thousand times, freed ten thousand slaves from the descendants of Ismā'īl, performed *Jihād* ten thousand times, fed ten thousand hungry Muslim beggars. And he is like one who clothed ten thousand naked Muslims. Ten good deeds are written for him for every word, and Allāh ﷻ will remove ten of his sins and would be with him in the grave until he is raised."[2]

Encouragement of the Qur'ān teacher

Muḥammad b. 'Alī b. Shahr Āshūb narrates that:

إِنَّ عَبْدَ الرَّحْمَنِ السُّلَمِيَّ عَلَّمَ وَلَدَ الْحُسَيْنِ الْحَمْدُ فَلَمَّا قَرَأَهَا عَلَى أَبِيهِ أَعْطَاهُ أَلْفَ دِينَارٍ وَ أَلْفَ حُلَّةٍ وَ حَشَا فَاهُ دُرّاً فَقِيلَ لَهُ فِي ذَلِكَ قَالَ وَ أَيْنَ يَقَعُ هَذَا مِنْ عَطَائِهِ يَعْنِي تَعْلِيمَهُ

[1] *Wasā'il al-Shī'ah*, vol. 3, p. 481.
[2] *Mustadrak al-Wasā'il*, vol. 1, p. 290.

'Abd al-Raḥmān al-Salmī taught Sūrah al-Ḥamd to one of Imām Ḥusain's ؏ children. When he recited it to his father, Imām ؏ gave his teacher a thousand dinars and a thousand garments and jewels.

It was protested to Imām ؏ that the teaching of one Sūrah did not deserve all these gifts and encouragement! Imām ؏ replied, "How can they equal the teaching he imparted!"[1]

Encouraging children to recite the Qur'ān

A) Training children to recite the Qur'ān

The Prophet ﷺ said:

أَدِّبُوا أَولادَكُم عَلى ثَلاثَ خِصالٍ : حُبِّ نَبِيِّكُمْ، و حُبِّ أَهلِ بَيتِهِ، وَاقَراءَةِ الْقُرآنِ؛ فَاِنَّ حَمَلَةَ القُرآنِ فى ظِلِّ اللهِ يَومَ لاظِلَّ اِلّا ظَلُّه مَعَ أنبِيائِهِ وَأَصفِيائِهِ

"Train your children on three virtues: loving your Prophet ﷺ, loving his family and reciting the Qur'ān; because the bearers of the Qur'ān are under the shade of Allāh ﷻ on that day when there is no shade, except that of Allāh's ﷻ; and they have a place next to His Prophets ؏ and chosen ones."[2]

B) Recitation of Sūrah Kāfirūn at the time of going to bed

It is narrated from the Holy Prophet ﷺ that he said to some of his companions:

إِذَا أَرَدْتَ الْمَنَامَ فَاقْرَأْ هَذِهِ السُّورَةَ يَعْنِي الْجَحْدَ ... وَ قَالَ ص: قُولُوا لِصِبْيَانِكُمْ إِذَا أَرَادُوا الْمَنَامَ أَنْ يَقْرَءُوا هَذِهِ السُّورَةَ حَتَّى لَا يَتَعَرَّضَ لَهُمُ الْجِنِ

---

[1] *Mustadrak al-Wasā'il*, vol. 4, p. 247.
[2] *Kanz al-'Ummāl*, vol. 16, p. 456.

"Recite this Sūrah at the time of going to bed; that is Sūrah Kāfirūn..."[1] He ﷺ also said, 'Tell your children that they must recite this Sūrah when they go to bed so that the jinn do not harm them.'"

C) Recitation of the Qur'ān at dawn

Imām Ṣādiq ؑ said:

كَانَ أَبِي كَثِيرَ الذِّكْرِ وَ كَانَ يَجْمَعُنَا فَيَأْمُرُنَا بِالذِّكْرِ حَتَّى تَطْلُعَ الشَّمْسُ وَ كَانَ يَأْمُرُ بِالْقِرَاءَةِ مَنْ كَانَ يَقْرَأُ مِنَّا وَ مَنْ كَانَ لاَ يَقْرَأُ مِنَّا أَمَرَهُ بِالذِّكْرِ

"My father used to recite the *Dhikr* (divine remembrance) very much... his routine was that he would gather us every day after the Prayer at dawn until sunrise and encourage those who knew the Qur'ān to read it, and whoever was younger and did not read the Qur'ān from among us would be instructed to recite the *Dhikr* of Allāh ﷻ."[2]

D) Advice of Imām Ṣādiq ؑ to his son Ismā'īl

Ḥurayz narrates regarding Imām Ṣādiq ؑ that:

كَانَ إِسْمَاعِيلُ بْنُ أَبِي عَبْدِ اللَّهِ عِنْدَهُ فَقَالَ يَا بُنَيَّ اقْرَأِ الْمُصْحَفَ فَقَالَ إِنِّي لَسْتُ عَلَى وُضُوءٍ فَقَالَ لاَ تَمَسَّ الْكِتَابَ وَ مَسَّ الْوَرَقَ

Once Ismā'īl, the son of Imām Ṣādiq ؑ was with his father, Imām said, "My son! Read the Qur'ān." Ismā'īl said: I am not with ablution. Imām ؑ said, "Don't touch the writing (while reading the Qur'ān); you may touch the (blank portion of the) pages."[3]

E) Loud recitation

Mu'awiyāh b. 'Ammār narrates that Imām Ṣādiq ؑ said:

---

[1] *Mustadrak al-Wasā'il*, vol. 4, p. 295.

[2] *Biḥār al-'Anwār*, vol. 46, p. 297, v. 93, p. 161; *Wasā'il al-Shī'ah*, vol. 4, p. 850, h. 3.

[3] *al-Istibṣār*, vol. 1, p. 113.

○ إِنَّ عَلِيَّ بْنَ الْحُسَيْنِ ع- كَانَ أَحْسَنَ النَّاسِ صَوْتاً بِالْقُرْآنِ- وَ كَانَ يَرْفَعُ صَوْتَهُ حَتَّى يُسْمِعَهُ أَهْلَ الدَّار

"'Alī b. al-Ḥusain ﷺ used to read the Qur'ānin the most melodious voice to the extent that folks of the house heard him."[1]

1. Effects of Qur'ān recitation at home

Good effects will appear in a house where the Qur'ān is recited, and the people of that house will be immersed in effulgence. So, how nice it is to teach our children to read some portion of Qur'ān at home every day and recite the divine verses in a sweet voice and become closely attached to them. Here are some of the good effects of reciting the Qur'ān:

A) From the Land of Blessings

The Prophet ﷺ says:

اجْعَلُوا لِبُيُوتِكُمْ نَصِيباً مِنَ الْقُرْآنِ- فَإِنَّ الْبَيْتَ إِذَا قُرِئَ فِيهِ الْقُرْآنُ يُسِّرَ عَلَى أَهْلِهِ وَ كَثُرَ خَيْرُهُ وَ كَانَ سُكَّانُهُ فِي زِيَادَةٍ

"Reserve a portion in your house for Qur'ān; because a house in which the Qur'ān is recited will be expanded for its folks and its well being will increase; occupants of that house will prosper."[2]

B) Place of arrival of the angels

Imām Ṣādiq ﷺ said:

الْبَيْتُ الَّذِي يُقْرَأُ فِيهِ الْقُرْآنُ وَ يُذْكَرُ اللَّهُ عَزَّ وَ جَلَّ فِيهِ تَكْثُرُ بَرَكَتُهُ وَ تَحْضُرُهُ الْمَلَائِكَةُ وَ تَهْجُرُهُ الشَّيَاطِينُ وَ يُضِيءُ لِأَهْلِ السَّمَاءِ كَمَا يُضِيءُ الْكَوْكَبُ الدُّرِّيُّ لِأَهْلِ

---

[1] *Wasā'il al-Shī'ah*, vol. 4, p. 858.

[2] *'Udat al-Dā'ī*, p. 269, *Wasā'il al-Shī'ah*, vol. 4, p. 851.

الأَرْضِ

"In a house where the Qur'ān is recited and Allāh ﷻ is remembered, goodness and blessings will increase, angels will be present there and devils will leave that place, and that house will shine for the people of heaven as the stars shine for the people of the earth."[1]

2. Effects of abandoning recitation of Qur'ān at home

Just as reading of the Qur'ān brings enlightenment and blessings to the people of the house and that house becomes the place where angels frequent, leaving recitation of the Qur'ān also has some negative effects, of which we will mention some here:

A) Decrease in blessings

The Holy Prophet ﷺ:

اجْعَلُوا لِبُيُوتِكُمْ نَصِيباً مِنَ الْقُرْآنِ- فَإِنَّ الْبَيْتَ ...إِذَا لَمْ يُقْرَأْ فِيهِ الْقُرْآنُ ضُيِّقَ عَلَى أَهْلِهِ وَ قَلَّ خَيْرُهُ وَ كَانَ سُكَّانُهُ فِي نُقْصَانٍ

"Set aside a portion for the Qur'ān in your house, because a house in which the Qur'ān is not recited will be a source of stress and hardship for its inhabitants, and its goodness will decrease, and its people will face scarcity."[2]

B) The place where devils frequent

Imām Ṣādiq ؑ said:

إِنَ الْبَيْتَ الَّذِي لَا يُقْرَأُ فِيهِ الْقُرْآنُ وَ لَا يُذْكَرُ اللَّهُ عَزَّ وَ جَلَّ فِيهِ تَقِلُّ بَرَكَتُهُ وَ تَهْجُرُهُ

[1] *Wasā'il al-Shī'ah*, vol. 4, p. 850, tr. 2; *Biḥār al-'Anwār*, vol. 93, p. 161.
[2] *'Udat al-Dā'ī*, p. 269; *Wasā'il al-Shī'ah*, vol. 4, p. 851.

الْمَلَائِكَةُ وَ تَحْضُرُهُ الشَّيَاطِين

"In a house where the Qur'ān is not recited and Allāh ﷻ is not remembered, its goodness and blessings will decrease, the angels will avoid it and it will become a place frequented by devils."[1]

K) Acquaintance with recommended acts

Another moral duty of parents towards their children is to acquaint them with recommended actions and deeds that are not obligatory in the *Sharī'ah* but are emphasized much; in such a way that they themselves become factors, practical preachers and worthy promoters of these good traditions to their children. They must encourage them to perform such desirable actions and follow those religious customs. For example, they should take their children by the hand to the *Masjid* and make them sit next to them and introduce them to the issues of congregational prayer and the importance of attending the *Masjid* and congregations. Also encourage them to wake up early, to pray at the first hour, perform the recommended Prayers and to pray the Midnight Prayer.

Some people may think that forcing children and teenagers to do what is recommended will cause them to get fed up and tired of obligations; but this perception is due to the lack of awareness of the teachings of Islamic teachers and scholars, because the teachings of the great leaders of Islam are not excessive, but rather, they arise from a complete familiarity with human characteristics and are also a ray of the light of heavenly revelation.

We learn from the Infallible *A'immah* ﷺ that familiarity with religious rules and recommended practices and acting according to them will purify the hearts and remove the rusts. The pure soul of the children flies in the light of connection with the Lord ﷻ and in the horizon of infinite perfection and finds effulgence and heavenly shine.

---

[1] *Wasā'il al-Shī'ah*, vol. 4, p. 850; *Biḥār al-'Anwār*, vol. 93, p. 161.

Of course - as we mentioned before - making children interested in obligatory and recommended issues should be done naturally and with principles of training, not by force, imposition, and violence.

Things children should be encouraged to do are as follows:

1. Attending congregational prayers

ʿAlī b. Ibrāhīm, in his commentary on the following verse:

فَٱصْدَعْ بِمَا تُؤْمَرُ...

"So proclaim what you have been commanded..."[1]

...writes: Once Abu Ṭālib came to the Prophet ﷺ accompanied by his son, Jaʿfar while the latter was praying and ʿAlī ؑ was following him in the Prayer. Abu Ṭālib said to Jaʿfar: My son! Stand next to your cousin and pray. So Jaʿfar stood on the left side of the Prophet ﷺ to pray.[2]

2. Encouragement for Midnight Prayer

The Prophet ﷺ said:

رَحِمَ اللهُ عَبْداً قامَ مِنْ اللَّيلِ فَصَلّى ، وَأيْقَظَ أهْلَه فَصَلّوا، ألا وَ اِنَّ أفْضَلَ الأعمالِ صَلاة الرَّجُلِ بِالليلِ ، وَالَّذى نَفسى بِيَدِه اِنَّ الرَّجُلَ اذا قامَ مِنَ الليلِ يُصَلّى ، تُسَبّحُ ثيابُه وَمنْ حَولَه

رَحِمَ اللَّهُ عَبْداً قَامَ مِنَ اللَّيْلِ فَصَلَّى وَ أَيْقَظَ أَهْلَهُ فَصَلَّوْا أَلَا وَ إِنَ أَفْضَلَ الْأَعْمَالِ صَلَاةُ الرَّجُلِ بِاللَّيْلِ وَ الَّذِي نَفْسِي بِيَدِهِ إِنَّ الرَّجُلَ إِذَا قَامَ مِنَ اللَّيْلِ يُصَلِّي تُسَبِّحُ ثِيَابُهُ وَ مَنْ حَوْلَه

"May Allāh ﷻ have mercy on the servant who wakes up in the middle of the night and prays and wakes up his family and friends so that they too pray the Midnight Prayer. Know that the best deed of

---

[1] Sūrah al-Ḥijr 15:94.

[2] *Mustadrak al-Wasāʾil*, vol. 6, p. 455.

man is to pray the Midnight Prayer. I swear by the one in whose hands my life is, when a person arises for the Midnight Prayer, his clothes and everything around him recites divine glorifications."[1]

'Alī ﷺ said:

وأُوصِيكم بقِيامِ اللَّيلِ مِن أوَّلِهِ إلى آخِرِهِ، فإنْ غَلَبَ عليْكُم النَّومُ ففي آخِرِهِ، ومَن مُنِعَ بِمَرَضٍ فإنَّ اللَّهَ يَعذِرُ بالعُذْرِ

"I advise you to pray the Midnight Prayer from midnight to the end of the night; and if sleep overtakes you, wake up at the end of the night and pray it. Whoever cannot do so due to his illness, Allāh ﷻ will forgive him as he has an excuse."[2]

Zayd b. 'Alī says:

كانَ أبى عَلىُّ بنُ الحُسَينِ-رَضى اللهُ عنه-لا يَفرُطُ فى صَلاة خَمسينَ رَكْعَة. قُلْتُ:وَكَيفَ صَلاة الْخَمسِينَ رَكعة قال:- صَلّى الله عليه وسَلَّم-سَبْعَة عَشَرَ رَكعَة الفرايِضُ وَثمَانٍ قَبْلَ الظُّهرِ، وَأربعٌ بَعْدَها وَأربعٌ قَبلَ الْعَصرِ، وَأربَعٌ بَعْدَ الْمَغرِبِ وَثَمان صَلاة السَّحَرَ وَثَلاثُ الوَتَرُ، وَرَكْعَتا الْفَجْرِ، قال رَضِى اللهُ عَنْه: وكانَ عَلىّ بن الحُسَينِ رَضِى اللهُ عَنه يَعْلّمُها أولادَه

My father 'Alī b. Al-Ḥusain ﷺ never shortened the prayers of fifty units (*Raka'h*); I asked: What is the meaning of fifty-unit prayer?

He said: Seventeen units are the obligatory daily prayers, eight units of Nafila before Ẓuhr Prayer and four units of *Nāfilah* after Ẓuhr and four units before 'Asr prayer and four units after Maghrib Prayer and eight units of Midnight Prayer and three units of *Witr* Prayer (two units with the intention of *Shaf'ah* Prayer and one unit with the intention of *Witr* Prayer) and two units of Fajr Prayer. Then he added:

---

[1] *Mustadrak al-Wasā'il*, vol. 6, p. 338.
[2] *Mustadrak al-Wasā'il*, vol. 3, p. 151.

My father (Imām Zayn al-'Ābidīn ﵇) used to teach these prayers to his children.[1]

3. Encourage the daily Nāfilah prayers

Imām Bāqir ﵇ says about the special qualities of his father Imām Sajjad ﵇:

وَكانَ يقضى مافاتَه مافاتَه مِنْ صَلاة نافِلَة النَّهار فى اللَيل، وَيقُولُ: يا بُنَىَّ، لَيس هذا عَلَيْكُمْ بِواجِبٍ، وَلكِناُحِبُّ لِمَن عَوَّدَ مِنْكُمْ نَفْسَه عادَة مِنْ الخَيْرِ أن يَدُومَ عَليها

"His Eminence ﵇ used to perform the *Qaḍā* of the *Nāfilah* prayers he had missed during the day, at night and said: My child! It is not obligatory for you to perform these *Nāfilah* prayers, but I would like you to continue doing something good you have got in the habit of."[2]

4. Two units of 'Ishā Nāfilah

Imām Ṣādiq ﵇ says:

كانَ أبى يُصلّى بَعدَ عِشاءِ الآخرِة رَكعَتَينِ وَهُوَ جالِسٌ يقرأ فيهما مائةَ آية، وكانَ يَقُولُ: مَنْ صلاّهما وَقَرَأ مِائة لَمْ تُكْتَبْ من الغافلينَ

◌َ كَانَ أَبِي يُصَلِّي بَعْدَ عِشَاءِ الْآخِرَةِ رَكْعَتَيْنِ وَ هُوَ جَالِسٌ يَقْرَأُ فِيهِمَا مِائَةَ آيَةٍ وَ كَانَ يَقُولُ مَنْ صَلَّاهُمَا وَ قَرَأَ مِائَةَ آيَةٍ لَمْ يُكْتَبْ مِنَ الْغَافِلِينَ

"My father ﵇ always prays two units after the 'Ishā prayer and after that sits and recites a hundred verses from the Qur'ān. And he used to say: Whoever prays these two units and recites a hundred verses will not be considered among the heedless."[3]

---

[1] *Musnad Zayd*, p. 118.
[2] *Kashf al-Ghummah*, vol. 2, p. 278.
[3] *Mustadrak al-Wasā'il*, vol. 4, p. 204.

5. Teaching the Wednesday eve Prayer to Fāṭimah Zahrā عليها السلام

It is narrated from Lady Zahrā عليها السلام that she said: The Prophet of Allāh ﷺ taught me the Wednesday eve Prayer and said: "There are six units of this prayer and in every unit after Sūrah al-Ḥamd, one should recite:

قُلِ ٱللَّهُمَّ مَٰلِكَ ٱلْمُلْكِ تُؤْتِى ٱلْمُلْكَ مَن تَشَآءُ وَتَنزِعُ ٱلْمُلْكَ مِمَّن تَشَآءُ وَتُعِزُّ مَن تَشَآءُ وَتُذِلُّ مَن تَشَآءُ ۖ بِيَدِكَ ٱلْخَيْرُ ۖ إِنَّكَ عَلَىٰ كُلِّ شَىْءٍ قَدِيرٌ ﴿٢٦﴾ تُولِجُ ٱلَّيْلَ فِى ٱلنَّهَارِ وَتُولِجُ ٱلنَّهَارَ فِى ٱلَّيْلِ ۖ وَتُخْرِجُ ٱلْحَىَّ مِنَ ٱلْمَيِّتِ وَتُخْرِجُ ٱلْمَيِّتَ مِنَ ٱلْحَىِّ ۖ وَتَرْزُقُ مَن تَشَآءُ بِغَيْرِ حِسَابٍ ﴿٢٧﴾

"Say, 'O Allāh, Master of all sovereignty! You give sovereignty to whomever You wish, and strip of sovereignty whomever You wish; You make mighty whomever You wish, and You abase whomever You wish; all good is in Your hand. Indeed You have power over all things. You make the night pass into the day and You make the day pass into the night. You bring forth the living from the dead and You bring forth the dead from the living, and You provide for whomever You wish without any reckoning.'"[1]

And after the prayer if he invokes blessings on the Prophet ﷺ as he deserves, Allāh عزّ وجلّ will forgive all his sins of seventy years and give him a reward that cannot be counted."[2]

6. Teaching the tasbih of Lady Fāṭimah Zahrā عليها السلام

Abū Ḥārūn Makfūf narrates from Imām Ṣādiq عليه السلام who said:

يَا أَبَا هَارُونَ إِنَّا نَأْمُرُ صِبْيَانَنَا بِتَسْبِيحِ فَاطِمَةَ ع كَمَا نَأْمُرُهُمْ بِالصَّلَاةِ فَالْزَمْهُ فَإِنَّهُ لَمْ يَلْزَمْهُ عَبْدٌ فَشَقِيَ

"O Abū Ḥārūn! We command our children to recite the *Tasbīḥ* of Fāṭimah Zahrā عليها السلام, just as we command them to pray, so be regular in

[1] Sūrah āl-'Imrān 3:26-27.
[2] *Mustadrak al-Wasā'il*, vol. 6, p. 371.

reciting the *Tasbīḥ* of Fāṭimah ﴿عليها السلام﴾, because one who recites this *Tasbīḥ* regularly will never go astray."[1]

7. Remaining awake the night of 15th Sha'bān

Zayd b. 'Alī says:

كَانَ عَلِيُّ بْنُ الْحُسَيْنِ ع يَجْمَعُنَا جَمِيعاً لَيْلَةَ النِّصْفِ مِنْ شَعْبَانَ- ثُمَّ يُجَزِّئُ اللَّيْلَ أَجْزَاءً ثَلَاثَةً فَيُصَلِّي بِنَا جُزْءاً ثُمَّ يَدْعُو فَنُؤَمِّنُ عَلَى دُعَائِهِ ثُمَّ يَسْتَغْفِرُ اللَّهَ وَ نَسْتَغْفِرُهُ وَ نَسْأَلُهُ الْجَنَّةَ حَتَّى يَنْفَجِرَ الْفَجْر

"My father, 'Alī b. Al-Ḥusain ﴿عليه السلام﴾, used to gather all of us on the eve of the 15th Sha'bān; then he divided that night into three parts: in the first part he would recite the Prayer for us, then he would supplicate, and we would say Amīn. Then he would ask for forgiveness and until dawn broke, we would also ask Allāh ﴿عز وجل﴾ for forgiveness and beseech Him for Paradise."[2]

8. Remaining awake during the Qadr Night

Qāḍī Nu'mān Miṣrī has narrated in *Da'im al-Islām* that the Messenger of Allāh ﴿صلى الله عليه وآله﴾ would fold up his beddings in the last part of the month of *Ramaḍān* and prepare himself for worship. He would awaken his family on the 23rd eve and (even) splash water on their faces. Lady Fāṭimah Zahrā ﴿عليها السلام﴾ did not let anyone from the family sleep on this night, and she shortened the sleep of her children by giving them lesser food. From the day she encouraged them to remain awake that night: asked them to sleep during the day so that they may remain awake at night, and she said, "Whoever is deprived of the good of this night is at a loss."[3]

9. Remaining awake the night of 'Īd al-Fiṭr

Sayyid b. Ṭāwūs narrates from Imām Bāqir ﴿عليه السلام﴾:

---

[1] *al-'Amālī al-Ṣadūq*, p. 518; *Wasā'il al-Shī'ah*, vol. 4, p. 1023.
[2] *Wasā'il al-Shī'ah*, vol. 5, p. 241.
[3] *Da'im al-Islām*, vol. 1, p. 282.

كَانَ عَلِيُّ بْنُ الْحُسَيْنِ ع يُحْيِي لَيْلَةَ عِيدِ الْفِطْرِ بِصَلَاةٍ حَتَّى يُصْبِحَ وَ يَبِيتُ لَيْلَةَ الْفِطْرِ فِي الْمَسْجِدِ وَ يَقُولُ يَا بُنَيَّ مَا هِيَ بِدُونِ لَيْلَةٍ يَعْنِي لَيْلَةَ الْقَدْرِ

"Imām Sajjad ؑ used to stay in the *Masjid* on the eve of 'Īd al-Fiṭr, praying until morning and saying to his children: My children, the virtue of tonight is no less than the night of *Qadr*."[1]

10. Memorizing some supplications

Imām Zayn al-'Ābidīn ؑ says, "During some battle, Jibra'īl ؑ descended on the Prophet ﷺ while the Prophet's ﷺ chest was covered with heavy armour, which was making him suffer. Jibra'īl ؑ said: O Muḥammad ﷺ! Your Lord ﷻ sends you greetings and says: Remove this armour and recite this supplication, which will be a source of security for you and your *Ummah*. Then Imām ؑ said: Imām Ḥusain ؑ said: My father instructed me to memorize and respect this supplication and advised me to write this prayer on his burial shroud and to teach it to my family and encourage them to read and teach it. Then he recited Du'a Jawshan al-Kabīr."

Bedtime supplication

Mu'awiyāh b. Wahab says: One of the children of Imām Ṣādiq ؑ came to his father one night when he was sleeping and said that he wanted to sleep. Imām ؑ said: My child; recite:

أَشْهَدُ أَنْ لَا إِلَهَ إِلَّا اللهُ وَ أَنَّ مُحَمَّداً ص عَبْدُهُ وَ رَسُولُهُ وَ أَعُوذُ بِعَظَمَةِ اللهِ وَ أَعُوذُ بِعِزَّةِ اللهِ وَ أَعُوذُ بِقُدْرَةِ اللهِ وَ أَعُوذُ بِجَلَالِ اللهِ وَ أَعُوذُ بِسُلْطَانِ اللهِ إِنَّ اللهَ عَلَى كُلِّ شَيْءٍ قَدِيرٌ وَ أَعُوذُ بِعَفْوِ اللهِ وَ أَعُوذُ بِغُفْرَانِ اللهِ وَ أَعُوذُ بِرَحْمَةِ اللهِ مِنْ شَرِّ السَّامَّةِ وَ الْهَامَّةِ وَ مِنْ شَرِّ كُلِّ دَابَّةٍ صَغِيرَةٍ أَوْ كَبِيرَةٍ بِلَيْلٍ أَوْ نَهَارٍ مِنْ شَرِّ فَسَقَةِ الْجِنِّ وَ الْإِنْسِ وَ مِنْ شَرِّ فَسَقَةِ الْعَرَبِ وَ الْعَجَمِ وَ مِنْ شَرِّ الصَّوَاعِقِ وَ الْبَرَدِ اللَّهُمَّ صَلِّ عَلَى

[1] *Iqbāl al-'Āmāl*, p. 27.

مُحَمَّدٍ عَبْدِكَ وَ رَسُولِك.

I bear witness that there is no god, except Allāh ﷻ and that Muḥammad ﷺ is His servant and messenger and I seek refuge in the greatness of Allāh ﷻ and I seek refuge in the honour of Allāh ﷻ and I seek refuge in the power of Allāh ﷻ and I seek refuge in the majesty of Allāh ﷻ and I seek refuge in the authority of Allāh ﷻ and indeed Allāh ﷻ is powerful over everything. And I seek refuge in the pardon of Allāh ﷻ and I seek refuge in the forgiveness of Allāh ﷻ and I seek refuge in the mercy of Allāh ﷻ from the evil of the *Jinn* and humans and from the evil of transgressors of Arabs and non-Arabs and from the evil of lightning and cold. Bless Muḥammad ﷺ Your servant and messenger.[1]

11. Encouraging children to give charity

Hārūn b. ʻIsā says:

Imām Jaʻfar Ṣādiq عليه السلام once said to his son, Muḥammad, 'Son, how much is left with you of that (money) for expenses?'

He replied, 'Forty dinars.' He said, 'You should go out and give it away as charity.' The son said, 'No more money is left with me besides this.' The Imām said, 'You should give it as charity, Allāh, the Most Majestic, the Most Glorious, will replace it. Have you not seen that for everything there is a key, and the key to greater means of sustenance is giving charity, so give it as charity.'

The son followed the instruction. Imām Jaʻfar Ṣādiq عليه السلام had to wait for only ten days when he received four thousand *dīnārs* from a certain place.

He said, 'Son, we gave Allāh forty *dīnārs*, and He has given us four thousand *dīnārs*.'[2]

Muḥammad b. ʻUmar Yazīd says: I informed Abū al-Ḥasan that I lost two sons and I have one young son left. Imām عليه السلام said, "Give *Sadaqah* on his behalf." He said: As soon as I wanted to get up and leave him, he said,

---

[1] *Mustadrak al-Wasā'il*, vol. 5, p. 42.
[2] *al-Kāfī*, Pg. 10.

"Ask your young son to give a piece of bread or something else as *Sadaqah* with his own hand, even if it is very little, because what is given as charity in the way of Allāh ﷻ, even if it is little, is great in the sight of Allāh ﷻ, provided that the giver of the charity has sincere intention. Almighty Allāh says: *So, he who has done an atom's weight of good shall see it...*"[1]

L) Commemoration of Islamic rites

Acquainting children with Islamic rites makes them interested in Islamic patterns and values and keeps religious teachings alive in their lives and minds.

Commemoration of the 'Āshūrā' uprising

One of the best and highest examples of honouring and remembering Islamic expressions is the commemoration of the epics and valour of the martyrs of Imām Ḥusain b. 'Alī ؑ and the children of his faithful companions in Karbalā'. Therefore, the committed parents are responsible to keep this great memory alive in the hearts of their children: because the survival and continuity of Islam and the pride of Muslims is to keep 'Āshūrā' of Imām Ḥusain ؑ alive.

Imām Ṣādiq and other *A'immah* ؑ have taught us to take our children to the assemblies to mourn the martyrdom of Imām Ḥusain ؑ and introduce them to the memory and name of Aba 'Abdullāh ؑ and introduce to them the fateful events of 'Āshūrā'.

The late Kolaynī has narrated through his chains of narrators from Abū Dāwūd Mustariq on the authority of 'Abdī that: When I came to meet Imām Ṣādiq ؑ. He said, "Tell Umm Farwah[2] and let her hear what calamities befell her grandfather (Ḥusain b. 'Alī ؑ)!"

Umm Farwah came and stood behind the curtain. Imām ؑ said, "('Abdī!) recite some of those verses to us." I recited the following:

---

[1] *Wasā'il al-Shī'ah*, vol. 6, p. 261, tr. 1.

[2] One of the daughters of Imām Ṣādiq ؑ, whose mother was Fāṭimah, daughter of Ḥusain ؑ, son of Imām Sajjad ؑ. (*Muntahī al-'Āmāl*, vol. 2, p. 158).

"Emancipate my existence with your tears..."

This poem was so heart-rending that suddenly Umm Farwah wailed and screamed, and all the ladies of the house of Imām Ṣādiq followed her and started crying.

Suddenly, Imām Ṣādiq said: At home...at home (be careful at home) we saw the people of Madinah gathered behind the door to see what happened. The Imām sent someone to that crowd to tell them: One of our children suddenly fainted and that is why the women screamed.[1]

Remembering the oppression of ʿAlī and Zahra

Among the best and lofty implications of commemorating Islamic rituals is to encourage the children to memorize the meaningful sermon of Lady Fāṭimah Zahrā.

This sermon - which has great themes and lofty knowledge - describes some of the events after the passing of the Prophet and defends the position of *Wilāyah* and *Imāmah*. The sermon is so eloquent that the reader can understand the oppressiveness of ʿAlī and Zahra after the Prophet by studying it carefully.

Zaynab Kubrā memorized this sermon at the age of seven, and the members of *Ahl al-Bayt* clan have narrated it from her.[2]

In the same way, they advised their children to memorize this sermon so that the memory of *Jihād* and martyrdom in the way of opposing tyranny and resistance against oppressors remains alive in their hearts and Islamic rituals are preserved.

Zayd b. ʿAlī, in a conversation with Aḥmad b. Abī Ṭāhir said regarding this sermon:

رأيتُ مَشايخَ آلِ أبى طالب يَرووُنَه عَن آبائهم ويُعلّمونه اولادهم

[1] *al-Kāfī*, vol. 8, pp. 215-216.
[2] *Safinat al-Biḥār*, vol. 1, 558.

I saw elders of the progeny of Abū Ṭālib narrate this sermon from their forefathers and teach it to their children.[1]

M) Teaching informative and epic poetry

We know that since ancient times beautiful religious and epic poems and verses have played an important role in communication. They had divine mission and were always considered among prominent examples of art and literature. In general, the use of artistic and literary formats is a condition for the influence and endurability of a message; because the fine edifying content is like a pure and beautiful soul that can be placed in a pure, strong, graceful and a beautiful body, and its value and importance and its way to hearts will increase a hundredfold.

The power of the art of writing lies in the fact that it can reshape the most complex content into the easiest form for everyone to understand. It can also give a beautiful shape to the realities and present their importance in the best way. Therefore, there is no doubt regarding the importance of familiarizing children and teenagers with the literary and artistic heritage of Islamic culture whose sophistication and greatness still has prominence in the world.

Teaching the instructive verses of Abū Ṭālib

Amīr al Mu'minīn 'Alī ﷺ advises the fathers to teach their children the instructive verses of Abū Ṭālib, which will instil in them both the Islamic teachings as well as glorious scenes of the early history of Islam. Also, the memory of Abū Ṭālib - the only true defender of the noble Prophet - would be preserved in their hearts and minds.

Imām Ṣādiq ﷺ used to say:

كَانَ اَمِيْرُ الْمُؤْمِنِيْنَ يُعْجِبُهُ أَنْ يُروى شِعرُ أبى طالبٍ و أن يُدَوَّنَ، و قال: تَعَلَّمُوهُ وَ

[1] *Sharḥ Nahj al-Balaghah*, vol. 4, p. 94.

عَلِّمُوْهُ اَوْلَادَكُمْ، فَاِنَّهٗ كَانَ عَلٰى دِيْنِ اللهِ وَ فِيْهِ عِلْمٌ كَثِيْرٌ

"Amīr al Mu'minīn (a) used to be extremely pleased when Abū Ṭālib's verses were quoted or written, and he said: Learn these verses and teach them to your children, because Abū Ṭālib trod the path of Allāh's ﷻ religion, and his compositions have useful content."[1]

Abū Ṭālib's poetic compositions are numerous and they have even been compiled into a *Dīwān*[2]. Abū Ṭālib composed verses on various topics, especially about the personality of the Noble Prophet of Islam ﷺ. But since it is beyond the scope of this book to present them here, we only suffice by quoting a few lines as follows:

مَليکُ النّاس ليسَ له شريک   هو الوهّابُ والمُبدى المعيدُ
وَمَنْ فَوْقَ السَّماءِ لَه بحقٍّ   وَمَنْ تَحت السَّماءِ لَه عَبيدُ

Allāh is most powerful and without an equal, He is the benefactor and creator; and resurrection of the creatures is in his hands. Whatever is in the heavens is His and whatever is under the sky is subservient to Him.[3]

Teaching 'Abdī's poems

Another advice that Imām Ṣādiq (a) gives us is to teach the verses of 'Abdī to children. His name was Sufyān b. Muṣ'ab 'Abdī Kūfī and he was one of the poets of *Ahl al-Bayt* (a) and a companion of Imām Ṣādiq (a). Most of his compositions are about the virtues of Amīr al Mu'minīn (a) and his illustrious successors.

'Allamah Amīnī says: Among 'Abdī's works; we have not seen any poetry other than poems related to *Ahl al-Bayt* (a).[4] All of 'Abdī's compositions were approved by Imām Ṣādiq (a) and he sometimes

[1] *Wasā'il al-Shī'ah*, vol. 12, p. 248; *Mustadrak al-Wasā'il*, Vol. 6, p. 101, v. 15, p. 166, *Abū Ṭālib Yagānih Mudāfi' Islām*, p. 64; *al-Ghadīr*, vol. 7, Pg. 393; *al-Ḥujjah Ala Al-Madhāhib*, p. 25.

[2] Collected works.

[3] *Kanz al-Fawā'id*, p. 79: *Abū Ṭālib Yagānih Mudāfi' Islām*, p. 125.

[4] *al-Ghadīr*, vol. 2, p. 294.

asked 'Abdī to recite poems at gatherings of *Azādārī* mourning to be read in memory of the martyrs.[1]

Imām Ṣādiq ﷷ said:

يا مَعْشَرَ الشيعَة، عَلِّموا أودكم شِعرَ العبدى؛ فَا ِنَّه عَلى دِينِ الله

"O Shī'ahfolks, teach 'Abdī's verses to your children; because he followed the religion of Allāh ﷻ."[2]

'Allāmah Amīnī has quoted many verses of 'Abdī in his book of *al-Ghadīr*. Here we present a few by way of example:

أُحبُّ النَّبيَّ الْمصطَفى وَابنَ عَمِّه   عَليّاً وَسِبْطَيه وَفاطِمَةَ الزهرا

هُمْ أَهْلَ بَيْتٍ أُذْهِبَ الرِجُس عَنْهُمْ   وَأطلعهم أُفقَ الهُدى أنجُماً زُهَرا

مولاتُهُمْ فَرْضٌ على كُلِّ مُسْلِمٍ   وَحُبُّهُمْ أسنى الذَّخائِرِ للأُخرى

وَما أنا لِلصحبِ الكِرام بِمُبْغِضٍ   فَا ِنِّىْ أرى البَعْضاءَ فى حَقِّهم كُفرا

Translation:

I love the Prophet ﷺ, the Chosen One (Muṣtafā), his cousin 'Alī ﷷ and his two grandsons عليهما السلام, and Fāṭimah Zahrā عليها السلام.

They are the people of a house from which filth is kept away, and they are shining stars brought forth in the horizon of guidance.

Their mastership is an obligation upon every Muslim, and their love is the best treasure trove for the Hereafter.

And I am not a hater of the noble ones, because I regard hatred to them as disbelief.[3]

---

[1] *Rijāl Kishī*, p. 254.
[2] *Rijāl Kishī*, p. 254.
[3] *al-Ghadīr*, vol. 2, p. 295.

N) Celebrating Islamic festivals

Islamic festivals are the unforgettable memories of important events in the history of Islam; especially the day of the festival of Ghadīr, in which ʿAlī عليه السلام was appointed by the Messenger of Allāh ﷺ as his caliph and successor. Thus the religion of Allāh was perfected, as *Imāmah* is the seamless continuation of Prophethood.

The day of ʿĪd al-Ghadīr is the day of culmination of the relentless efforts of the Messenger of Allāh ﷺ. For this reason, this auspicious day has been one of the greatest Islamic festivals for the holy A'immah عليهم السلام.

Imām Ṣādiq عليه السلام considered this day very important and as compared to other days, he attached greater importance and virtue to it.

Qasim b. Yaḥyā narrates from his grandfather, Ḥasan b. Rāshid as follows:

Imām Ṣādiq عليه السلام was asked: Is there any other ʿĪd for the believers besides ʿĪd al-Fiṭr and ʿĪd al-Aḍḥā and Friday? He said:

نَعَمْ، لَهُم ما هُوَ أظَمُ مِنْ هذا. يَومٌ أُقيمَ أميرُ الْمُومنينَ عليه السلام، فَعَقَد لَه رَسُولُ
الله اَلوِلايَة فى أعْناقِ الرّجال وَالنّساءِ بِغَديرِ خُمًّ. فَقُلْتُ: وَأىّ يَومٍ ذاكَ؟ قال:
...يَوْمُ ثمانية عَشَرَ مِنْ ذى الْحِجّة. قالَ: ثُمَّ قالَ: وَالْعَمَلُ فيه يَعْدِلُ العَمَلَ فى ثمانين
وَيَنبَغى أن يُكثرَ فيه ذِكْرُ اللهِ عَزَّوجَلَّ، وَالصَّلاة عَلَى النَّبىّ وَيُوَسِّعَ الرَّجُلُ فيه عَلى
عِياله

"Yes, there are ʿĪd's for the believers and there is an ʿĪd greater than them; it is the day when Amīr al Mu'minīn عليه السلام was appointed as the caliph of the Prophet ﷺ.

Then the Holy Prophet ﷺ had made his love compulsory on believing men and women at Ghadīr al-Khum."

I asked: What day is that?

He replied, "It is on 18th of Dhu al-Ḥijjah."

Then he said, "A good deed performed on this day is equal to the deeds of eighty months. Muslims should remember Allāh ﷻ in excess on this day and recite *Durūd* and *Salām* on the Holy Prophet ﷺ many times and every person should treat his family with nice things on this day."

Yes, the commemoration of Islamic occasions and especially the auspicious 'Īd al-Ghadīr is to revive Islam and follow the orders of the purified *Ahl al-Bayt* (a), and how nice it is to give small and big gifts to the family members and especially the children on this day to cheer them up. At the same time, we explain to them what Imamat and *Wilāyah* mean and what these commemorations are for.

O) Preparing for Friday

The leaders of Islam have shown sensitivity and attached special importance to the celebration of Friday and have determined special programs for it.

On this day, it is recommended to perform rituals such as: reciting supplications of Imām Mahdī (aj): Du'a Nudbah, Du'a Simāt; and also the Friday Prayer. One should take care of personal hygiene and bathing, etc. Most importantly, it is emphasized to devote this day for religious education. The Holy Prophet ﷺ said:

"Woe to the Muslim, who does not free himself on Friday every week to learn the divine commands."[1]

Moreover, it has also been advised to provide necessities of life to one's family; as the Prophet ﷺ is reported to have said:

اِشْتَرو لِصِبيانِكمُ اللَّحْمَ وَذكّروهُم يومَ الجُمُعَة

"Buy meat for your children and explain the importance of Friday to them."[2]

[1] *Biḥār al-'Anwār*, vol. 59, p. 36.
[2] *Mustadrak al-Wasā'il*, vol. 6, p. 99.

Also, Amīr al Mu'minīn عليه السلام said:

أطرِفُوا أهاليكم فى كُلّ لَيلَة جُمعَة بِشَىءٍ مِنْ الْفاكِهة كَىْ يَفْرَحُوا با لجُمُعَة

"Procure some fruit every Friday eve for your families, so that they are happy at the arrival of Friday."[1]

"In a narration, Friday is mentioned, instead of Friday eve."[2]

---

[1] *'Udat al-Dā'ī*, p. 75.
[2] *Mustadrak al-Wasā'il*, vol. 6, p. 99.

Part Six

Children and society

Children and society

A) Social interactions

Since human nature is based on attachment and relationship with each other, the child also prefers to live in a group and hates isolation.

Social life has customs and conditions to prepare the environment for a healthy and peaceful life and eliminate the grounds of conflict and enmity. Therefore, the divine leaders ﷺ, have given recommendations to strengthen human relationships and to realize a desirable and sublime life, which doubtlessly, if done properly, will guarantee the overall health of the society and good human relationships.

Children and teenagers form a huge part of society. Their personality and their familiarity with manners and relationships and different types of social interactions take place during childhood and adolescence, and it is the parents who determine the path of their lives with their vital role and influence. If parents teach children that they have self-respect and dignity, and others also have it in the same way, respect for one's own personality and others will become part of a child's permanent character, and they would turn away from meaningless boasting and violation of other people's rights and anger towards them and acquire numerous good moral qualities that are the foundation of success and happiness in social life and coexistence with others.

To summarise, positive and negative values visible in the society are mainly rooted in the behaviour and speech of parents and seen in the conduct of children and the type of education inspired and instilled by the family to children, for it is they who will shape the present and future society. The seeds planted in the house and family will bear fruit in the hearts of human beings.

Knowing one's personality

The first lesson that parents should impart to their children is to teach them about themselves; let them know that Allāh ﷻ has created human beings as honoured, dignified, free, pure and heavenly; and He does not want them to be humiliated and degraded by their own selves.

Divine prophets also arrived to guide man to reach the heights of perfection and dignity. Therefore, it is up to the parents to explain to their child that: you live in the society with human dignity, and if Allāh ﷻ forbid, you destroy this dignity one day, people will not value you. Then they should make the children aware of what humiliates their character and harms their honour and dignity.

Expression of poverty

Luqmān the Wise said to his son:

يَا بُنَيَّ ذُقْتُ الصَّبِرَ وَ أَكَلْتُ لِحَاءَ الشَّجَرِ فَلَمْ أَجِدْ شَيْئاً هُوَ أَمَرُّ مِنَ الْفَقْرِ فَإِنْ بُلِيتَ بِهِ يَوْماً وَ لاَ تُظْهِرِ النَّاسَ عَلَيْهِ فَيَسْتَهِينُوكَ وَ لاَ يَنْفَعُوكَ بِشَيْءٍ ارْجِعْ إِلَى الَّذِي ابْتَلاَكَ بِهِ فَهُوَ أَقْدَرُ عَلَى فَرَجِكَ وَ سَلْهُ مَنْ ذَا الَّذِي سَأَلَهُ فَلَمْ يُعْطِهِ أَوْ وَثِقَ بِهِ فَلَمْ يُنْجِهِ

My child! I tasted the bitter plant of patience and ate the bark of the tree and found nothing more bitter than poverty.

So, if one day you lament about your poverty to the people, they will consider you base and lowly and will not support you.

My child - in this situation - return to the one who made you suffer from poverty and put you to the test (and ask Him to remove your imprisonment), because He is more capable of making an opening for you. My child! Ask Allāh ﷻ for your needs. Who has ever asked Allāh ﷻ for something, but Allāh ﷻ did not give it to him or trusted Allāh ﷻ and He did not save him?![1]

Vying what others have

Abū Ḥamzah al-Thumālī says:

[1] *al-Kāfī*, Vol. 4, p. 22, (*Sabr* is also a yellow and bitter plant).

دَعَا حُذَيْفَةُ بْنُ الْيَمَانِي ابْنَهُ عِنْدَ مَوْتِهِ فَأَوْصَى إِلَيْهِ وَ قَالَ يَا بُنَيَّ أَظْهِرِ الْيَأْسَ مِمَّا فِي أَيْدِي النَّاسِ فَإِنَّ فِيهِ الْغِنَى وَ إِيَّاكَ وَ طَلَبَ الْحَاجَاتِ إِلَى النَّاسِ فَإِنَّهُ فَقْرٌ حَاضِرٌ

In his last moments, Ḥuḍaifah b. al-Yamānī summoned his son and advised: My son! Despair of what is in the hands of others; because your needlessness lies in that (you ignore the wealth of others). Do not ask for your needs from others, because poverty is nothing other than this.[1]

The honour of the believer

'Alī ؑ says to his son, Imām Ḥusain ؑ:

أَيْ بُنَيَّ عِزُّ الْمُؤْمِنِ غِنَاهُ عَنِ النَّاسِ

"My child, the greatness of a believer lies in his lack of need from others."[2]

Avoid humiliation.

Luqmān the Wise says to his son:

يَا بُنَيَّ إِيَّاكَ أَنْ تَسْتَذِلَ فَتُخْزَى

My child! Don't humiliate yourself and you will be disgraced.[3]

Honouring the world

It is narrated from Imām Ṣādiq ؑ that Luqmān said to his son:

فَإِنْ أَرَدْتَ أَنْ تَجْمَعَ عِزَّ الدُّنْيَا فَاقْطَعْ طَمَعَكَ مِمَّا فِي أَيْدِي النَّاسِ فَإِنَّمَا بَلَغَ الْأَنْبِيَاءُ وَ الصِّدِّيقُونَ مَا بَلَغُوا بِقَطْعِ طَمَعِهِم

---

[1] *al-'Amālī al-Ṣadūq*, p. 287.
[2] *Tuḥaf al-'Uqūl*, p. 84.
[3] *al-Ikhtiṣāṣ*, p. 332.

"...if you want the respect of the world to be gathered for you, get rid of your greed and vying for what others have, because the prophets and righteous people reached every position due to giving up of greed."[1]

Respecting the personality of others

Just as it is obligatory for everyone to protect their reputation and personality and not to simply ignore it, it is also necessary to respect the personality of others in the society. Therefore, parents should make their children understand that others have the same personality and dignity as them. All members of the society have the same expectation in return and should not be mocked. Therefore, let us have a better understanding of others and strengthen the spirit of love, brotherhood, and cooperation in the society, and this will not be possible except by following the social customs of Islam. Some of these good practices include:

Healthy behaviour

Luqmān the Wise said to his son:

يَا بُنَيَّ ابْدَأِ النَّاسَ بِالسَّلَامِ وَ الْمُصَافَحَةِ قَبْلَ الْكَلَامِ

My child! Before you start speaking to people, you must take precedence in greeting (*Salām*) and shaking hands.[2]

Controlling the tongue

Also, Luqmān said to his son:

يَا بُنَيَّ مَنْ لَا يَكُفَّ لِسَانَهُ يَنْدَم

My child! Anyone who does not control his tongue and does not guard it will regret.[3]

Avoiding rudeness

---

[1] *Biḥār al-'Anwār*, vol. 13, p. 419.
[2] *al-Ikhtiṣāṣ*, p. 333.
[3] *al-Ikhtiṣāṣ*, p. 333.

Amīr al Mu'minīn ﷺ advised Imām Ḥasan Mujtabā ﷺ:

قُولُو اللِنّاسِ حُسناًكَما أمَرَكُمُ الله

"Speak kindly to people as Allāh ﷻ has commanded you."[1]

'Alī ﷺ says to his son, Imām Ḥusain ﷺ:

وَ اعْلَمْ أَيْ بُنَيَّ أَنَّهُ مَنْ لاَنتْ كَلِمَتُهُ وَجَبَتْ مَحَبَّته

"My child! Know that whoever's speech becomes gentle and sweet, his love and affection will become necessary for everyone."[2]

Good manners

Luqmān said to his son:

يا بُنَىَّ ، اِيّاکَ وَالضَّجْرَ وَسُوءَ الْخُلقِ وَقِلَّة الصَّبرِ. فَلا يَستَقيمُ عَلى هذِه الخِصالِ صاحِبٌ وَألْزِمْ نَفسَکَ التَّودة فى اُمورِکَ وصَبرِّ عَلى مُووناتِ الاخوان نَفسَکَ.وَحسِّنْ مَعَ جَميعِ الناسِ خُلقَکَ، يا بُنَىّ اِن عَدمَکَ ما تَصِلُ بِه قِرابَتَکَ وَتَتَفَضَّلُ بِه عَلى اِخوانکَ، فَلا يَعدِم مَنّکَ حُسنَ الْخُلقِ وَبَسْطُ البِشرِ؛ فَا نَّه مِنْ أحسَنَ خُلْقَه، أحَبَّه الأخيارُ وَجانَبَه الْفُجّارُ

My child! Don't be restless, moody, and impatient, because you will not have any friends left with these traits. Persuade yourself to be patient so that you remain patient in hard times. In the same way, be patient in solving the problems of your brothers and behave nicely with others.

My child! Even if you are not able to bond with your relatives and do a good turn to your brothers, never give up good nature and generosity, because whoever improves his manners and conduct, good people will love him and bad people will avoid him.[3]

---

[1] *Tuḥaf al-'Uqūl*, p. 195.
[2] *Tuḥaf al-'Uqūl*, p. 87.
[3] *Biḥār al-'Anwār*, vol. 13, p. 419.

Avoiding vices and bad morals

'Alī ﷺ said to his son, Muḥammad b. al-Hanafiyyah:

إيَّاكَ والعُجْبَ، وسُوءَ الخُلُقِ، وقِلَّةَ الصَّبرِ، فَإنَّهُ لا يَستَقِيمُ لكَ علَى هذهِ الخِصالِ الثَّلاثِ صاحِبٌ، ولا يَزالُ لكَ علَيها مِنَ النَّاسِ مُجانِب

"Avoid selfishness, misconduct and impatience; because with these traits, you won't have any friends left, and a number of people will always avoid you."[1]

Also, that honourable person said to his son, Imām Ḥasan Mujtabā ﷺ:

ولَبَعضُ إمساكِكَ على أخِيْكَ مَعَ لُطفٍ خَيْرٌ من بَذْلٍ مَعَ عُنْفٍ

"Undoubtedly, withholding something from your brother kindly is better than giving it to him resentfully."[2]

Imām Ḥusain ﷺ said to his son:

مَنْ تَكَبَّرَ عَنْ النّاس ذَلَّ

"Whoever shows arrogance to others is disgraced."[3]

His Eminence, Sulaymān ﷺ used to say to his son:

يا بُنَيّ، اِيّاکَ والْمِراءَ؛ فا ِنّه لَيْسَتْ فيه مَنْفَعة وَهُوَ يُهَيِّجُ بَيْنَ الاِ خوانِ الْعِداوَة

My child! Do not quarrel, because quarrelling does not benefit you, besides, it will cause enmity between brothers.[4]

[1] *Mustadrak al-Wasā'il*, vol. 1, p. 136.
[2] *Biḥār al-'Anwār*, vol. 74, p. 209.
[3] *Tuḥaf al-'Uqūl*, p. 84.
[4] *Majmu'ah Warrām*, p. 340.

'Alī ﷺ said to his son, Imām Ḥasan Mujtabā ﷺ:

يا بُنَيَّ، لا تَسْتَخِفَّنَّ بِرَجُلٍ تَراه أبداً، إن كانَ اكبَرَ مِنک فَعُدَّ أبُوکَ ، وَإنْ مِنک فَهُوَ أخُوکَ، وَإنْ كانَ أصْغَرَ مِنک فَاَحْسِبْ اَنَّه ابنُکَ

"My child! Never (in your encounters) humiliate anyone, because he is either older than you: so, you must consider him as your father, or he is the same age as you: that is: he is as your brother, or younger than you; so you should consider him as your child."[1]

Ābī in his book of *Nathr al-Durār* narrates from Imām Bāqir ﷺ that he said to his son, Imām Ja'far Ṣādiq ﷺ:

إنَ اللَّهَ خَبَأَ ثَـلاَثَةَ أَشْيَاءَ فِي ثَـلاَثَةِ أَشْيَاءَ خَبَأَ رِضَاهُ فِي طَاعَتِهِ فَلاَ تُحَقِّرَنَّ مِنَ الطَّاعَةِ شَيْئاً فَلَعَلَّ رِضَاهُ فِيهِ وَ خَبَأَ سَخطَهُ فِي مَعْصِيَتِهِ فَلاَ تُحَقِّرَنَّ مِنَ الْمَعْصِيَةِ شَيْئاً فَلَعَلَّ سَخطَهُ فِيهِ وَ خَبَأَ أَوْلِيَاءَهُ فِي خَلْقِهِ فَلاَ تُحَقِّرَنَّ أَحَداً فَلَعَلَّ الْوَلِيَّ ذَلِك

"Allāh ﷻ has concealed three things in three things:

1. He has hidden His pleasure in His obedience, so do not consider any obedience insignificant as perhaps divine pleasure lies in that only.

2. He has hidden His anger in His disobedience, so don't consider any disobedience insignificant as perhaps divine anger lies in that only.

3. He has concealed His friends among his creatures, so do not humiliate anyone; perhaps he is Allāh's ﷻ friend."[2]

Luqmān the Wise said to his son:

يا بُنَيَّ، لا تُشمِتْ بِالمُوتِ، اَلا تَسخَر بِالمُبتَلى، وَلا تَمنَعْ بَالمَعروفِ

---

[1] *Kanz al-'Ummāl*, p. 217.

[2] *Biḥār al-'Anwār*, vol. 75, pp. 187 and 27; *Kashf al-Ghummah*, vol. 2, p. 360.

My child! Don't blame death, don't make fun of someone who is sick and do not avoid doing good deeds.[1]

It is narrated about Imām Ṣādiq ؑ:

ن: أَتَاهُ مَوْلًى لَهُ فَسَلَّمَ عَلَيْهِ وَ مَعَهُ ابْنُهُ إِسْمَاعِيلُ فَسَلَّمَ عَلَيْهِ وَ جَلَسَ فَلَمَّا انْصَرَفَ أَبُو عَبْدِ اللَّهِ ع انْصَرَفَ مَعَهُ الرَّجُلُ فَلَمَّا انْتَهَى أَبُو عَبْدِ اللَّهِ ع إِلَى بَابِ دَارِهِ دَخَلَ وَ تَرَكَ الرَّجُلَ وَ قَالَ لَهُ ابْنُهُ إِسْمَاعِيلُ يَا أَبَهْ أَلَّا كُنْتَ عَرَضْتَ عَلَيْهِ الدُّخُولَ فَقَالَ لَمْ يَكُنْ مِنْ شَأْنِي إِدْخَالُهُ قَالَ فَهُوَ لَمْ يَكُنْ يَدْخُلُ قَالَ يَا بُنَيَّ إِنِّي أَكْرَهُ أَنْ يَكْتُبَنِي اللَّهُ عَرَّاضا

One of the cothere andf Imām Ṣādiq ؑ came to him and greeted the Imām and also greeted Ismā'īl, Imām's ؑ son, who was also present there, and sat down. After a while, Imām ؑ left that place and that man also accompanied him. When Imām ؑ reached his place, he separated from that man, Ismā'īl said: Father, why did you not ask him to come inside? Imām ؑ said, "I was not prepared to receive him." Ismā'īl said: He would not have actually come into the house. The Imām ؑ said, "My son, I did not want Allāh ﷻ to record a fault of mine."[2]

It is narrated that:

'Alī ؑ said to his son, Imām Ḥasan ؑ:

واقْبِل عُذْرَ مَن اعْتَذَر إليْك، وخُذْ العَفْوَ من النَّاس

"Accept the excuse of someone, who apologizes to you, and accept forgiveness from the people."[3]

'Alī b. Ja'far has narrated from his honourable brother, Imām Kāẓim ؑ as follows:

اَخَذَ أبی بِيَدی ثُمّ قَالَ: يا بُنَیّ، اِنَّ أبی مُحَمّدَ بنَ عَلیٍّ أخَذَ بِيَدی، كَما أخَذتُ

---

[1] *Majmu'ah Warrām*, p. 421.
[2] *Biḥār al-'Anwār*, vol. 75, p. 457.
[3] *Kanz al-'Ummāl*, vol. 16, p. 269.

بیدکَ قالَ: وَإِنَّ أبی عَلیَّ بْنَ الحُسَینِ أخَذَ بِیَدی وَقالَ : یا بُنَیّ،وَإِن شَتَمَکَ رَجُلٌ عَنْ یَمینِکَ ثُمَّ تَحَوَّلَ إِلی یَسارِکَ وَاعتَذَرَ إِلَیکَ فَاقبَل مِنه

"My father took my hand and said: My son! My father - Imām Bāqir ﷺ – once held my hand in the same way as I hold your hand and said: My father 'Alī b. Al-Ḥusain ﷺ held my hand and said...If a person sitting on your right curses, you and then goes to sit on your left and apologizes, you must accept his apology."[1]

Keeping the secrets of others

One of the important issues that a child should observe in his social relations with others is keeping the secrets of his brothers and friends; as disrespect and disloyalty to friends causes weakness in friendships; on the contrary it takes away one's dignity and self-esteem.

'Alī ﷺ said to Imām Ḥasan ﷺ:

... ولا تُذِعْ سِرَّهُ وإن أذاعَ سِرَّك

"Do not divulge the secrets of your friend, even if he has exposed yours."[2]

'Alī ﷺ said to Imām Ḥusain ﷺ:

وَ مَنْ هَتَكَ حِجَابَ غَيْرِهِ انْكَشَفَتْ عَوْرَاتُ بَيْتِه

"Whoever exposes the veil (of reputation and personality) of another, the faults of his family members will also be exposed."[3]

Avoid cruelty.

Cruelty and oppression are major sins. Oppressing others leads to the deprivation of peace and security of the society and destroys the limits and boundaries of relationships and social rights of individuals and becomes the source of large disturbances.

---

[1] *Majmu'ah Warrām*, p. 351; *Wasā'il al-Shī'ah*, vol. 11, p. 528.
[2] *Biḥār al-'Anwār*, vol. 74, p. 208.
[3] *Tuḥaf al-'Uqūl*, p. 84.

In the family, children should learn from their parents' behaviour to respect the rights of others, their personality, property, wealth, and belongings and not to encroach on anyone's rights, even if they are weak and cannot defend their rights. Especially during childhood and adolescence, they must avoid every kind of harassment and annoyance of others and consider the displeasure and suffering of others as their own suffering and displeasure and displeasure of the Almighty.

Abū Ḥamzah Thumālī narrates from Imām Bāqir ﵇:

لَمَّا حَضَرَ عَلِيَّ بْنَ الْحُسَيْنِ ع الْوَفَاةُ ضَمَّنِي إِلَى صَدْرِهِ ثُمَّ قَالَ يَا بُنَيَّ أُوصِيكَ بِمَا أَوْصَانِي بِهِ أَبِي ع حِينَ حَضَرَتْهُ الْوَفَاةُ وَ بِمَا ذَكَرَ أَنَّ أَبَاهُ أَوْصَاهُ بِهِ قَالَ يَا بُنَيَّ إِيَّاكَ وَ ظُلْمَ مَنْ لَا يَجِدُ عَلَيْكَ نَاصِراً إِلَّا اللَّه

"When my father was on the verge of death, he clasped me to his chest and said: My son! I advise you to what my father said to me at the time of his passing, and it was a bequest that his forefathers had also made. Then Imām ﵇ said: My son! Do not oppress one who has no helper, except Allāh ﷻ."[1]

Luqmān the Wise said to his son:

يا بُنَيَّ، الفَقْرُ خَيْرٌ مِنْ أن تَظْلِمَ وَتَطغىٰ

My child! Poverty and destitution are better than oppressing others.[2]

He also said:

يَا بُنَيَّ لَا تَرْثِ لِمَنْ ظَلَمْتَهُ وَ لَكِنِ ارْثِ لِسُوءِ مَا جَنَيْتَهُ عَلَى نَفْسِكَ وَ إِذَا دَعَتْكَ الْقُدْرَةُ إِلَى ظُلْمِ النَّاسِ فَاذْكُرْ قُدْرَةَ اللَّهِ عَلَيْكَ

My child! Do not cry for someone you have wronged; rather, weep for the crime you have carried on your soul, and when your power and

[1] *Biḥār al-'Anwār*, vol. 75, p. 308, *Majmu'ah Warrām*, p. 366; *Tuḥaf al-'Uqūl*, p. 251.
[2] *al-Ikhtiṣāṣ*, p. 332.

position make you inclined to oppress others, remember the power that Allāh Almighty has over you.¹

Avoid enmity.

'Alī said to Imām Ḥasan:

$$\text{يَا بُنَيَّ بِئْسَ الزَّادُ إِلَى الْمَعَادِ الْعُدْوَانُ عَلَى الْعِبَادِ}$$

"My child! The worst provision for the Hereafter is enmity with others."²

Luqmān the Wise says to his son:

$$\text{يَا بُنَيَّ لَا تُكَالِبِ النَّاسَ فَيَمْقَتُوكَ وَ لَا تَكُنْ مَهِيناً فَيُذِلُّوكَ وَ لَا تَكُنْ حُلْواً فَيَأْكُلُوكَ وَ لَا تَكُنْ مُرّاً فَيَلْفِظُوكَ}$$

My child! Do not clash with people in the world, because they will harbor grudge against you; and do not insult anyone as they will regard you debased, and neither be so sweet that they eat you up (take undue advantage) nor be so bitter that they throw you away.³

Refrain from confrontation.

The practice of the Infallibles was that they never repaid the oppression or lack of politeness of others in the same currency, except when Allāh's commandments were disregarded. On the contrary they were forgiving when it came to personal issues, because forgiveness is tastier than revenge.

'Alī said to Imām Ḥasan:

$$\text{وَلَا تَطْلُبَنَّ مُجَازَراةَ أَخِيكَ وَإِن حَثَا الترابَ بِفِيكَ}$$

---

¹ *Biḥār al-'Anwār*, vol. 13, p. 426; *Majmu'ah Warrām*, p. 422.
² *Tuḥaf al-'Uqūl*, p. 86.
³ *al-Ikhtiṣāṣ*, p. 333.

"My child! Don't seek revenge from your brother, even if he has cast dust into your mouth."[1]

'Alī ﷺ says to his son, Imām Ḥasan ﷺ:

أطِع أخاك وإنْ عَصاك، وصَلْه وإنْ جَفاك

"Obey your brother even if he disobeys you and remain attached to him even if he persecutes you."[2]

'Alī ﷺ said to Imām Ḥasan ﷺ:

احْمِلْ نَفْسَكَ مَعَ أَخِيكَ عِنْدَ صَرْمِهِ عَلَى الصِّلَةِ وَ عِنْدَ صُدُودِهِ عَلَى اللُّطْفِ وَ الْمَسْأَلَةِ وَ عِنْدَ جُمُودِهِ عَلَى الْبَذْلِ وَ عِنْدَ تَبَاعُدِهِ عَلَى الدُّنُوِّ وَ عِنْدَ شِدَّتِهِ عَلَى اللِّينِ وَ عِنْدَ جُرْمِهِ عَلَى الِاعْتِذَارِ حَتَّى كَأَنَّكَ لَهُ عَبْدٌ وَ كَأَنَّهُ ذُو نِعْمَةٍ عَلَيْكَ وَ إِيَّاكَ أَنْ تَضَعَ ذَلِكَ فِي غَيْرِ مَوْضِعِه وَ أَنْ تَفْعَلَهُ بِغَيْرِ أَهْلِه

"When your brother drives you away, persuade yourself to bond with him, and when he turns away from you, turn towards him with grace and kindness and aim for interaction with him and his friendship. When he shows rudeness and miserliness, forgive him and be benevolent, and when he stays away, you approach him, and when he is rude to you, you be kind to him, and when he commits a mistake, ask forgiveness for him, as if you are his saviour and he is the bestower of blessings on you, and do not use these good manners inappropriately and don't use them on one undeserving of them."[3]

Trustworthiness

One of the most desirable qualities in a person is his trustworthiness. Trustworthiness with the people of the society bestows trust and peace. When everyone trusts each other and suspicion disappears, life becomes sweeter, and people help each other more than before.

---

[1] *Biḥār al-'Anwār*, vol. 74, p. 209.

[2] *Tuḥaf al-'Uqūl*, p. 82; *Kanz al-'Ummāl*, vol. 16, p. 182 (with a slight difference).

[3] *Biḥār al-'Anwār*, vol. 74, p. 209.

It is narrated from Imām Kāẓim ﷺ that he said to his son:

يَا بُنَيَّ أَدِّ الْأَمَانَةَ يَسْلَمْ لَكَ دُنْيَاكَ وَ آخِرَتُكَ وَ كُنْ أَمِيناً تَكُنْ غَنِيّاً

"My child! Return the trust to its owner so that your world and the Hereafter remain good and be trustworthy so that you become wealthy and needless."[1]

Imām ʿAlī ﷺ said to his son, Imām Ḥasan Mujtabā ﷺ:

وَ لَا تَخُنْ مَنِ ائْتَمَنَكَ وَ إِنْ خَانَك

"My child! Don't betray someone who trusted you, even if he betrayed you."[2]

Luqmān the Wise said to his son:

يَا بُنَيَّ إِيَّاكَ أَنْ تَسْتَدِينَ فَتَخُونَ مِنَ الدَّيْن

My child! Don't borrow from others and then betray in returning it.[3]

Precedence in goodness

When your child understands the sweetness and pleasure of community life, he rushes to the help of his comrades, takes care of the shortcomings of their lives, and removes sadness of his brothers from their hearts.

Now, it is your responsibility as parents, to introduce and encourage your children for good deeds and cooperation and collaboration with other Muslim brothers.

The Holy Qur'ān and the words of the Infallibles ﷺ as well as the life of those nobles are emphatic about this issue. Amīr al Mu'minīn ﷺ used to dig wells with his own hands, cultivate palm trees and distribute them among the poor in the way of Allāh ﷻ. At night, he himself and his sons used to knock the doors of the poor and deliver

---

[1] *Biḥār al-'Anwār*, vol. 75, p. 117 and v. 13, p. 416; *Majmuʿah Warrām*, p. 421.

[2] *Biḥār al-'Anwār*, vol. 74, p. 208.

[3] *al-Ikhtiṣāṣ*, p. 332.

them bread and food, while concealing their identities. The Holy Qur'ān says:

$$...وَتَعَاوَنُواْ عَلَى ٱلْبِرِّ وَٱلتَّقْوَىٰ وَلَا تَعَاوَنُواْ عَلَى ٱلْإِثْمِ وَٱلْعُدْوَٰنِۚ...$$

> "...Cooperate in piety and God wariness, but do not cooperate in sin and aggression..."[1]

Marāzim b. Ḥakīm narrates from Imām Ṣādiq that he said: My father used to say:

$$اِذا هَمَمْتَ فَبَادِرْ فَاِنَّكَ لا تَدري ما يَحْدُثُ$$

"If you want to do a good deed, do it immediately; you don't know what may happen (later)."[2]

'Alī b. Ja'far narrates from his brother, Imām Mūsā Kāẓim that:

$$أَخَذَ أَبِي بِيَدِي ثُمَّ قَالَ يَا بُنَيَّ- إِنَّ أَبِي مُحَمَّدَ بْنَ عَلِيٍّ ع أَخَذَ بِيَدِي كَمَا أَخَذْتُ بِيَدِكَ وَ قَالَ إِنَّ أَبِي عَلِيَّ بْنَ الْحُسَيْنِ ع أَخَذَ بِيَدِي وَ قَالَ يَا بُنَيَّ افْعَلِ الْخَيْرَ إِلَى كُلِّ مَنْ طَلَبَهُ مِنْكَ فَإِنْ كَانَ مِنْ أَهْلِهِ فَقَدْ أَصَبْتَ مَوْضِعَهُ وَ إِنْ لَمْ يَكُنْ مِنْ أَهْلِهِ كُنْتَ أَنْتَ مِنْ أَهْلِه$$

"(Once) my father took my hand and said: My son! My father, Muḥammad b. 'Alī also held my hand as I have held your hand and said: My father, 'Alī b. al-Ḥusain held my hand and said: My son! Whoever asks you to do a good deed for him, do it for him; if he is worthy of it, you have reached your goal, and if he is not worthy, you will be worthy of it."[3]

Imām Ṣādiq used to say to his son:

---

[1] Sūrah al-Mā'idah 5:2.
[2] *Wasā'il al-Shī'ah*, vol. 1, p. 84.
[3] *Wasā'il al-Shī'ah*, vol. 11, p. 528; *Tuḥaf al-'Uqūl*, p. 290; *Majmū'ah Warrām*, p.351.

يا بُنَيَّ، اِجْعَل مَعْرُوفَكَ فى أهْلِه، وَكُنْ فيه طالباً لِثَوابِ الله ، وكُنْ مُقتَصِداً، وَلا تَمْسِكْه تَقتيراً، وَلا تُعطِه تَبْذيراً

"My child, direct your goodness and benevolence to those who are worthy of it and through it seek Allāh's ﷻ pleasure and reward. Be moderate in good deeds; neither be parsimonious nor be wasteful."[1]

B) Interaction with scholars and intellectuals

One of the moral and educational duties of fathers towards their children is to familiarize them with Islamic scholars and intellectuals. Because being in their company and getting to know them has many educational and moral effects and blessings, and it is obvious that the principle of closeness and intimacy with each person has a positive effect on transferring his traits and morals to others. Especially, that person should be a committed scholar and a pious intellectual and must be treading the path of Islam. Therefore, it is up to the father to make the child familiar with the real image of the true scholars and to make him interested in them, and this itself will play a significant role in the future of the child's life.

What are the signs of the scholar?

Imām Ṣādiq ؑ said: Luqmān said to his son:

يا بُنَيَّ...وَ لِلْعَالِمِ ثَلَاثُ عَلَامَاتٍ الْعِلْمُ بِاللَّهِ وَ بِمَا يُحِبُّ وَ مَا يَكْرَهُ

"My son! Three signs of a scholar are that (1) He should have knowledge of Allāh ﷻ (2) and what is pleasing to Him and (3) what He dislikes."[2]

Explanation

[1] *Biḥār al-'Anwār*, vol. 13, p. 420.
[2] *Biḥār al-'Anwār*, vol. 13, p. 415.

A scholar and an intellectual is worthy of friendship and companionship, and from the point of view of education, it is considered a true guiding ethic that he must be God-knowing and God-fearing. His knowledge of the Creator causes him to obey His commands and adhere to divine obligations and values, and to avoid taboos and unlawful things. Such a person can be a role model.

Therefore, we should introduce our children to such divine scholars, not every intellectual who has only memorized a little terminology.

Benefits of the company of scholars

Imām ʿAlī ؑ, in his will to his son, Imām Ḥusain ؑ says:

وَ مَنْ خَالَطَ الْعُلَمَاءَ وُقِّرَ

"Whoever associates with scholars should be treated with dignity and respect."[1]

Luqmān the Wise says to his son:

أَيْ بُنَيَّ صَاحِبِ الْعُلَمَاءَ وَ جَالِسْهُمْ وَ زُرْهُمْ فِي بُيُوتِهِمْ لَعَلَّكَ أَنْ تُشْبِهَهُمْ فَتَكُونَ مِنْهُمْ

My child! Be friends and with scholars and cultivate their company, visit them in their homes; perhaps you will start resembling them and become one with them.[2]

He also said to his son:

جَالِسِ الْعُلَمَاءَ أَوْ زَاحِمْهُمْ بِرُكْبَتَيْكَ فَإِنَّ اللَّهَ يُحْيِي الْقُلُوبَ بِنُورِ الْحِكْمَةِ كَمَا يُحْيِي الْأَرْضَ بِوَابِلِ السَّمَاءِ

---

[1] *Tuḥaf al-ʿUqūl*, p. 84.
[2] *Biḥār al-ʾAnwār*, vol. 13, p. 432, v. 75, p. 458.

Interact with scholars and sit with folded knees before them (politely), because Allāh ﷻ revives hearts with the light of wisdom, just as He revives the earth with the heavy rains of the sky.[1]

It is indeed meant to encourage them to attend the gatherings of scholars and intellectuals and cultivate their company to acquire Islamic knowledge and learn what one is ignorant of and to understand the ways and customs of life. And that to make them their practical model and tap into the source of divine knowledge through their graceful channel.

Again, one of the advice of Luqmān the Wise to his son is that he said:

يَا بُنَيَّ تَعَلَّمْ مِنَ الْعُلَمَاءِ مَا جَهِلْتَ وَ عَلِّمِ النَّاسَ مَا عَلِمْتَ

My child! Learn what you don't know from scholars and teach people what you have learned.[2]

Amīr al Mu'minīn ؑ says in his will to his son, Muḥammad b. al-Hanafiyyah:

يَا بُنَيَّ اقْبَلْ مِنَ الْحُكَمَاءِ مَوَاعِظَهُمْ وَ تَدَبَّرْ أَحْكَامَهُمْ

"My child! Accept the advice of the wise and ponder upon their judgments."[3]

And that wise sage also says:

يَا بُنَيَّ تَعَلَّمِ الْحِكْمَةَ تَشَرَّفْ بِهَا فَإِنَّ الْحِكْمَةَ تَدُلُّ عَلَى الدِّينِ وَ تُشَرِّفُ الْعَبْدَ عَلَى الْحُرِّ وَ تَرْفَعُ الْمِسْكِينَ عَلَى الْغَنِيِّ وَ تُقَدِّمُ الصَّغِيرَ عَلَى الْكَبِيرِ وَ تُجْلِسُ الْمِسْكِينَ مَجَالِسَ الْمُلُوكِ وَ تَزِيدُ الشَّرِيفَ شَرَفاً وَ السَّيِّدَ سُؤْدُداً وَ الْغَنِيَّ مَجْداً وَ كَيْفَ يَظُنُّ ابْنُ آدَمَ أَنْ يَتَهَيَّأَ لَهُ أَمْرُ دِينِهِ وَ مَعِيشَتِهِ بِغَيْرِ حِكْمَةٍ وَ لَنْ يُهَيِّئَ اللَّهُ عَزَّ وَ جَلَّ أَمْرَ

---

[1] *Majmu'ah Warrām*, p. 59.
[2] *Majmu'ah Warrām*, p. 422; *Biḥār al-'Anwār*, vol. 13, p. 426.
[3] *Nūr al-Thaqlayn*, vol. 4, p. 20.

الدُّنْيَا وَ الْآخِرَةِ إِلَّا بِالْحِكْمَةِ وَ مَثَلُ الْحِكْمَةِ بِغَيْرِ طَاعَةٍ مَثَلُ الْجَسَدِ بِغَيْرِ نَفْسٍ وَ مَثَلُ الصَّعِيدِ بِغَيْرِ مَاءٍ وَ لَا صَلَاحَ لِلْجَسَدِ بِغَيْرِ نَفْسٍ وَ لَا لِلصَّعِيدِ بِغَيْرِ مَاءٍ وَ لَا لِلْحِكْمَةِ بِغَيْرِ طَاعَة

My child! Learn wisdom by which you will find honour and greatness; because learning wisdom is an indicator of a person's religion, and it is wisdom and knowledge that makes the slave superior to the freemen, and the poor and the helpless superior to the rich, and puts the small before the great, and puts the poor in the place of kings and increases the honour of the honourable and greatness of the great, and grants prosperity and greatness to the wealthy.

(My child) How one imagines that the needs of his religion and livelihood will be provided to him without wisdom, while Allāh ﷻ never entrusts the affairs of this world and the Hereafter to anyone without wisdom.

(My child) The example of wisdom without obedience and service is like a body without life and earth without water. Just as a body without a soul has no value and no land is settled without water, so no wisdom is effective without obedience and service.[1]

Luqmān says to his son:

يَا بُنَيَّ لَا تُجَادِلِ الْعُلَمَاءَ فَيَمْقُتُوك

My child! Don't argue and fight with people, as they would become inimical to you.[2]

C) Foresight

Foresight and thinking before doing anything is the most desirable trait. Parents should make their children familiar with it; because many people were trapped or were exposed to difficult problems due to only a single moment of negligence.

---

[1] *Biḥār al-'Anwār*, vol. 75, p. 458.
[2] *Majmu'ah Warrām*, p. 77.

In his will to his son, Imām Ḥasan ﷺ, Amīr al Mu'minīn ﷺ says:

... التَّدْبِيرُ قَبْلَ الْعَمَلِ يُؤْمِنُكَ النَّدَم

"Contemplation and forethought secure you from regret."[1]

He also said:

أَيْ بُنَيَّ الْفِكْرَةُ تُورِثُ نُوراً وَ الْغَفْلَةُ ظُلْمَةٌ وَ الْجَهَالَةُ ضَلاَلَة

"My son! Contemplation brings light, neglect and argumentation lead astray."[2]

He also said:

ومَن اعتبَرَ اعتزَلَ، ومَن اعتزَلَ سَلِم

"Whoever contemplates, learns a lesson, whoever learns a lesson, chooses isolation, and whoever isolates remains safe (from the seditions of the times)."[3]

He also said:

وَ الطُّمَأْنِينَةُ قَبْلَ الْخِبْرَةِ ضِدُّ الْحَزْم

"Trusting (someone) before testing him is opposed to foresight."[4]

And he said:

وَ أَنْهَاكَ عَنِ التَّسَرُّعِ بِالْقَوْلِ وَ الْفِعْلِ وَ إِذَا عَرَضَ شَيْءٌ مِنْ أَمْرِ الْآخِرَةِ فَابْدَأْ بِهِ وَ إِذَا عَرَضَ شَيْءٌ مِنْ أَمْرِ الدُّنْيَا فَلاَ تَأْتِهِ حَتَّى تُصِيبَ رُشْدَكَ فِيه

---

[1] *Tuḥaf al-'Uqūl*, p. 86.
[2] *Tuḥaf al-'Uqūl*, p. 85.
[3] *Tuḥaf al-'Uqūl*, p. 84.
[4] *Tuḥaf al-'Uqūl*, p. 85.

"I forbid you to be hasty in speech or action, and if you are faced with an issue of the Hereafter, deal with it. And if you are faced with a worldly matter, don't do it until you think it is good for you and you become aware of its reality."[1]

He also said:

وَمَنْ تَوَرَّطَ فِي الْأُمُورِ غَيْرَ نَاظِرٍ فِي الْعَوَاقِبِ، فَقَدْ تَعَرَّضَ لِمُفْضِحَاتِ النَّوَائِبِ

"Whoever engages in work without thinking about the consequences would be exposed to difficult problems."[2]

He also said:

وأَمْسِكْ عن طَريقٍ إذا خِفْتَ ضَلالَتَه، فإنَّ الكَفَّ عند حَيْرَةِ الضَّلالِ خَيْرٌ من رُكُوبِ الأَهْوال

"Refrain from going on the path whose misguidance you fear, because avoiding the abyss of deviation is better than getting caught in the vortex of horror."[3]

1. Dealing with problems of life

Ever since man stepped on the earth and recognized himself, he has always struggled with the problems and bitterness of life and sometimes he overcame them and sometimes he has been defeated by them.

Parents carry a collection of diverse life experiences; they are familiar with the problems and hardships of the past for many years and its bitter and sweet blessings. Therefore, they should pass on their experiences to their children and prepare them for the problems they might face in the summers and winters of life. Their gradual and guided instruction with the different aspects of life will save them from

[1] *Majmu'ah Warrām*, p.378.
[2] *Tuḥaf al-'Uqūl*, p. 86.
[3] *Biḥār al-'Anwār*, vol. 84, p. 200.

laziness and carelessness. In that case, if one day children face a problem - in any relationship - they will not give up; they will not be overcome fear and terror, but they would gather courage and like a strong mountain remain steadfast and patient and try to get out of that tight corner; because they have the experience of their parents as a useful tool and they are well prepared. Unlike a child who grew up pampered, who does not have any kind of familiarity with hardships and problems, and therefore, when faced with the smallest adversity, he quickly loses hope and self-confidence and feels defeated.

In some traditions, it is mentioned that you should sometimes pressurize children when they are young so that they will be patient when they grow up.

Ṣāliḥ b. ʿUqbah says:

سَمِعْتُ الْعَبْدَ الصَّالِحَ ع يَقُولُ يُسْتَحَبُّ غَرَامَةُ الْغُلَامِ فِي صِغَرِهِ لِيَكُونَ حَلِيماً فِي كِبَرِهِ

I heard Imām Mūsā Kāẓim say, "It is recommended to discipline a boy in his childhood so that he will be patient when he is grown up."[1]

1. Hope in Allāh and supplication

The foremost and the only way a person can make his problems and pains bearable, is to trust in his Creator and Lord and to pray to Him.

He is the Lord in whose control everything lies, and the problem of humans is nothing as compared to His power. When we regard Him as our custodian and put our reliance on Him, the heavy burden of problems will automatically be removed from our shoulders; because:

...مَن يَتَوَكَّلْ عَلَى ٱللَّهِ فَهُوَ حَسْبُهُۥ...

"Allāh will suffice for whoever that trusts in Him."[2]

---

[1] *Wasāʾil al-Shīʿah*, vol. 5, p. 126.
[2] Sūrah al-Ṭalāq 65 : 3.

Even if the whole world turns its back on them, since they have Allāh ﷻ with them, they have no sorrow. Those who have no support in the world, but regard Allāh ﷻ as their support and rely on Him, are not few and they became the perfect exemplars of humanity.

In his youth, Ibrāhīm ﵇ was thrown into the midst of a burning fire by the tyrant, Namrūd, but by trusting in Allāh ﷻ and taking refuge in him, in front of the stunned Namrūd and his followers that boundless fire turned into a blooming garden and made everyone aware that it was only Allāh ﷻ who defended Ibrāhīm against all his enemies and he did not need any other support.

During his childhood Prophet Yūsuf ﵇ was thrown into a well by his brothers, and he had no hope except for Allāh ﷻ, and this very attachment and reliance became a factor for Allāh ﷻ to save him from the dark well and grant him power and greatness.

There are many such examples in the history of Islam and Islamic traditional reports, among which is the following:

Ibrāhīm's ﵇ conversation with Ismā'īl ﵇ on a difficult mission

Qutub Rāwandī says:

رُوِىَ أنَّ اِبراهيم قالَ لاِسماعيلَ عليه السلام فى حالِ الذِّبحِ: اُدعُ أنتَ بِالفَرَجَ ؛ لأنّكَ الْمُضطَر (أمَّن يُجيبُ الْمُضطَرَّاِذا دَعاه) فَلَمّا رَأى الْكَبش خَرَجَ لِيَاخُذَه، فَلمَّا رَجَع رَأى يَدَى اِسماعيلَ مُطلقَتينِ،، قال: وَمَنْ أطْلَقَكَ؟ قالَ: رَجُلُ مَنْ صِفَتُه كَذا، قالَ: هُو جِبْرَئيلُ. وَهَلْ قالَ لَكَ؟ قالَ: نَعَمْ قالَ لى: اُدعُ اللهَ فَدَعُوَتُكَ الآنَ مستجابَة. قالَ اِبراهيمُ: وأىُّ شَىءٍ دَعَوْتَ؟ قالَ: قُلتُ: اَللّهمَّ اغفِرْلِلمُؤمِنينَ وَالمُؤمِناتِ. قالَ : يا بُنَىّ، اِنَّكَ لَمُوَفَّقٌ

It is narrated that when Ibrāhīm ﵇ (had tied up the hands and feet of Ismā'īl ﵇) and was ready to slaughter him, he said to Ismā'īl: Pray for an opening, because now you are in real distress.

أَمَّن يُجِيبُ ٱلْمُضْطَرَّ إِذَا دَعَاهُ وَيَكْشِفُ ٱلسُّوٓءَ...

"Is He who answers the call of the distressed [person] when he invokes Him and removes his distress..."[1]

Just then he noticed a big ram. He immediately left his place and went to the ram. When he returned, he saw that the rope tying the hands of Ismāʿīl ﷺ was undone. He asked in amazement: Who untied your hands?

Ismāʿīl ﷺ said: A man of such and such description. Ibrāhīm ﷺ said: He was Jibra'īl ﷺ. Did he tell you something?

Ismāʿīl ﷺ replied: Yes, he said to me: Pray, because your prayer is now being answered.

Ibrāhīm ﷺ said: My son, what did you pray? Ismāʿīl ﷺ said: I said: Allāh ﷻ, forgive all believing men and women. Ibrāhīm ﷺ said: My son, (this is Allāh's ﷻ blessing and) you are a fortunate person.[2]

By surrendering to his father, Ismāʿīl ﷺ had surrendered to the will of Allāh ﷻ, and at that crucial time, when he apparently saw no way out for himself, he only trusted in and took refuge in Allāh ﷻ and Allāh ﷻ never forsakes a servant who has taken refuge in Him, especially in a sensitive situation, and He helps him immediately.

If you have a problem, recite...

Imām Riḍā ﷺ said:

رَأيتُ أبى فى المَنامِ فَقالَ: يا بُنَىَّ، اذا كُنتَ فى شِدَّة فَأكْثِرْ مِن أن تَقولَ: يا رَؤُفُ يا رَحيمُ

"I saw my father in dream, and he told me: My son! If you have a problem, repeat in excess: O, Gentle one, O Merciful (*Yā Rawufu Yā Raḥīmu*).[3]

[1] Sūrah al-Naml 27:62.
[2] *Mustadrak al-Wasā'il*, p. 247.
[3] *Biḥār al-'Anwār*, vol. 93, p. 272.

Never despair of supplicating

Imām Ṣādiq (a) said:

قال لُقمان : يَا بُنَي وَ لاَ تَضْجَرَنَّ بِطَلَبِ حَاجَةٍ فَإِنَّ قَضَاءَهَا بِيَدِ اللَّهِ وَ لَهَا أَوْقَاتٌ وَ لَكِنِ ارْغَبْ إِلَى اللَّهِ وَ سَلْهُ وَ حَرِّكْ إِلَيْهِ أَصَابِعَك

"Luqmān said to his son: My son, don't get tired of praying for your needs, because fulfillment of your needs is only in the hands of Allāh (swt), who has a specific time and place; but turn to Allāh (swt) with inclination and ask Him for your needs and move your fingers towards Him while praying."[1]

In the letter of Imām 'Alī (a) to his son, Imām Ḥasan Mujtabā (a), it is mentioned as follows:

ثُم جَعَلَ بِيَدِكَ مَفَاتِيحَ خَزَائِنِه فَأَلْحِحْ فِي الْمَسْأَلَةِ يَفْتَحْ لَكَ بَابَ الرَّحْمَةِ بِمَا أَذِنَ لَكَ فِيهِ مِنْ مَسْأَلَتِهِ فَمَتَى شِئْتَ اسْتَفْتَحْتَ بِالدُّعَاءِ أَبْوَابَ خَزَائِنِهِ فَأَلْحِحْ وَ لاَ يُقَنِّطْكَ إِنْ أَبْطَأَتْ عَنْكَ الْإِجَابَةُ فَإِنَّ الْعَطِيَّةَ عَلَى قَدْرِ الْمَسْأَلَةِ وَ رُبَّمَا أُخِّرَتْ عَنْكَ الْإِجَابَةُ لِيَكُونَ أَطْوَلَ لِلْمَسْأَلَةِ وَ أَجْزَلَ لِلْعَطِيَّةِ وَ رُبَّمَا سَأَلْتَ الشَّيْءَ فَلَمْ تُؤْتَاهُ وَ أُوتِيتَ خَيْراً مِنْهُ عَاجِلاً وَ آجِلاً أَوْ صُرِفَ عَنْكَ لِمَا هُوَ خَيْرٌ لَكَ فَلَرُبَّ أَمْرٍ قَدْ طَلَبْتَهُ فِيهِ هَلاَكُ دِينِكَ لَوْ أُوتِيتَهُ

"Then Almighty Allāh has placed the keys of His treasuries in your hands in the sense that He has shown you the way to ask Him. Therefore, wherever you wish, open the doors of His favour with prayer. And let the abundant rains of His mercy fall on you. Delay in acceptance of the prayer should not disappoint you because the grant of prayer is according to the measure of (your) intention. Sometimes acceptance (of prayer) is delayed with a view to its being a source of greater reward to the asker and of better gifts to the expectant.

[1] *Biḥār al-'Anwār*, vol. 13, p. 420.

Sometimes you ask for a thing, but it is not given to you, and a better thing is given to you later or a thing is taken away from you for some greater good of yours, because sometimes you ask for a thing, which contains ruin for your religion if it is given to you."[1]

2. Prayers to solve problems

Abū Ḥamzah al-Thumālī narrates from Imām al-Bāqir ﵇, he said:

كَانَ أَبِي يَقُولُ لِوُلْدِهِ يَا بَنِيَّ إِذَا أَصَابَتْكُمْ مُصِيبَةٌ مِنَ الدُّنْيَا وَ نَزَلَتْ بِكُمْ فَاقَةٌ فَلْيَتَوَضَّأِ الرَّجُلُ فَلْيُحْسِنْ وُضُوءَهُ فَلْيُصَلِّ أَرْبَعَ رَكَعَاتٍ أَوْ رَكْعَتَيْنِ فَإِذَا انْصَرَفَ مِنْ صَلَاتِهِ فَلْيَقُلْ

My father, Imām ʻAlī b. Ḥusain ﵇ used to say to his children: My children, if you are afflicted with a calamity or poverty, need, or a difficult matter, one of you should perform ablution for prayer and pray four or two units and after the prayer recite this supplication:

يَا مَوْضِعَ كُلِّ شَكْوَى يَا سَامِعَ كُلِّ نَجْوَى يَا شَافِيَ كُلِّ بَلَاءٍ يَا عَالِمَ كُلِّ خَفِيَّةٍ وَ يَا كَاشِفَ مَا يَشَاءُ مِنْ بَلِيَّةٍ يَا نَجِيَّ مُوسَى يَا مُصْطَفِيَ مُحَمَّدٍ ص يَا خَلِيلَ إِبْرَاهِيمَ أَدْعُوكَ دُعَاءَ مَنِ اشْتَدَّتْ فَاقَتُهُ وَ ضَعُفَتْ قُوَّتُهُ وَ قَلَّتْ حِيلَتُهُ دُعَاءَ الْغَرِيبِ الْغَرِيقِ الْفَقِيرِ الَّذِي لَا يَجِدُ لِكَشْفِ مَا هُوَ فِيهِ إِلَّا أَنْتَ يَا أَرْحَمَ الرَّاحِمِينَ لَا إِلَهَ إِلَّا أَنْتَ سُبْحَانَكَ إِنِّي كُنْتُ مِنَ الظَّالِمِينَ

O one, Who is the object of all complaints! O listener of every whispered supplication! O healer of every sorrow! O knower of every secret! O remover of the evils that He wills! O saviour of Mūsā ﵇, the chooser of Muḥammad ﷺ, O one who took Ibrāhīm ﵇ as His friend! I call You like one, who is starving and helpless, whose strength is depleted, whose solutions are reduced. I pray to you like a drowned person, a stranger, and a poor man, who has no other

---

[1] *Tuḥaf al-ʻUqūl*, vol. 73; *Biḥār al-'Anwār*, vol. 74, p. 205.

way or solution to solve his problem except You, O Most merciful of the merciful ones. Glory be to You; I was among the wrong doers!

قَالَ عَلِيُّ بْنُ الْحُسَيْنِ ع لَا يَدْعُو بِهَا رَجُلٌ أَصَابَهُ بَلَاءٌ إِلَّا فَرَّجَ اللَّهُ تَعَالَى عَنْه

'Alī b. Ḥusain ﷺ then said: No one who is in trouble will recite this supplication except that Allāh ﷻ will create an opening for him.[1]

3. Patience and endurance

Another way to deal with problems is patience and stability and not backing down in the face of problems.

Sa'dī says:

Patience (*Ṣabr*) and victory (*Ẓafar*) are two old friends; victory is achieved due to patience.

'Alī ﷺ said:

لَا يَعْدَمُ الصَّبُورُ الظَّفَرَ وَ إِنْ طَالَ بِهِ الزَّمَان

"A patient person is not deprived of victory, even though the time of patience may be prolonged."[2]

Imām 'Alī ﷺ said in his will to Imām Ḥusain ﷺ:

وَ مِنْ كُنُوزِ الْإِيمَانِ الصَّبْرُ عَلَى الْمَصَائِب

"Patience in adversity is one of the treasures of faith."[3]

He also said:

الصَّبْرُ جُنَّةٌ مِنَ الْفَاقَة

"Patience is a shield against poverty and misery."[4]

---

[1] Ibn. Ṣabbāgh Mālikī, *al-Fuṣūl al-Muhimmah*, p. 188, *Mustadrak al-Wasā'il*, vol. 6, p. 392.
[2] *Nahj al-Balaghah*, Saying 145.
[3] *Tuḥaf al-'Uqūl*, p. 85.
[4] *Tuḥaf al-'Uqūl*, p. 86.

Also, in his will to Imām Ḥasan Mujtabā ﷺ, he said:

اطْرَحْ عَنْكَ وَارِدَاتِ الأُمُورِ بِعَزَائِمِ الصَّبْرِ وَ حُسْنِ الْيَقِين

"Cast away the problems and troubles that befall you through good faith and certainty."[1]

Muḥammad b. Ḥawab says: Imām Sajjād ﷺ said to Imām Muḥammad Bāqir ﷺ in his will:

يَا بُنَيَّ اصْبِرْ لِلنَّوَائِبِ وَ لاَ تَعَرَّضْ لِلْحُتُوفِ وَ لاَ تُعْطِ نَفْسَكَ مَا ضَرُّهُ عَلَيْكَ أَكْثَرُ مِنْ نَفْعِهِ لِغَيْرِك

"My child! Be patient in problems and misfortunes and don't expose yourself to death and don't do anything that has more harm than benefit."[2]

Of course, it goes without saying that patience means perseverance, determination, effort and confronting problems, not as commonly believed that it implies stagnation, giving up and doing nothing, which is a wrong notion.

Luqmān's Advice to his son

It is said that Luqmān had a son who sometimes complained about the troubles of the times. Although his father told him: 'There is wellbeing in this only', he was not satisfied and content. Luqmān wanted a situation where he could actually show this point practically to his son, until one day he decided to travel with him to one of the villages. They rode on a donkey and were travelling for some time when the donkey's leg broke and he could not move further. The son complained! The father said: 'There is wellbeing in this only'. Then they started walking, but after walking some distance, the boy's injured his foot and he could not walk further. So they had to spend the night on the road with the hope that some help might arrive the following morning. The son began to complain but the father said: 'There is wellbeing in this only'. In the morning, a caravan passed from there

[1] *Biḥār al-'Anwār*, vol. 70, p. 181.
[2] *al-Fuṣūl al-Muhimmah*, p. 188.

and along with it they reached that village. As soon as they reached there, they were confronted with a strange and bitter sight! Human corpses were strewn all around! When they asked what the story was, they were told that night before the enemy had attacked and killed them all. Luqmān said to his son: I told you: 'There is wellbeing in this only'.

If those problems had not befallen us and we had entered this place the previous night, we would also be lying among these corpses.[1]

4. Concealing pain and sorrow

One of the things that our children should be familiar with is perseverance against pain. They should be taught not to show impatience and leave the field with a little discomfort and pain; Ḥāfiẓ says:

بادل خونین لب خندان بیاور همچو جام

نی گرت زخمی رسد آیی چو چنگ اندر خروش

Though heart is sorrowful, you smile with the lips on the goblet.

Likewise, when grief overcomes, don't emit a scream, and start crying, (but be patient).

Imām Bāqir ﷺ said to his noble son, Imām Ṣādiq ﷺ:

يَا بُنَيَ مَنْ كَتَمَ بَلَاءً ابْتُلِيَ بِهِ مِنَ النَّاسِ وَ شَكَا ذَلِكَ إِلَى اللَّهِ عَزَّ وَ جَلَّ كَانَ حَقّاً عَلَى اللَّهِ أَنْ يُعَافِيَهُ مِنْ ذَلِكَ الْبَلَاء

"My child! Whoever hides his illness and discomfort from people and shares his pain and suffering only with Allāh ﷻ and grieves only to Him, it is the right upon Allāh ﷻ to heal him from that illness and affliction."[2]

Only Allāh ﷻ

---

[1] *Chehel Ḥadīth wa Chehel Dāstān*, p. 11.

[2] *Makārim al-'Akhlāq*, p. 389; *Mustadrak al-Wasā'il*, vol. 2, p. 69; *Biḥār al-'Anwār*, vol. 93, p. 296.

Mas'ada b. Ṣadaqah narrates from Imām Ja'far Ṣādiq ﷺ that:

اشْتَكَى بَعْضُ وُلْدِ أَبِي فَمَرَّ بِهِ فَقَالَ لَهُ قُلْ عَشْرَ مَرَّاتٍ يَا اللَّهُ يَا اللَّهُ يَا اللَّهُ فَإِنَّهُ لَمْ يَقُلْهَا أَحَدٌ مِنَ الْمُؤْمِنِينَ قَطُّ إِلَّا قَالَ لَهُ الرَّبُّ تَبَارَكَ وَ تَعَالَى لَبَّيْكَ عَبْدِي سَلْ حَاجَتَكَ

"Once, one of my father's ﷺ children was complaining about pain. My father passed by him and said: My son! Say: Ya Allāh ﷻ, ten times, because no believer ever uttered these words except that the mighty and the blessed Lord ﷻ said in reply: Here I am, O My servant; ask Me what you need."[1]

Ḥasan b. Abī Nu'aym says: Once, one of the children of Imām Ṣādiq ﷺ complained to his father about pain and discomfort of his illness. Imām ﷺ said to him, "My son! Recite:

اللَّهُمَّ اشْفِنِي بِشِفَائِكَ وَ دَاوِنِي بِدَوَائِكَ وَ عَافِنِي مِنْ بَلَائِكَ فَإِنِّي عَبْدُكَ وَ ابْنُ عَبْدَيْكَ

"O Allāh ﷻ! Grant me cure through Your treatment, heal me with your medicine, and protect me from your affliction; I am your servant and the son of your servant."[2]

Imām Sajjād's ﷺ conversation with his father

Imām Bāqir ﷺ said: My father, 'Alī b. Al-Ḥusain ﷺ said:

مَرِضْتُ مَرَضاً شَدِيداً فَقَالَ لِي أَبِي ع مَا تَشْتَهِي فَقُلْتُ أَشْتَهِي أَنْ أَكُونَ مِمَّنْ- لَا أَقْتَرِحُ عَلَى اللَّهِ رَبِّي مَا يُدَبِّرُهُ لِي فَقَالَ لِي أَحْسَنْتَ ضَاهَيْتَ إِبْرَاهِيمَ الْخَلِيلَ صَلَوَاتُ اللَّهِ عَلَيْهِ حَيْثُ قَالَ جَبْرَئِيلُ ع هَلْ مِنْ حَاجَةٍ فَقَالَ لَا أَقْتَرِحُ عَلَى رَبِّي بَلْ حَسْبِيَ اللَّهُ وَ نِعْمَ الْوَكِيلُ

"I was very sick; my father asked: My son! Do you want something? I said: I want to be of those who do not suggest what Allāh

[1] *Wasā'il al-Shī'ah*, vol. 4, p. 1132; *Mustadrak al-Wasā'il*, vol. 5, p. 219.

[2] *Makārim al-'Akhlāq*, p.392; *Mustadrak al-Wasā'il*, vol. 2, p. 85; *Wasā'il al-Shī'ah*, vol. 4, p. 1099.

ﷻ has planned and destined. Imām ﷺ said: Well done to you for becoming like Ibrāhīm ﷺ, the friend of the Lord ﷻ; when Jibra'īl ﷺ asked him: Do you need anything? He answered: No, I do not suggest anything to my Lord; because sufficient for us is Allāh ﷻ, and [He is] the best disposer of affairs."[1]

5. Contentment and surrender

Imām 'Alī ﷺ said to Imām Ḥusain ﷺ:

وَمَن رَضِيَ بِقِسَمِ اللَّهِ لَمْ يَحْزَن على ما فاتَه

"A person who is satisfied with Allāh's ﷻ distribution will never grieve for what he has lost."[2]

It is also narrated from Amīr al Mu'minīn ﷺ that one of Luqmān's advice to his son was:

"My child! One whose certainty has decreased and his intention to seek sustenance has weakened, should learn from the fact that Allāh ﷻ has taken him through three stages and sent him his sustenance, while he had nothing to do in any of those situations. He neither worked nor made any effort. So, the one who did not forget him in those three situations will send him sustenance in the fourth stage as well.

The first stage: When he was in the womb and Allāh ﷻ provided him with sustenance in a place where neither heat nor cold bothered him.

The second stage: When he emerged from the womb and was fed his mother's milk, while he had no will power of his own.

The third stage: After he was weaned, he lived upon his parents, who were so devoted to him that they put him before themselves. They made sacrifices for him until he reached the age of reason and started working and striving in life. At that time his life became difficult. He completely forgot all those favours of Almighty Allāh and made unreasonable assumptions about his Lord ﷻ and denied the rights of

---

[1] *Biḥār al-'Anwār*, vol. 46, p. 67, quoting *Da'wat Rāwandī.*
[2] *Tuḥaf al-'Uqūl*, p. 84.

others in his property. He was hard on himself and his family, fearing shortage of sustenance and that it will not be replaced by Allāh ﷻ. My child! How wicked this person was![1]

4. The practice of the Prophet ﷺ and his family ؑ

The best practical way to fight problems is to learn and gain experience from the conduct of the Infallibles ؑ; because the practical way of Purified *Ahl al-Bayt* ؑ is the manifestation and embodiment of Allāh's ﷻ teachings and the surest and easiest way to gain experience of fighting against the hardships of life, which is referred to in two examples:

A) The Prophet ﷺ and the command to pray

Yūsuf b. ʿAbdullāh b. Salām says:

أَنَّ النَّبِيَّ ص كَانَ إِذَا نَزَلَ بِأَهْلِهِ شِدَّةٌ أَمَرَهُمْ بِالصَّلَاةِ ثُمَّ قَرَأَ وَ أْمُرْ أَهْلَكَ بِالصَّلاةِ وَ اصْطَبِرْ عَلَيْها

Whenever a problem arose for the family of the Prophet ﷺ, he would order his family members to pray to solve that problem; then he would recite this verse:

وَأْمُرْ أَهْلَكَ بِٱلصَّلَوٰةِ وَٱصْطَبِرْ...

"And bid your family to prayer and be steadfast in its maintenance..."[2][3]

It is mentioned in the book of *Makārim al-'Akhlāq* that:

كَانَ النَّبِيُّ ص إِذَا أَصَابَتْ أَهْلَهُ خَصَاصَةٌ نَادَى أَهْلَهُ يَا أَهْلَاهْ صَلُّوا صَلُّوا

---

[1] *Biḥār al-'Anwār*, vol. 13, p. 414 (translation and summary).
[2] Sūrah ṬāḤā 20:132.
[3] *Mustadrak al-Wasā'il*, vol. 6, p. 395; *Majmuʿah Warrām*, p. 162.

The practice of the Prophet ﷺ was that whenever a problem beset his family, he would say: Pray, pray![1]

B) The method of Amīr al Mu'minīn ؑ

Imām Zayn al-'Ābidīn ؑ said:

مَا أُصِيبَ أَمِيرُ الْمُؤْمِنِينَ ع بِمُصِيبَةٍ إِلَّا صَلَّى فِي ذَلِكَ الْيَوْمِ أَلْفَ رَكْعَةٍ وَ تَصَدَّقَ عَلَى سِتِّينَ مِسْكِيناً وَ صَامَ ثَلَاثَةَ أَيَّامٍ وَ قَالَ لِأَوْلَادِهِ إِذَا أُصِبْتُمْ بِمُصِيبَةٍ فَافْعَلُوا بِمِثْلِ مَا أَفْعَلُ فَإِنِّي رَأَيْتُ رَسُولَ اللَّهِ ص هَكَذَا يَفْعَلُ فَاتَّبِعُوا أَثَرَ نَبِيِّكُمْ وَ لَا تُخَالِفُوهُ فَيُخَالِفَ اللَّهُ بِكُمْ إِنَّ اللَّهَ تَعَالَى يَقُولُ

"No calamity befell Amīr al Mu'minīn ؑ, except that he prayed a thousand units of Prayer on that day, gave charity to sixty poor people, fasted for three days, and said to his children: If you are afflicted with a calamity, do as I do, because I saw the Prophet of Allāh ﷺ act like this. So follow the Sunnah of the Prophet ﷺ and do not oppose it as Allāh ﷻ will also turn away from you. Allāh, the Almighty says for the one who makes patience and forgiveness his practice:

وَلَمَن صَبَرَ وَغَفَرَ إِنَّ ذَٰلِكَ لَمِنْ عَزْمِ ٱلْأُمُورِ ﴿٤٣﴾

"As for him who endures patiently and forgives —that is indeed the steadiest of courses."[2]

ثُمَّ قَالَ زَيْنُ الْعَابِدِينَ ع فَمَا زِلْتُ أَعْمَلُ بِعَمَلِ أَمِيرِ الْمُؤْمِنِينَ ع

Then Imām Zayn al-'Ābidīn said, "I have always acted upon the way of Amīr al Mu'minīn ؑ."[3]

---

[1] *Makārim al-'Akhlāq*, p. 334.
[2] Sūrah al-Shūrā 42:43.
[3] *Mustadrak al-Wasā'il*, vol. 2, p. 481.

5. Avoiding attachment to the world

Living in the world and enjoying its pleasures and blessings is a natural thing and no one can stop people from using this legitimate right. The Holy Qur'ān has also mentioned the use of this legitimate privilege in a number of verses, and Infallible *A'immah* vehemently opposed those who imagined that piety in the world implies living in seclusion and depriving themselves of lawful blessings. But it goes without saying that they also mentioned an important issue that is the subject of our discussion:

While the Infallible *A'immah* advised us to improve the life of this world by exploiting its possibilities and using the blessings of Allāh, they also warned us against relying on and depending solely on the world, because unconditional attachment to the world means being seduced by hopes and wallowing in material manifestations and insatiable desires which endangers life and blinds people, limiting their cognition to appearances.

Attachment to the world means relying on dreams and falling behind the convoy of goodness and happiness, and it is clear how much this insatiable attachment can become a barrier to charity and prevent people from evolving and discharging religious duties. Therefore, the Prophet ﷺ and the Infallibles strictly forbade us from attachment to the world; and themselves, while they continued to live in the world, they did not care for it even for a moment. Even if all the treasures of the world were to be placed in their hands, they would not become happy, and even if all the people of the world turn their backs to them and they lose all possibilities of life, they would not feel regret, and this is the true meaning of piety in the world and the Qur'ān has also mentioned it:

لِّكَيْلَا تَأْسَوْاْ عَلَىٰ مَا فَاتَكُمْ وَلَا تَفْرَحُواْ بِمَآ ءَاتَىٰكُمْ ۗ...

"so that you may not grieve for what escapes you, nor exult for what comes your way, and Allāh does not like any swaggering braggart..."[1]

[1] Sūrah al-Ḥadīd 57:23.

The world is a deep sea

Imām Kāẓim ﷺ said to Hishām: Hishām! Luqmān said to his son:

يَا بُنَيَّ إِنَّ الدُّنْيَا بَحْرٌ عَمِيقٌ وَ قَدْ هَلَكَ فِيهَا عَالَمٌ كَثِيرٌ فَاجْعَلْ سَفِينَتَكَ فِيهَا الْإِيمَانَ بِاللَّهِ عَزَّ وَ جَلَّ وَ اجْعَلْ شِرَاعَهَا التَّوَكُّلَ عَلَى اللَّهِ وَ اجْعَلْ زَادَكَ فِيهَا تَقْوَى اللَّهِ فَإِنْ نَجَوْتَ فَبِرَحْمَةِ اللَّهِ وَ إِنْ هَلَكْتَ فَبِذُنُوبِك

My dear son! The world is a deep sea, and many worlds are drowned in it. Your ship in this deep sea must be fear of Allāh ﷻ and its interior rich in faith, its sail is trust, its captain is wisdom, its guide is knowledge, and its anchor is patience. So, if you are saved, in the light of grace it was divine mercy, and if you perished, it was the result and punishment of your sins.[1]

The deception of world worshipers

Imām 'Alī ﷺ said in his will to his son, Imām Ḥasan Mujtabā ﷺ:

"Beware lest, you become deceived by the leanings of the people towards worldly attraction and their rushing upon it. Allāh has warned you about it and the world has informed you of its mortal character and unveiled to you, its evils. Surely those chasing it are like barking dogs or devouring carnivores, who hate each other. The stronger among them eat away the weaker and the big among them tramples the small. The world has put them on the track of blindness and taken away their eyes from the beacons of guidance. They have therefore been perplexed in its bewildering's and sunk in its pleasures.

They took it as a god, but it played with them. They too played with it and forgot what is beyond it. Beware, O my child lest, the abundance of its flaws dishonours you. Some are like tied cattle and some like stray cattle who have lost their wits and are running in unknown directions. They are flocks of calamities wandering in rugged valleys. There is no herdsman to control them.

---

[1] *Makārim al-'Akhlāq*, p. 254.

They are perplexed, fallen into calamities in a barren desert and extremely exhausted. They are without a shepherd or leaders who may lead and guide them. Slowly they continue to move forward till they enter into absolute darkness where they are on the verge of stampeding and losing their way.

Know, O my child, that everyone, who is riding on the carriage of night and day is being carried by them even though he may be stationary, and he is traversing distance even though he is resting. Allāh has accepted nothing but ruining this world and prospering the next world.[1]

Luqmān the Wise said to his son:

يا بُنَيّ لا تَأمَنْ الدَّنيا وَالذُّنوبَ وَالشَّيطانَ فيها

My child! Never in your life should you imagine that you are safe from the world, the sinners, and the Satan.[2]

Do not depend on the world

Imām Ṣādiq ﷺ says: Luqmān's advice to his son was:

يَا بُنَيَّ لَا تَرْكَنْ إِلَى الدُّنْيَا وَ لَا تَشْغَلْ قَلْبَكَ بِهَا فَمَا خَلَقَ اللَّهُ خَلْقاً هُوَ أَهْوَنُ عَلَيْهِ مِنْهَا أَ لَا تَرَى أَنَّهُ لَمْ يَجْعَلْ نَعِيمَهَا ثَوَاباً لِلْمُطِيعِينَ وَ لَمْ يَجْعَلْ بَلَاءَهَا عُقُوبَةً لِلْعَاصِينَ.

My child! Do not make the world your support and do not occupy your heart with it, because Allāh ﷻ has not created a baser creation than the world. Don't you see that Allāh ﷻ has not deemed His blessings to be the reward of the obedient and the righteous, and His calamities as punishments for the sinners?[3]

---

[1] *Tuḥaf al-'Uqūl*, p. 74.
[2] *al-Ikhtiṣāṣ*, p. 332.
[3] *Biḥār al-'Anwār*, vol. 13, p. 412.

Amīr al Mu'minīn ﷺ advised his son, Muḥammad b. al-Hanafiyyah as follows:

يا بُنَيَّ إيَّاكَ والاتِّكالَ علَى الأمَانِيِّ، فَإنَّها بَضَائعُ النَّوكى، وتثبيطٌ عَنِ الآخِرَةِ

"My child! Don't rely on hopes, which are the merchandise of fools, and they hinder a person from the path of the Hereafter."[1]

The warning of Imām Zayn al-'Ābidīn ﷺ

Imām Sajjād ﷺ said in his advice to his son, Imām Muḥammad Bāqir ﷺ:

وَ اعْلَمْ أَنَ السَّاعَاتِ تُذْهِبُ عُمُرَكَ وَ أَنَّكَ لَا تَنَالُ نِعْمَةً إِلَّا بِفِرَاقِ أُخْرَى فَإِيَّاكَ وَ الْأَمَلَ الطَّوِيلَ فَكَمْ مِنْ مُؤَمِّلٍ أَمَلًا لَا يَبْلُغُهُ وَ جَامِعِ مَالٍ لَا يَأْكُلُهُ وَ مَانِعٍ مَا سَوْفَ يَتْرُكُهُ وَ لَعَلَّهُ مِنْ بَاطِلٍ جَمَعَهُ وَ مِنْ حَقٍّ مَنَعَهُ أَصَابَهُ حَرَاماً وَ وَرَّثَهُ احْتَمَلَ إِصْرَهُ وَ بَاءَ بِوِزْرِهِ- ذلِكَ هُوَ الْخُسْرانُ الْمُبِينُ

"My child! The passage of hours and minutes depletes your life, and it will take you away. Without a doubt you will not get any blessing unless you have missed another. Beware of long hopes, because there are many who wish, but do not reach them and gatherers of wealth who do not enjoy it, and the misers who withhold their property from the needy and leave it and die. Perhaps they accumulated that wealth in an unlawful manner and did not pay its dues; a wealth that they acquired in a forbidden way and bequeathed to others. They carry its heavy responsibility, and the sin caused by that property; and they leave the world, and this is manifest waste and loss."[2]

---

[1] *Nūr al-Thaqlayn*, vol. 4, p. 211.
[2] *Biḥār al-'Anwār*, vol. 46, pp. 231-230.

Moderation in life

Luqmān the Wise says to his son:

يَا بُنَيَّ لَا تَدْخُلْ فِي الدُّنْيَا دُخُولًا يُضِرُّ بِآخِرَتِكَ وَ لَا تَتْرُكْهَا تَرْكاً تَكُونُ كَلًّا عَلَى النَّاس

My child! Don't get involved in the affairs of this world so much that it will harm you in the Hereafter, and don't neglect the affairs of this world in such a way that you become a burden to others (use the blessings of this world so that you don't become a burden to others and don't be attached to it).[1]

Think about the future

He also said:

وَ لَا تُكْثِرْ مِنَ الدُّنْيَا فَإِنَّكَ عَلَى غَفْلَةٍ مِنْهَا وَ انْظُرْ إِلَى مَا تَصِيرُ مِنْهَا

Do not increase material assets in the world; because you are unaware of its reality, look at what you are moving towards.[2]

Bitterness of this world is sweetness of the Hereafter

He also says:

يَا بُنَيَّ اجْعَلِ الدُّنْيَا سِجْنَكَ فَتَكُونَ الْآخِرَةُ جَنَّتَك

[1] *Majmu'ah Warrām*, p. 56; *Biḥār al-'Anwār*, vol. 13, p. 411 (with some difference).
[2] *al-Ikhtiṣāṣ*, p. 335.

My child! Make this world your prison so that the Hereafter will be your Paradise.[1]

He also told his son:

يَا بُنَيَّ بِعْ دُنْيَاكَ بِآخِرَتِكَ تَرْبَحْهُمَا جَمِيعاً وَ لَا تَبِعْ آخِرَتَكَ بِدُنْيَاكَ تَخْسَرْهُمَا جَمِيعا

"Sell your world for your Hereafter, you will benefit from both, but don't sell your Hereafter for your world, as you will make loss in both."[2]

[1] *al-Ikhtiṣāṣ*, p. 332.
[2] *Majmuʿah Warrām*, p. 97.

Part Seven

Puberty and youth

Puberty and youth

A) Celebrating adulthood

One of the best and sweetest times that children spend is the sweet and memorable period of their adulthood. At this stage, children feel a great excitement blowing into their souls and it is as if they are stepping into a new world. With the changes they find in their body and soul, they note that Allāh ﷻ has blessed and invited them by handing over heavy responsibility of their duties; so they are on the threshold of prosperity and growth and moving towards infinite perfection and approaching their holy threshold.

The celebration ceremony is also a positive and effective response to the inner states and emotions of teenagers. This ceremony validates the pure and energetic personality of teenagers and makes them more capable for accepting religious and human responsibilities.

Therefore, the honourable fathers should thank Allāh ﷻ for this gift and benevolence and celebrate that day. It is appropriate that this day should be celebrated, and public and private gatherings and feasts should be organized for it, and the father or elder of the family or one of the teachers or clergymen should talk about the greatness of the task and responsibility. How good it would be if those flowers and gifts brought on birthdays are also brought for this celebration. How nice it is that gifts of books and tapes [in form of lectures, *latmiyah* or a *nashīd*] are so useful. If it is mentioned to the teenager that since you have reached the age of responsibility and from this moment onwards, Allāh ﷻ has special care, attention, and kindness for you, and because of the merit hidden in you, He has placed this heavy responsibility on you and opened the path of perfection, progress, and the highway of eternal Paradise for you, he would transform himself.

The greatest feast of man

Sayyid b. Ṭāwūs, who lived about six hundred years ago, paid a lot of attention to this issue. He not only accorded importance to the day of his adulthood, but also remembered that day as the greatest 'Īd.

On the contrary, he thought of organizing a celebration for his child's coming of age and celebrating that unforgettable day. And in the book of *Kashf al-Muḥajjah* he hopes that if he remains alive until the day of adulthood of his son he will consider that day as an Eid and give 150 gold coins in charity in the way of Allāh ﷻ.[1]

Statements Sayyid b. Ṭāwūs in the ceremony of his son's adulthood

When his son, Muḥammad stepped into the sixteenth year of his life, Sayyid b. Ṭāwūs, first called an astrologer to determine the time of his child's birth. After the moment of Muḥammad's birth became clear, he thanked Allāh ﷻ and spoke to his son.

Sayyid expressed the responsibility of a responsible person in a simple and powerful expression and vivid and interesting simile. He said: A person who has reached the age of responsibility is like a slave, who does the lowest jobs for his master. But his master's decision is to raise his servant from that humble position to a royal and great position and entrust him with the keys of the dominions. Now, Allāh ﷻ has invited this servant to His door to do him a good turn and entrust him with the keys of this world and the Hereafter and give him the keys of the palaces of heaven.[2]

Then father and son prostrate to thank Allāh ﷻ for this great blessing. After that the father greets the guardian angel and also persuades his child to greet the two angels - Raqīb and ʿAtīd - and seek help from them for his happiness and success. Then he turns his attention to the enemy of humans (*'Iblīs*) and asks Allāh ﷻ to keep him away, and at the end he prays two units of thanksgiving prayer.[3]

Complain of Ibn. Ṭāwūs to the parents

Sayyid b. Ṭāwūs complains about parents in his exquisite writing:

---

[1] *Kashf al-Muḥajjah*, p. 87.
[2] *al-Tashrīf bi Taʿrīf wa Waqt Taklīf*, p. 6.
[3] *al-Tashrīf bi Taʿrīf wa Waqt Taklīf*, pp. 8-10.

As far as we have seen and heard, if someone reaches the kingdom of a country or is entrusted with a province, position, and responsibility, he cherishes that day very much and records that unforgettable moment that he will never forget. He makes that day a day of celebration with his loved ones, but it is amazing regarding the day of adulthood: when a boy reaches the position of divine servitude and undertakes heavy responsibility, that it should be disregarded and ignored so much that it is considered a nameless day!

So far, I have not met anyone who valued this very great and unforgettable day and fulfilled the right of this day or was saddened for a moment because of the loss of such a day. Therefore, I advise myself, my children, and my friends to honour this day and try to respect it. [1]

B) Choosing a spouse

Another right that the children have upon their father is that he must choose a suitable spouse for them. Of course, fathers are well aware that the issue of marriage and choosing a spouse for the child is not the only issue in this regard, but what has a defining role in the matter of marriage is the culture and rules governing marriage and its style. In this regard, parents and children have serious responsibilities, and it is very important to get to know them and pay attention to all aspects of marriage in fulfilling these responsibilities.

The Prophet of Islam ﷺ, while enumerating some of the rights of children over their parents also considered the issue of marriage as one of these rights and said:

مِنْ حَقِ الْوَلَدِ عَلَى وَالِدِهِ ثَلَاثَةٌ يُحَسِّنُ اسْمَهُ وَ يُعَلِّمُهُ الْكِتَابَةَ وَ يُزَوِّجُهُ إِذَا بَلَغَ

[1] Translation and adaptation from the book of *al-Tashrīf bi Taʿrīf wa Waqt Taklīf*, p. 15.

"Among the rights that a child has over his father are three: choose a good name for him; teach him reading and writing; and choose a wife for him when he reaches puberty."[1]

Getting a spouse for the child is a right, but choosing a good spouse is a duty. Parents who have tasted the ups and downs of life and gained much experience regarding marriage and the twists and turns of its issues, are obliged not to be careless and take a simplistic approach to matters related to marriage. They should overlook wealth and external standards as it would make their child a victim of fleeting desires. They should not be selfish but should carefully consider the authentic Islamic standards and be well informed about the ethics, behaviour, and religion of the other party. Failure to pay attention to these issues causes irreparable damage to children's lives. In this way, marriages take place which are the beginning of many problems, and instead of being a comforting sweet life with the pleasure of Allāh ﷻ, the spouse becomes the cause of suffering, torture, and unhappiness. Here are some of the characteristics of a good spouse:

1. He should be righteous and honest

A man brought his son to the Messenger of Allāh ﷺ and asked:

مَا حَقُ ابْنِي هَذَا قَالَ تُحَسِّنُ اسْمَهُ وَ أَدَبَهُ وَ تَضَعُ مَوْضِعاً حَسَنا

What right does this child of mine have over me? The Prophet said, "Give him a good name, train him well and place him in a good place."[2]

As mentioned in the footnote of Late Ibn. Fahd al-Ḥillī's book, *'Udat al-Dā'ī*[3] perhaps it implies choosing a righteous spouse for the child.

---

[1] *Makārim al-'Akhlāq*, p. 220; *Kanz al-'Ummāl*, vol. 16, p. 417; *Wasā'il al-Shī'ah*, vol. 15, p. 200, quoted from Ibn. Fattāl Nishāpūrī, *Rauḍa al-Wai'zīn*; *Mustadrak al-Wasā'il*, vol. 15, p. 161.

[2] *'Udat al-Dā'ī*, p. 76; *Makārim al-'Akhlāq*, p. 443, *Wasā'il al-Shī'ah*, vol. 15, p. 123, 124, and 198; *Kanz al-'Ummāl*, vol. 16, p. 417.

[3] *'Udat al-Dā'ī*, p. 76.

2. He should be God-fearing and pious

A man came to Imām Ḥasan ﷺ to consult about his daughter's marriage. He said:

زَوِّجْهَا مِنْ رَجُلٍ تَقِيٍ فَإِنَّهُ إِنْ أَحَبَّهَا أَكْرَمَهَا وَ إِنْ أَبْغَضَهَا لَمْ يَظْلِمْهَا

"Give her hand to a pious and God-fearing man, because if he loves her, he will respect her, and if he is angered, he will not oppress her."[1]

(That is: He would not attack or harass her.)

It is mentioned in *Kitāb al-'Ayāl* that the Prophet ﷺ said:

زَوِّجْهَا مَنْ يَخافُ اللهَ

"Get your daughter married to someone who fears Allāh ﷻ."[2]

It is natural that a person who has piety and fears Allāh ﷻ, always sees himself in the presence of Allāh ﷻ, therefore, he never allows himself to fall into the abyss of sin by oppressing others and by annoying and oppressing his wife, who is a trust with him. He would not become a target of divine wrath. God-fearing people are patient and they overcome problems through patience and perseverance. They are also kind and forgiving, and if they are angry and displeased with their spouse's actions and words, they forgive and pardon with dignity; and they make their spouse aware of their ugly mistakes in a pleasant manner and words.

3. He should be religious and trustworthy

Amīr al Mu'minīn ﷺ narrates from the Messenger of Allāh ﷺ as follows:

[1] *Makārim al-'Akhlāq*, p. 204.
[2] *Kitāb al-'Ayāl*, vol. 1, p. 273.

إِذَا أَتَاكُمْ مَنْ تَرْضَوْنَ دِينَهُ وَ أَمَانَتَهُ فَزَوِّجُوهُ فَإِنْ لَمْ تَفْعَلُوا تَكُنْ فِتْنَةٌ فِي الْأَرْضِ وَ فَسادٌ كَبِير

"If a person comes proposing for your daughter and you are satisfied with his religion and trustworthiness, marry your daughter to him; but if you don't, great sedition and corruption will arise in the society."[1]

Ḥusain b. Bashar says:

كَتَبْتُ إِلَى أَبِي جَعْفَرٍ الثَّانِي ع أَسْأَلُهُ عَنِ النِّكَاحِ فَكَتَبَ ع مَنْ خَطَبَ إِلَيْكُمْ فَرَضِيتُمْ دِينَهُ وَ أَمَانَتَهُ فَزَوِّجُوهُ إِلَّا تَفْعَلُوهُ تَكُنْ فِتْنَةٌ فِي الْأَرْضِ وَ فَسادٌ كَبِير

I wrote to Imām Bāqir ﵇: A man proposed for my daughter. Imām ﵇ wrote in response: Whoever proposed for your daughter; if you are satisfied with his religion and trustworthiness, and you like him; then whatever may happen marry your daughter to him and if you don't, there will be great sedition and corruption on earth.[2]

In these two narrations, three basic points and one bitter warning have been emphasized, which can be considered carefully and explained: first of all, if the spouse is religious and his/her religiosity is liked, because religion as a factor that controls the person and prevents him from transgressing divine limits and does not allow a person to fall into wrongdoing, which will be the beginning of the breakup of the warm centre of the family. A person is devoid of commitment and religion that does not adhere to any principles, neither to the principles of the family nor to the principles of society. Whenever he wants to come home, he allows himself to be contaminated by every ugly act and sometimes he may end up in prison; because either he has cooperated with the merchants of death, or he has been involved in corruption, and these things will cause the heart of the family to disintegrate, and your daughter will be homeless.

---

[1] *Mustadrak al-Wasā'il*, vol. 14, p. 188.
[2] *Makārim al-'Akhlāq*, p. 204.

Second: A man must be trustworthy. A cheater can never be a good husband for your daughter and a worthy father for his children, because an irresponsible and dishonest person cannot look after his family in a trusted manner. But if a trustworthy person looks after his family, he will take good care of his wife and children and try not to fail in guarding these divine trusts. In addition to that, a trustworthy person in the society will achieve a favourable name and reputation, and it would also be an honour for his family.

Another point that stands out in the narration of Amīr al Mu'minīn ﵇ is the phrase of 'whatever it is'. Imām ﵇ said: The spouse must be religious and faithful, whatever may happen. It means whether he is poor or rich; whether he has a well-paid job or not, whether he is handsome and beautiful, dark-skinned and ugly, whether his father is rich or poor, none of these external titles have any effect on a person's worthiness for marriage.

The bitter fruit mentioned at the end of the two above mentioned narrations is that if you reject a religious and reliable son-in-law and do not marry your daughter to such a person, you have fuelled seditions and social corruption. Perhaps it implies that when you overlooked the criterion of faith and trustworthiness, pious and decent people will be pushed aside, and corrupt people will take their place. In that case, a family will be formed with non-Islamic and inhuman standards, and if this happens, it will lead to greater corruption, and an unworthy and irresponsible spouse will easily play with the fate of the family and contaminate it with his false hopes. Yes, wheat must be separated from the chaff.

4. He should have good morals

'Alī ﵇ narrates from the Prophet ﷺ, who said:

إِذَا جَاءَكُمْ مَنْ تَرْضَوْنَ خُلُقَهُ وَ دِينَهُ فَزَوِّجُوهُ قَالَ قُلْتُ يَا رَسُولَ اللَّهِ وَ إِنْ كَانَ دَنِيّاً فِي نَسَبِهِ قَالَ إِذَا جَاءَكُمْ مَنْ تَرْضَوْنَ خُلُقَهُ وَ دِينَهُ فَزَوِّجُوهُ إِنَّكُمْ إِلَّا تَفْعَلُوهُ تَكُنْ فِتْنَةٌ فِي الْأَرْضِ وَ فَسَادٌ كَبِيرٌ

"If a person, whose morals and honesty you like, proposes for the hand of your daughter, accept it and marry your daughter to him." I said: Even if he is inferior in terms of lineage? The Prophet ﷺ once again repeated the same sentence and said, "If a person whose morals and religion are pleasing to you proposes for the hand of your daughter, marry your daughter to him and if you do not do this, great sedition and corruption will be created on the earth."[1]

In this narration also, the Holy Prophet ﷺ has relied on the two criteria: of religion and morals, and he regards them to be factors of happiness and stability of the family and neglecting them as cause of corruption of the society and prevalence of sedition. However, lineage or ancestry that was mentioned in the question, is not considered a criterion.

'Alī b. Asbāṭ and Imām Bāqir ؑ

'Alī b. Mahziyār says:

كَتَبَ عَلِيُ بْنُ أَسْبَاطٍ إِلَى أَبِي جَعْفَرٍ ع فِي أَمْرِ بَنَاتِهِ وَ أَنَّهُ لَا يَجِدُ أَحَداً مِثْلَهُ فَكَتَبَ إِلَيْهِ أَبُو جَعْفَرٍ ع فَهِمْتُ مَا ذَكَرْتَ مِنْ أَمْرِ بَنَاتِكَ وَ أَنَّكَ لَا تَجِدُ أَحَداً مِثْلَكَ فَلَا تَنْظُرْ فِي ذَلِكَ رَحِمَكَ اللَّهُ فَإِنَّ رَسُولَ اللَّهِ ص قَالَ- إِذَا جَاءَكُمْ مَنْ تَرْضَوْنَ خُلُقَهُ وَ دِينَهُ فَزَوِّجُوهُ إِلَّا تَفْعَلُوهُ تَكُنْ فِتْنَةٌ فِي الْأَرْضِ وَ فَسادٌ كَبِير

'Alī b. Asbāṭ wrote a letter to Imām Bāqir ؑ and raised the issue of marrying his daughters that he can't find anyone of his standard. Imām ؑ wrote in reply: Regarding what you wrote to me about your daughter, that you can't find anyone of your level to give her hand in marriage. May Allāh ﷻ have mercy on you. Do not think much regarding this, because the Prophet ﷺ said, "If someone asks for the hand of your daughter in marriage and his morals and honesty you

[1] *Wasā'il al-Shī'ah*, vol. 14, p. 52; *Kitāb al-'Ayāl*, vol. 1, p. 264; *Kanz al-'Ummāl*, vol. 16, p. 318.

like, marry your daughter to him, and if you don't, there will definitely be a big sedition and corruption in the society."[1]

5. Do not use poverty as an excuse

Poverty and wealth are in the hands of Allāh ﷻ. In addition, wealth alone does not bring happiness and what is the basis of felicity and peace in life is the faith of men and women.

It is mentioned in *Fiqh ar-Riḍā* that:

إِنْ خَطَبَ إِلَيْكَ رَجُلٌ رَضِيتَ دِينَهُ وَ خُلُقَهُ فَزَوِّجْهُ وَ لَا يَمْنَعْكَ فَقْرُهُ وَ فَاقَتُهُ قَالَ اللَّهُ تَعَالَى وَ إِنْ يَتَفَرَّقَا يُغْنِ اللَّهُ كُلًّا مِنْ سَعَتِهِ وَ قَوْلُهُ

"If a man, whose religion, and morals are satisfactory to you comes to ask you for the hand of your daughter, give her in marriage to him, and his poverty should not be an obstacle to this marriage. Allāh Almighty says:

...إِن يَكُونُواْ فُقَرَآءَ يُغْنِهِمُ ٱللَّهُ مِن فَضْلِهِۦ وَٱللَّهُ وَٰسِعٌ عَلِيمٌ ﴿٣٢﴾

"If they are poor, Allāh will enrich them out of His grace, and Allāh is all-bounteous, all-knowing."[2][3]

Same religion and caste

Never give your daughter to someone of other than your sect or religion; because with this act, you would have pushed her away from your religion and led her to another religion, and in fact, you would have severed her kinship bond.

Imām Ṣādiq ؑ said:

مَنْ زَوَّجَ ابْنَتَهُ مُخَالِفاً لَهُ عَلَى دِينِهِ فَقَدْ قَطَعَ رَحِمَهَا

[1] *al-Kāfī*, Vol. 5, Pg. 347.
[2] Sūrah al-Nūr 24:32.
[3] *Mustadrak al-Wasā'il*, vol. 16, p. 188.

"A person who marries his daughter to someone who is opposed to his religion has definitely cut off her kinship bond."[1]

Don't marry your daughters to transgressors

There are many narrations of the Prophet ﷺ that a father should be careful and not give his daughter to a drunkard, a fornicator, a hot-tempered person etc., as it will lead to terrible consequences.

For more information, we refer to some warnings of the Holy Infallibles ﷺ.

The Messenger of Allāh ﷺ said:

مَنْ شَرِبَ الْخَمْرَ بَعْدَ مَا حَرَّمَهَا اللَّهُ عَلَى لِسَانِي فَلَيْسَ بِأَهْلٍ أَنْ يُزَوَّجَ إِذَا خَطَبَ

"Anyone who drinks wine, even though Allāh ﷻ has forbidden it, does not deserve that a girl be given to him in marriage, when he proposes."[2]

Imām Ṣādiq ؑ said:

مَنْ زَوَّجَ كَرِيمَتَهُ مِنْ شَارِبِ الْخَمْرِ فَقَدْ قَطَعَ رَحِمَهَا

"Whoever marries his daughter to a drunkard has severed relations from her."[3]

The Prophet of Islam ﷺ said:

مَنْ زَوَّجَ كَرِيمَتَهُ بِفَاسِقٍ نَزَلَ عَلَيْهِ كُلَّ يَوْمٍ أَلْفُ لَعْنَةٍ وَ لاَ يَصْعَدُ لَهُ عَمَلٌ إِلَى السَّمَاءِ وَ لاَ يُسْتَجَابُ لَهُ دُعَاؤُهُ وَ لاَ يُقْبَلُ مِنْهُ صَرْفٌ وَ لاَ عَدْلٌ

[1] *Wasā'il al-Shī'ah*, vol. 17, p. 249, tr. 7.
[2] *Makārim al-'Akhlāq*, p. 204; *Wasā'il al-Shī'ah*, vol. 14, p. 53; *Mustadrak al-Wasā'il*, vol. 4, p. 190.
[3] *Wasā'il al-Shī'ah*, vol. 14, p. 53.

"Whoever marries his daughter to a wicked person, a thousand curses will fall on him every day, and no deed of his will rise to the heavens, and his prayers will not be answered, and no charity and ransom will be accepted from him."[1]

He also said:

$$\text{مَنْ زَوَّجَ كَرِيمَتَهُ مِنْ فَاسِقٍ فَقَدْ قَطَعَ رَحِمَه}$$

"Whoever marries his daughter to a transgressor has cut off his relations from her."[2]

Through his chains of narrators, Shaykh Ṣadūq has narrated from Yaʿqub b. Yazīd from Ḥusain b. Bashār Wāsṭī, who said:

$$\text{كَتَبْتُ الى أبى الحَسَنِ الرِّضا عليه السلام: اِنَّ قِرابَة قَدْ خَطَبَ وَفى خُلقِه سُوءٌ قال:}$$
$$\text{لا تُزَوِّجْه اِنْ كانَ سِيّءُ الخُلقِ}$$

I wrote a letter to Imām Riḍā ؑ that I have a relative and he has proposed for my daughter, but he is a bit rude. Imām ؑ said, "If he is rude, don't give him the hand of your daughter."[3]

Consulting ladies of the family

The Prophet ﷺ said:

$$\text{آمِرُوا النِّساءَ في بناتِهن}$$

"Consult your ladies in matters related to their daughter."[4]

---

[1] *Mustadrak al-Wasāʾil*, vol. 5, p. 279, v. 14, p. 192.
[2] *Makārim al-ʾAkhlāq*, p. 204; *Kitāb al-ʿAyāl*, vol. 1, p. 270.
[3] *Wasāʾil al-Shīʿah*, vol. 14, p. 54; *Makārim al-ʾAkhlāq*, p. 203; *Mustadrak al-Wasāʾil*, vol. 14, p. 192.
[4] *Nahj al-Faṣāḥah*, p. 2.

Consulting the girl

Among the important issues that a father should consider in choosing a spouse for his child is that he should consult with the child. He should ask his child's opinion about his future spouse, especially in the case of girls; it is more emphasized to seek their view.

Prophet ﷺ consulted with Lady Fāṭimah Zahrā عليها السلام

It is narrated from 'Aṭā b. Abī Rabāḥ that he said:

لَمَّا خَطَبَ عَلِيٌ فَاطِمَةَ أَتَاهَا رَسُولُ اللَّهِ ص فَقَالَ إِنَّ عَلِيّاً قَدْ ذَكَرَكِ فَسَكَتَتْ فَخَرَجَ فَزَوَّجَهَا

When 'Alī عليه السلام proposed for Fāṭimah عليها السلام to the Prophet ﷺ, the latter came to Fāṭimah عليها السلام and said, "Fāṭimah عليها السلام dear, 'Alī عليه السلام has asked me for your hand in marriage." Fāṭimah عليها السلام remained silent and did not say anything (since silence is a sign of approval). The Prophet ﷺ came out and married her to 'Alī عليه السلام.[1]

Abū Mūsā narrates from the Messenger of Allāh ﷺ that he said:

اِذَا أَرَادَ أَحَدُكُمْ أَنْ يُزَوِّجَ ابْنَتَه فَلْيَسْتَأْمِرْها

"When one of you wants to marry off his daughter, he should consult with her first."[2]

The Prophet ﷺ said:

تُسْتَامَرُ الْأَيِّمُ فى نَفْسِها قالُوا: فَاِنَّ الْبِكْرَ تَسْتَحيى قالَ: اِنَّها صُماتُها

---

[1] *Biḥār al-'Anwār*, vol. 43, p. 136.
[2] *Kanz al-'Ummāl*, vol. 16, p. 311.

In the matter of the daughter's marriage, she must herself be consulted. It was said: But she would be ashamed and keep quiet? The Prophet ﷺ said, "Her silence is her assent."[1]

No compulsion

Many fathers think that as fathers and guardians of the family, they feel empowered to take any decision they want and implement it. Hence, the consent and desire of their son or daughter is not important and they will forcefully marry their child to anyone they choose. This is a forced marriage, and it will soon fall apart, and bear bitter and harmful fruits that no one can tolerate.

Ibn. Abī Ya'fūr complained to Imām Ṣādiq ؑ regarding his parents and said: I want to marry a woman, but my parents are against it; they have another girl in mind.

Imām ؑ said: "Marry the woman you want and leave the one your parents have in mind."[2]

Urgency in marriage of the girl

The Messenger of Allāh ﷺ said:

حَقُّ الْوَلَدِ عَلَى ... إِذَا كَانَتْ أُنْثَى ...يُعَجِّلَ سَرَاحَهَا إِلَى بَيْتِ زَوْجِهَا

"If the child is a girl, her father has the right to marry her as soon as possible."[3]

C) Future of children

Children's future is one of the important issues that sometimes make parents think where the future destiny of their children will lead in terms of education and career? Of course, it is one of the important

---

[1] *Musnad Zayd*, p. 272.
[2] *Makārim al-'Akhlāq*, p. 237.
[3] *Wasā'il al-Shī'ah*, vol. 15, p. 199.

responsibilities of parents to think about the future of their children and to plan tactfully according to high Islamic values and to create a bright and successful future for them. They should use views and experiences of others and not to neglect this important task, because the future of children takes shape at the hands of parents.

Parents should study all the issues related to their child that they have to deal with in the future. It is not something that can be postponed. They should think about it now, as tomorrow would be late.

The duty of the parents is not only to provide food, clothes, housing, and material needs to their children. Whether we want it or not, these things are accomplished due to natural affection, because the parents cannot see their child naked or hungry. Rather, the foresight and vigilance of parents and their sensitivity to the child's future requires them to pay more attention to his future career, morals, behaviour, and character. This means that our youth should not be idle and a burden on society in the future. He should be spirited and happy and should not grow up without any character. He should not be needy of others but should have a suitable occupation and earn enough to manage his own life.

1. Choosing a profession

The problem of choosing a job and ensuring the future of a child's career is one of the problems that every parent faces, and on the other hand, it can be said that it is the parents who can, better than anyone else, suggest to their child the most suitable career and render him effective help to strengthen his God-given talents and make them reach perfection.

If they see that their child is interested in a career suitable for that family, they should never make him a subject of ridicule and mockery. Rather, with the advice of teachers and mentors, they should let his talent grow to the level he is interested in. They should never force the child to follow the father's profession or that of the family's favourite person or take up a profession desired by parents and make more money and gain material and social benefits, because if he doesn't succeed in his forced career, he will lose hope and self-confidence and will not show interest in any other line of work also.

Parents should just pay attention that the line the child chooses or expresses interest in is not unlawful or disliked by *Sharī'ah*. They should encourage and help him to grow and advance in that direction.

Isḥāq b. 'Ammār says: I met Imām Ṣādiq and informed him that I had a child...I asked Imām : What occupation should I choose for him when he grows up?

Imām said:

إِذَا عَدَلْتَهُ عَنْ خَمْسَةِ أَشْيَاءَ فَضَعْهُ حَيْثُ شِئْتَ لَا تُسْلِمْهُ صَيْرَفِيّاً فَإِنَّ الصَّيْرَفِيَّ لَا يَسْلَمُ مِنَ الرِّبَا وَ لَا تُسْلِمْهُ بَيَّاعَ أَكْفَانٍ فَإِنَّ صَاحِبَ الْأَكْفَانِ يَسُرُّهُ الْوَبَاءُ إِذَا كَانَ وَ لَا تُسْلِمْهُ بَيَّاعَ طَعَامٍ فَإِنَّهُ لَا يَسْلَمُ مِنَ الِاحْتِكَارِ وَ لَا تُسْلِمْهُ جَزَّاراً فَإِنَّ الْجَزَّارَ تُسْلَبُ مِنْهُ الرَّحْمَةُ وَ لَا تُسْلِمْهُ نَخَّاساً فَإِنَّ رَسُولَ اللَّهِ ص قَالَ شَرُّ النَّاسِ مَنْ بَاعَ النَّاسَ

Keep your child away from five vocations and put him in any other profession you want.

Don't let him become a money changer because the money changer is not safe from usury. Don't let him become a burial shroud seller, because a shroud seller becomes extremely happy when there is epidemic of cholera (or other diseases so that the death rate increases, and he will sell more burial shrouds).

In the same way, don't make him a butcher, because (because of repeatedly cutting off the heads of animals), he would lose compassion and affection from his nature. Also, do not make him a slave trader, because the Prophet said: The lowest of people is one who buys and sells human beings.[1]

In a tradition narrated by Imām Mūsā b. Ja'far [2] from the Prophet , instead of money changer, goldsmith is mentioned and instead of grocer, wheat merchant is mentioned.

---

[1] *Wasā'il al-Shī'ah*, vol. 12, p. 97.
[2] *Wasā'il al-Shī'ah*, vol. 12, p. 98.

In any case, all these occupations, prohibited or regarded abhorrent by the Infallibles ﷺ have a negative effect on a person in some way, although engaging in these occupations is not basically illegal or prohibited by *Sharī'ah*, unless the person himself - regarding some professions like that of a money changer etc. - is sure that he will fall into usury, in which case choosing that line will be unlawful, because it would be a preface to unlawful business of usury.

2. Transferring life experiences to children

Human generations, on the basis of transfer of experiences and information to each other develop culture and civilization and make them flourish.

A major part of this is the responsibility of families and parents who have to pass on their many life experiences to their children.

In his letter to Imām Ḥasan Mujtabā ﷺ, Amīr al Mu'minīn ﷺ writes:

"Indeed, the heart of a teenager is like a land ready and empty of cultivation, and it accepts what is thrown into it, therefore, I have gone ahead to nurture you before your heart is hard and your mind is busy, so that you can work diligently and learn from experiences. From the learned experiences, you will find out the things that you are trying to test, and you will not seek refuge in suffering, and you are exempted from the experience of learning (again) and the knowledge that I have reached may reach you and it becomes clear to you what we used to see darkly.

My son! Although I have not lived as long as all those who have been before me, but I have observed their deeds and thought about their end, and I have investigated what they left until I became one of them, rather, the knowledge that I have gained from their deeds. It is as if I have lived with them from the beginning to the end, and I have known the bright and dark points of their lives, and I have known its benefits and losses, and for you, I have separated its excellence from everything, and I have searched for its goodness...[1]

---

[1] *Tuḥaf al-'Uqūl*, pp. 67 and 68.

3. Financial aid

Children are part and parcel of a person, so helping them is helping your own self, and denying them financial help leads to unfortunate mental and emotional consequences that cannot be compensated and sometimes causes them to be humiliated in front of friends and society. Of course, financial aid should not be taken to extremes, which may cause corruption and devastation of children.

Abū Hurairah narrates from the Prophet ﷺ, who said:

تَصَدَّقوا، فَقال رَجُلٌ: عِنْدی دینارٌ؟ قالَ: أنفِقه أو تَصَدَّقْ به عَلی نَفْسِکَ، قالَ: عِندی دینارٌ آخَر، قالَ : تَصَدَّق بِه عَلی امْرَأتِکَ، قالَ : عِنْدی دینارٌ آخَر قالَ : تَصَدَّقْ بِه عَلی وَلَدِکَ. قالَ عِنْدی دنیارٌ آخَر، قالَ: تَصَدَّقْ بِه عَلی خادِمِکَ. قالَ : عِنْدی دینارٌ آخَر.قالَ: أنتَ أبْصَرُ بِه

'Spend in charity.' A man who heard the Prophet ﷺ, said: I have one dinar. The Prophet ﷺ said, 'Spend it on yourself.' He said again: I have another *dīnār*. The Prophet ﷺ said, 'Spend it on your wife.' He said: I have another *dīnār*. The Prophet ﷺ said, "Give it to your child." He said: I have another *dīnār*. The Prophet ﷺ said, "You are more aware how to spend it."[1]

4. Protecting children from the burden of society

'Āmir b. Sa'd narrates from his father that the Prophet ﷺ said:

إنَّکَ إنْ تَتْرُکْ وَرَثتکَ أغنیاءَ خَیرٌ مِنْ أنْ تَترُکَهُمْ عالَة

"If you make your heirs and survivors needless after yourself, it is better than leaving them poor and in need of others and to be a burden on society."[2]

[1] *Kitāb al-'Ayāl*, vol. 1, p. 141.
[2] *Kitāb al-'Ayāl*, vol. 1, p. 149.

The Holy Prophet of Islam ﷺ said about a man from the *Anṣār* who freed his five or six slaves at the time of his death though he possessed nothing else; and left nothing for his young children:

لَوْ اَعْلَمْتُمُونيي أمْرَهُمْ ما تَرَكْتُكُمْ تُدْفِنُونَه مَعَ الْمسلِمِينَ، تَرَكَ صَبيَة صِغاراً يَتَكفَّفُونَ النَّاسَ

"Had you informed me about their situation, I would not have let you bury him in the Muslim cemetery. He left some young children to take up begging in the society."[1]

[1] *Tuḥaf al-'Uqūl*, p. 365.

Bibliography

1. *al-Ikhtiṣāṣ*, Shaykh Mufīd, Baseerati, Qom.
2. *al-Istibṣār*, Shaykh Ṭūsī, Daar Sa-ab, Beirut.
3. *al-Imām al-Ḥusain*, Ibn Asākir, Mausisa Al-Mahmudi, Beirut.
4. *al-'Amālī*, Shaykh Ṣadūq, Haidariya, Najaf.
5. *al-'Amālī*, Shaykh Ṭūsī, Haidariya, Najaf.
6. *Ikhtiyār Ma'rifat Rijāl*, Abū 'Amr Kishī, Aalami, Beirut.
7. *Akhlāq Islāmī*, Sayyid Mahdī Shams al-dīn, Intisharat Shafaq, Qom.
8. *Iqbāl al-'Āmāl*, Sayyid b. Ṭāwūs, Old edn, Tehran.
9. *Abū Ṭālib Yagānih Muda'fi Islām*, Muḥammad Riḍā Ṭabasī, Nashr Qaim, Tehran.
10. *Biḥār al-'Anwār*, Muḥammad Bāqir Majlisī, Islami, Tehran.
11. *Tuḥaf al-'Uqūl*, Ibn. Shu'bah Ḥarrānī, Islamiya, Tehran.
12. *al-Tashrīf bi Ta'rīf wa Waqt Taklīf*, Sayyid b. Ṭāwūs, Saadi, Tehran.
13. *Tafsīr al-Ṣāfī*, Fayḍ al-Kāshānī, Islamiya, Tehran.
14. *Tafsīr Namūnih*, Nāṣir Makārim Shirāzī and a group of scholars, Darul Kutubul Islamiya, Tehran.
15. *Tawẓīḥ al-Masā'il*, (Bakhsh Istiftaat), Āyatullāh Arākī, Daftar Tablighat, Qom.
16. *Thawāb al-'Āmāl*, Shaykh Ṣadūq, Haidariya, Najaf.
17. *al-Jawāhir as-Saniyah*, Shaykh Ḥurr 'Āmilī, Tus, Qom/Tehran.
18. *Chehel Ḥadīth wa Dāstān*, Mahdī Mu'tamadī, Mushtaqi, Isfahan.
19. *al-Ḥujjah 'Alā' Dhahab*, Fakhar b. Sa'd Mūsawī, Intisharat Nahza, Baghdad.

20. *al-Ḥadīth*, Muḥammad Taqi Falsafī, Daftar Nashr Farhang Islami, Tehran.

21. *Ḥilyat al-'Awliyā*, Abū Nu'aym Iṣfahānī, Dar al-Kitab, Beirut.

22. *Hayāt Imām al-'Askarī*, Muḥammad Jawād Ṭabasī, Daftar Tablighat, Qom.

23. *Dar al-Akhbār*, Muḥammad Riḍā Ṭabasī, Najaf.

24. *Da'im al-Islām*, Qāḍī Nu'mān Miṣrī, Aal al-Bayt, Qom.

25. *Rabiṭa Dosti wa Muḥabbat*, Aḥmad Muṭahharī, Jami Mudarriseen, Qom.

26. *Rijāl*, Shaykh Ṭūsī, Haidariya, Najaf.

27. *Rawḍāt al-Jannāt*, Sayyid Muḥammad Bāqir Khwansārī, Ad-Durar al-Islamiya, Beirut.

28. *Rawḍāt al-Wā'iẓīn*, Ibn Fattāl Nishāpūrī, Ar-Radi, Qom.

29. *Safīnat al-Biḥār*, Shaykh 'Abbās Qomī, Sanai, Tehran.

30. *Sharāī' al-Islām*, Muḥaqqiq Ḥillī, Azwa, Beirut.

31. *Sharḥ Nahj al-Balaghah*, Ibn. Abī al-Ḥadīd, Dar al-Ahya Turath, Beirut.

32. *Ṣaḥīfah Imām Riḍā*, Astan Quds Razavi, Meshed.

33. *Ṣaḥīfah Sajjādiyah*, Fayḍ Kāshānī, Tehran.

34. *'Udat al-Dā'ī*, Ibn. Fahd Ḥillī, Qom.

35. *'Uyūn Akhbār al-Riḍā*, Shaykh Ṣadūq, Tus.

36. a*l-Ghadīr*, 'Allāmah Amīnī, Dar al-Kutub al-Islamiya, Tehran.

37. *Furū' al-Kāfī*, Muḥammad b. Ya'qūb Kolaynī, Daar Sa-Abdul, Beirut.

38. *Farhang Jāmi'*, Aḥmad Sayyaḥ, Kitab Faroshi Islam.

39. *al-Fuṣūl al-Muhimmah*, Ibn. Ṣabbāgh Mālikī, Al-Adl.

40. *Qāmūs ar-Rijāl*, Muḥammad Taqī Shūshtarī, Jami Mudarriseen, Qom.

41. *al-Kāfī*, Thiqat al-Islām Shaykh Kolaynī, Daar Sa-Abdul, Beirut.

42. *Kitāb al-'Ayāl*, Ibn Abī al-Duniyā, Ibn Qayyim, Saudi.

43. *Kashf al-Ghummah*, 'Alī b. 'Isā Irbilī, Dar al-Kitab.

44. *Kashf al-Muḥajjah*, Sayyid b. Ṭāwūs, Dawari, Qom.

45. *Kanz al-'Ummāl*, Muttaqī al-Hindī, Mausisa ar-Risala, Beirut.

46. *Kanz al-Fawā'id*, Muḥammad b. 'Alī Karāchī, Lithograph, Tehran.

47. *Guftār Falsafī (Kūdak)*, Muḥammad Taqi Falsafī, Nashr Marif, Tehran.

48. *Mabanī Takmīlatah al-Minhāj*, Sayyid Abū al-Qāsim Khū'ī, Ilmiya, Qom.

49. *al-Maḥāsin*, Barqī, Dar al-Kutub, Qom.

50. *Al-Muḥajjat al-Baiḍā*, Fayḍ Kāshānī, Aalami, Beirut.

51. *Majmu'ah Warrām*, Warrām b. Abī Farās, Qom.

52. *Mardān 'Ilm dar Maydān 'Amal*, Sayyid Ni'matallāh Ḥusainī, Jami Mudarriseen, Qom.

53. *Mustadrak al-Wasā'il*, Mirzā Ḥusain Nūrī, Aal al-Bayt, Qom.

54. *Musnad Zayd*, Zayd b. 'Alī b. Ḥusain, Dar al-Kitab, Beirut.

55. *Makārim al-'Akhlāq*, 'Allāmah Ṭabarsī, Aalami, Beirut.

56. *Manāqib Āl Abī Ṭālib*, Ibn. Shahr Āshub, Allamah, Qom.

57. *Muntahī al-'Āmāl*, Shaykh 'Abbās Qomī, Islamiya, Tehran.

58. *al-Mīzān*, 'Allāmah Ṭabāṭabāī, Ismailiyan, Qom.

59. *Naqsh Mādar dar Tarbiyat*, 'Alī Qā'imī, Daar Tabligh, Qom.

60. *Nahj al-Balaghah*, Sayyid Raḍī, Beirut.

61. *Nahj al-Faṣāhah*, Abū al-Qāsim Payndah.

62. *Nūr al-Thaqalayn*, 'Abd 'Alī b. Jumu'ah Ḥuwayzī, Ismailiyan, Qom.

63. *Wasā'il al-Shī'ah*, Shaykh Ḥurr al-'Āmilī, Islamiya, Tehran.

www.ingramcontent.com/pod-product-compliance
Lightning Source LLC
Chambersburg PA
CBHW030107100526
44591CB00009B/312
* 9 7 8 1 9 2 2 5 8 3 4 9 9 *